HAND IN HAND
WITH TIME

By the same author

Tempus
Highgate and Muswell Hill (with Joan Schwitzer)
Hornsey and Crouch End
Muswell Hill: History and Guide
Muswell Hill Revisited

Hornsey Historical Society
From Forest to Suburb: The Story of Hornsey Retold
Palace on the Hill
A Walk Around Muswell Hill
Hornsey Village: A Walk
Stroud Green: A Walk
Crouch End: A Walk (with Bridget Cherry)
A History of Muswell Hill

S.B. Publications
From Highgate to Hornsey

CONTENTS

ILLUSTRATIONS

Hobart House, Grosvenor Place, London, my office for over thirty years

With Elwyn Jones in August 1950

Walking in Lower Regent Street in 1950 with Agnes and Teresa Coughlan

Between pages 192 and 193

Teresa at Camber Sands, Rye, in 1953, just before our engagement

Me outside the National Gallery in the 1950s

Upton Avenue with post-war pre-fab houses built on the V1 bomb site

Teresa with Richard, our first child, and Olu, our lodger

On location at Rawdon Colliery, August 1953, with John Reid, Tony
    Maher, John Shaw Jones and Donald Alexander

Unconscious in a field at Rawdon!

At Calverton Colliery, Nottinghamshire, with Charlie Burgess

My press pass to the 1958 festival in Belgium

At my film unit desk

Francis Gysin, the third NCB Films Officer, in 1992 after retirement

Photograph taken in 1955 by Lionel Griffiths, who was testing his lighting
    skills at the time

Father and Mother outside 77 Upton Avenue in 1965

Sam Goodman in Germany in 1965

West German Short Film Festival at Oberhausen, February 1965

Film Festival banquet in Rouen with Gloria Tessler and Ken Myer

Stanley Bloom, his wife Salome with Teresa on a visit to Cambridge in 1963

On the Rhine on the Ruhrkhole boat

German mining apprentices at Cardiff University, 1972, with Bill Cleaver

Colleagues John Quin and Bob Roberts on a visit to Gullick Dobson
    mining machinery company in Wigan, Lancashire, 1973

Mining machinery exhibition at NCB Swadlincote, 1974

A research visit to South Wales, 1977, while writing *Basic Mechanical
    Engineering*, a training manual

Demonstating fire-fighting at Grassmoor Training Centre, Chesterfield, 1982

Retirement day for Irving Halle and me, 1 March 1984

My mother with Teresa and our children, Oonagh and Richard, 1974

Hornsey Historical Society on a weekend visit to Portsmouth in 1991

Leading a local history walk in Muswell Hill, September 1979

My mother celebrating her ninetieth birthday with sons Ernest and me, 1983

Family group with my five granddaughters, 1994

One of the local-history books I have published in retirement

Photographed at home in 2009

My thanks go to Antonia Owen, Simon Smith
and Nick Pearson for their help in the
preparation of this book

'Let me embrace thee, good old Chronicle,
That hast so long walk'd hand in hand with Time.'
William Shakespeare, *Troilus and Cressida*

1

CHILDHOOD

I WAS BORN on 18 August 1923 in the front upstairs bedroom of No. 12 White Road, Stratford, at about one o'clock in the afternoon, during a thunderstorm. My parents named me Kenneth David, and I was to be the second son in a family of four. My brother Ernest Edgar had been born in the same room on 22 November 1920.

White Road led off Vicarage Lane in Stratford, part of the County Borough of West Ham. It was an East London postal district and was sometimes described as being in Metropolitan Essex. There was no longer a vicarage in Vicarage Lane, but the winding road led from Romford Road up to the parish church of All Saints, a surviving medieval building with a long-lost rural past. I was to attend this church very regularly until I was sixteen years old. White Road was part of an estate of terraced houses, each built with a railed forecourt very close to the bay window. The estate had been erected in the late nineteenth century to help accommodate the vast influx of working people needed to serve the railways, docks and factories that had transformed the small Essex hamlets and villages close to the rivers Lea and Thames, five miles east of the City of London.

My father, Edgar Charles Gay, had been born in Stratford like his forebears and had worked all his life for the Post Office, most of it as a sack-carrying postman at the Stratford sorting office. My father worked shifts, sometimes leaving before six in the morning and returning at two in the afternoon and sometimes on a late shift, returning between nine and ten at night. There was a hall stand near the front door where he placed his 'shako' helmet, the headgear postmen wore before the peaked cap came into use in the 1930s. So when my brother and I came home from school, our father was often there to greet us. My mother Clara Jane (née Adams) was always there, too, of course, because in those days most married women did not go out to work.

Do nostalgic memories depend upon places staying the same? Perhaps it is best to hold them in the mind, where they can remain unchanged. When I returned to my childhood street I found that Nos. 2 to 12 had disappeared, cleared away after a wartime bomb had fallen on them. The streetlamps were now electric rather than gas, the metal railings were no longer there, having been removed during the war in a propaganda move to gather metal for the war effort (with little practical value, although it changed the face of London), and the bare, short street was inevitably lined with vehicles – there were none when I was young.

I vividly remember my lost house. When you entered the front door you came into a short corridor, not directly into the front living-room as in many earlier working-class houses. A door on the left led into the front downstairs room, which was the 'best' room, mainly used for visitors or on Sundays. The corridor led into our living-room, in which were a table, where we ate, and chairs. The left-hand wall consisted of two alcoves each side of a kitchen range set under a chimney. The range comprised a black metal oven, heated by a small coal fire. Pots or irons were heated on the oven's flat metal top. The alcove on the left held a cupboard; I kept my toys and books at the bottom of it. The other alcove was occupied by a tall dresser for china. On this we kept a radio, powered by an accumulator.

The window was next to this dresser and looked out on to a yard. A door next to it led down into the scullery, a single-storey rear extension provided with a sink served by a cold-water tap. There was no piped hot water. In the scullery was a built-in brick copper, lit by a fire and filled with water when the washing had to be done, which was always on Mondays. My mother pounded the clothes with a dolly, a copper dome at the end of a wooden handle. In the yard outside the scullery door was an iron mangle with wooden rollers, and I often had to turn the stiff wheel, helping my mother to push the clothes through the rollers to squeeze out the water.

Our scullery back door faced the scullery and window of No. 14 but was screened from it by a tall wooden fence. If you turned right into our yard, you came to the WC situated at the back of the scullery extension. There was no bathroom in the house. (Chamber pots were kept under the beds for night use.) The yard was small, with tiny flowerbeds, and was much frequented by pigeons and sparrows. It contained a wooden shed, and I remember standing on this to watch an airship pass over, probably the ill-fated R101.

On the wooden fence outside the scullery door hung a metal bath which was brought in and placed in front of the kitchen range when we had our weekly dip. Matters improved when Went Ham Borough Council opened the public baths in Romford Road in 1934. These contained not only swimming pools but slipper baths: a line of separate cubicles, each containing a huge bath. The attendant would use his key to turn on the taps so that the bath filled with hot steaming water enabling one to stretch full out. It became the custom for my father to take my brother and myself there each week.

A latched door in our living-room led up a short staircase to a small landing and the two bedrooms. My parents had the front one and my brother and I the back one. The space under the stairs was used to store a pram or a pushchair. Some nights after we had gone to bed my brother and I would creep down the stairs to listen to the radio from the other side of the living-room door. The floor of the living room was covered with linoleum and rugs. We had gas lighting, the amount of light from the mantle being controlled by little chains. It was a soft comforting light without the brilliance of electricity, to which we changed when a cable was laid along the street, in about 1933.

My mother cooked on a gas stove in the scullery as well as using the range. She was a good cook and served the old-fashioned meals that my father liked, such as joints with vegetables and heavy puddings to follow, although an egg custard dish was also his favourite. Nothing was wasted and sometimes I had dripping in a bread sandwich and I was also allowed to suck the marrow out of the bones. There was no fridge, so shopping was frequent, and in hot weather perishables were stored in a zinc-grated wooden box that kept away any flies that had escaped the sticky flypaper hanging from the ceiling.

My mother would fill a large earthenware pot with eggs when they were cheap in summer, preserving them for the winter with a substance called waterglass. A sewing machine, operated by a treadle, stood in the living-room. Here my mother would mend and make clothes, altering my brother's shirts when he had grown out of them so they would fit me. In short our family lived a way of life lived by millions of others; it was a typical British working-class home of the 1920s and 1930s. Of course, as a boy I never looked upon myself as being working-class. I had shelter, food and entertainment and lived among respectable people and not in poverty, my father always being in work and the local authority providing me with a good education and other services. Disparities between my upbringing and that of others were only to be recognised later on.

In searching back for my earliest recollections I have uncovered little cameos from the past, long forgotten. They come like free-floating and coloured balloons not tethered to date or day. How old was I when that happened? It seems impossible ever to know. And with what intensity did I live that experience? With far more feeling than now. The anxieties and miseries of childhood seem trivial decades later as one grows older and puts them into perspective. I remember thinking as a child that adults seemed to live in a completely different world and not understand us, and I promised that when I grew up I would remember what children thought; of course I never did. Nothing is more easily lost than the child's point of view.

Perhaps my first recollection is of sitting in a high chair and turning a plate over my head – but only, I think, because in later years my parents often reminded me of it. I recall being carried home by my father up a long gas-lit road after a visit to my grandparents. He wore a black-and-white herringbone overcoat, and I particularly remember it because of the fuss that was made when it was discovered that I had trod in something and it had been transferred from my shoe to his coat during the journey.

I remember being ill with an infectious disease and being sent to a fever hospital. I think I had scarlet fever and had to be isolated. Perhaps I was five years old, because my mother later told me that when I went to school I contracted all the illnesses, such as mumps, measles and whooping cough, and had my tonsils taken out. While I was at this strange hospital I was walking in a crocodile of children near some woods when a tree suddenly fell. On another occasion we raced across a field to watch a train go by, and sometimes we sat at tables playing with big, old wooden toys. My worst memory of that time is of being made, like others, to stand on a chair in the dormitory with a urine-stained sheet over my head because I had wet my bed. It seemed very unjust: I had not intended to wet the bed and never did so at home.

I vividly recall the toy soldiers and other playthings I kept at the bottom of the kitchen cupboard and playing in the street with some of them, such as a top and marbles, throwing cigarette cards and comparing my soldiers with another boy's on the doorstep of his house near by. *Alice in Wonderland* was the first book I was able to read all on my own, without assistance. I remember its details to this day, probably because I read it so many times – those little songs, the jokes and strange characters still linger in my mind.

I must have been about eight years old when I was taken by my mother to join the public library which stood near by in Romford Road. I was given a junior ticket, and I selected a book about Dr Dolittle by Hugh Lofting. The library, which I was to use so much, was part of a grand Edwardian building that also contained a college and the Passmore Edwards Museum with its intriguing showcases. My father had joined the library there in 1898 when the building opened, and books were borrowed by using a display board not by open access.

Living near the library was a great childhood blessing. I began by steadily working my way through the junior section, which seemed stuffed with books about boys in public boarding-schools, whose way of life – if the fiction gave a true impression – I became familiar with. Talbot Baines Reed was a particularly prolific author, with books such as *The Willoughby Captains*, *Master of the Shell*, *Tom, Dick and Harry*, and *The Adventures of a Three Guinea Watch*, and there was also Frank Richards and the world of Greyfriars School, better known through comics. I also came across Captain Marryat's adventure stories, W.E. Johns, F.E. Anstey and the usual classics, such as *Tom Brown's Schooldays*, *Little Lord Fauntleroy*, *The Swiss Family Robinson* and *The Water Babies*, as well as *Eric, or Little by Little*. In time I crept surreptitiously, feeling guilty, around the end bay of the junior section and browsed the nearest adult shelves which contained huge bound volumes of *Strand* magazine. In due course I had an adult ticket, and I moved on to Zane Grey and the Wild West, Leslie Charteris and the Saint, Agatha Christie and the orange covers of the Crime Club volumes and humorists such as A.A. Armstrong, A.P. Herbert, W.W. Jacob and Stephen Leacock.

Of course I cannot forget the day, a few weeks after my fifth birthday, when I was taken by my mother to school for the first time. This was Park Elementary, a huge board school built in 1889 in the architectural style devised to meet the needs of compulsory education. It was ten minutes' walk away in Ham Park Road. I approached with trepidation and nervousness – and what a relief it was for me when we discovered that they had too many children to take in on that first day, and that I had to come back a few days later. When I returned I had lost my fear, as I knew what to expect.

At school I joined a mixed infants class. This was in a huge room divided into two by a blue striped curtain with a class on each side. The room was heated by an open fire protected by a wire fire-guard. Here I made my first efforts at reading, writing and adding up, and here, too, I first became aware that girls could be beautiful. There was a girl of my own age who sat in the front row and who had golden hair in plaits, which were a lovely sight.

From ages five to eleven I progressed from form to form, each with a different teacher for the year. One painful memory is when a teacher stopped next to me when we were singing together as a class and asked me if I minded listening to the others instead. I have always loved singing but I cannot sing in tune. However, I still recall with pleasure a song that Mr Woodward taught us with the lines 'over the meadows, over the plains whispers the music and whispers again'. It was Mr Woodward who took us out into West Ham Park, opposite the school, and told us the names of the different trees. In break times we raced and chased in the playground and bought home-made sweets from a gypsy-like woman who hovered the other side of the railings holding a wicker basket of goodies. On the way home, we bought water ices from an Italian ice-cream vendor who pitched his barrow by the park.

With school came new friendships. My chief one was with a boy called George Green. It was a proud day when my mother let me go, aged about eight, round to his house to spend Saturday morning with him. This meant I had to cross busy West Ham Lane with its trams on my own to reach Widdin Street. George was a studious boy who had a chemistry set and a model steam engine and was a great one for inventing things. He was the youngest of the family, and his brothers and sisters seemed enormous to me. One occasion I particularly remember was a Guy Fawkes night when his mother came crying into the house because she had burned her hand letting off a firework.

The front room of their house, which was identical to mine, contained a gramophone player, a pouffe and a shelf of books, one of which was Jack London's *Call of the Wild*. Poor George developed a chest complaint and was sent to an open-air school in Essex. I remember him telling me that it was so cold that the ink froze in the inkwells. He did not sit the examination for secondary school, and we lost touch.

Otherwise my friends were those I played with in the street. West

Ham Park was near, but we rarely went there because there were no concrete patches and walls suitable for bouncing balls. We would gather in a gang in the road playing Cowboys and Indians, soldiers, leap-frogging, skipping, swinging around the lamppost and the like. At that time I had a pedal car, which I rode up and down the pavement. The wooden steering wheel had come off, but the car could be steered by using the three metal spikes that once had held the wheel. One of our games was to pedal or to be pushed into the lamppost. Great laughter all round. One day a passing horse and cart dropped a horse's nosebag and I found that this made a good cushion for my car seat. But, as a result, when I drove the car into the lamppost my knee was higher than usual and one of the metal spikes drove itself deeply into my leg. My mother said she vividly remembered examining the wound and seeing the bone. I was carried to Queen Mary's Hospital in West Ham Lane, where the injury was stitched up. She later told me that I had been left with a large scar because the stitches had been taken out too soon.

Motor vehicles were not often seen in our road, although a postman my father worked with sometimes called on his motor cycle and sidecar, a form of transport I now rarely see, if at all. So there was no problem when we had a street party for King George V's Jubilee and later for King George VI's coronation. Tables were laid out in the middle of the street, and we all sat round it for a meal, followed by songs such as 'Knees Up Mother Brown', aided by a piano brought out of one of the houses. There were no parked cars to get in the way.

Horse carts and handcarts were commonly used and any horse dung was quickly gathered up by gardeners off the road. Coal carts came round, and in the summer council water carts arrived to spray the dusty streets, their tanks being filled up again from tall standpipes positioned by the pavement kerb. Refuse collection was by cart, also drawn by horses. The gas lighter, with his long pole for turning on and off the street gas lamps, came round by bicycle; itinerant traders, such as a muffin seller, walked on foot. Some men would sing in the street and hold out a cap for coins, making their way around the various neighbourhoods as a way of dealing with unemployment and poverty.

The milk came by handcart. You hung a metal can on a hook high up on your front door frame, and the milkman took this, filled it from the churn on his cart and replaced it on the hook. If my mother ran out of milk she would sometimes send me to a yard in Vicarage Lane where a cow was kept. I would enter the yard, walk up wooden steps to a gallery and a woman would sell me milk fresh from the cow, using the jug I had brought. This yard escaped war damage but was swept away later by the planners.

Livestock was slaughtered by butchers in their backyards. One such place stood in Vicarage Lane opposite the end of White Road. On one terrifying day of my childhood a cow or bullock escaped and ran down our road, galloping along the pavement while I swiftly sheltered in my house doorway.

I was quite often out on the streets where a favourite occupation was roller-skating. Skates cost five shillings a pair, quite a lot of money for us. But soon I was skating around neighbouring streets seeking out those with the smoothest tarmac surface.

When I was home from school at the dinner hour I would sometimes be sent by my mother to the shops in Vicarage Lane. This usually took me to the Co-op, and here you stood in a crowd at the counter waiting your turn to be served. How annoyed I would be when a woman who had come in after me got served first, as it was more of a rush to get back to school in time. Serving was sometimes a long process; butter was taken off a mound, moulded into a block and weighed; cheese was sliced off a huge piece using a wire cutter. Weighing and packaging were an important part of a grocer's trade. I would rush back home hoping my mother had cooked my hot meal so that I could walk back for afternoon lessons without being penalised.

We would often do our main shopping as a family on a Saturday evening. This meant walking the ten minutes or so to Stratford Broadway where on the north side stalls clustered along the kerb selling produce of all kinds. We would go towards the end of the day because prices came down then, as stallholders were anxious to get rid of their meat, fruit and vegetables while they were still fresh. Behind these stalls were the chain stores, Woolworth's, Marks and Spencer and British Home Stores. To the east were the local department stores of J.R. Roberts and Boardman's as well as the Co-op; indeed, the headquarters of the London Co-operative Society was in Stratford. From the Broadway a narrow street called Angel Lane formed a shopping core and was lined with stalls selling every kind of produce from cat's meat to leather belts. On a Saturday night the Broadway and Angel Lane were bright with light from the acetylene lights or naphtha flares used by the stallholders.

Angel Lane was a very East End sort of place with an old court-yard of slum-like houses. Near the top end was the Theatre Royal, a Victorian building made famous in the post-war period by Joan Littlewood who, with Gerry Raffles, brought new playwrights such as Brendan Behan on to the London scene. My father told us how, as a young man in the Edwardian period, he had visited it to see shows such as *Sweeney Todd, the Demon Barber*.

On Sundays no shops opened and, as far as our family was concerned, Victorian values dominated. We did not play in the street. Either in the morning or the evening we went to church as a family of four, wearing our best clothes. We entered from Church Street through the long porch that stretched to the south door. In the afternoon was Sunday school.

When I look back I realise what a mark this religious upbringing made upon me. With a God-fearing, Victorian father occupied in church work, regular attendance at church and Sunday school lead-ing to confirmation as an Anglican, I absorbed the Christian ethic, especially the tenets of the Sermon on the Mount and the doctrine to love God and your neighbour. These moral messages were made powerful by the beauty of the language, as the cadences of the Jacobean Holy Bible sounded in my ears Sunday after Sunday. It was great prose that came close to poetry, and, without being conscious of it, listening to it made me aware of what the English language could achieve and made me love the sheer sound of words. It saddens me that in most churches this beautiful prose is no longer spoken. Religion is, after all, a form of magic; it lives in the world of the inexplicable, and the old Bible language, companion to Prospero and Hamlet in its power to enter common parlance, carried this magic forward and worked on the emotions of the listener.

I owed this to my father, and perhaps I should speak of him and his background at this point. After all, it is your parents who make you what you are – as Philip Larkin bitterly expressed in his famous line. Or perhaps they set their mark from which you move away as you become your own person. A child loves his parents but learns later to look at them with a more dispassionate eye in an attempt to understand them.

My father was a man of average height, about five feet nine inches, my own height now. He was of slim build, with ginger hair and a hollow kind of face that I was to see later in life replicated in a stranger I spied in a North German street. He was an emotional man with a great deal of nervous energy and a charisma that came across when he preached. When I was small my father was chosen to play Christian in a church production of Bunyan's *Pilgrim's Progress*. The professional producer brought in praised the way be transmitted strong emotion and said he had the qualities of a good actor.

He was a man of intelligence who could not use it in his manual work and so had found an outlet in church work, running a youth club, qualifying as a lay-preacher and writing sermons. He had inherited a trait, common in the Gay family, of being able to talk fluently and emotionally, often reducing others to silence. He always spoke in a Cockney accent and had trouble sounding the letter 'H' in the right place. He loved books and reading, mostly works of moral character.

Despite his persuasive charm there was a morbid side to him. He seemed to turn his emotions inwards. He was a nervous man, fearful of what might happen. If he found two knives crossed on the table he took it as a sign of trouble. When he felt he was ageing hetold us that 'it was the beginning of the end'. He suffered from an occasional tremble or shudder and would awake from sleep with a start. He would make mumbling noises as a sort of nervous expression. When we paddled in the sea on holiday he would suddenly grip my arm, fearful of the wide open space of sea and sky. He could not go up ladders or stand heights. He became a hypochondriac, visiting the doctor frequently, consuming pills and imagining all sorts of things wrong with him. After his death boxes of pills were found hidden in a cupboard. His health was not helped by his practice of rolling cigarettes and smoking. But he lived until he was seventy-eight years old. And of course I loved him.

My father's family lived in Stratford for several generations. My great-grandfather was named Isaac Gay. He was born in 1824 in Norwich and died in 1878. He married an Elizabeth Johnson who lived from 1818 until 1913. They were residents in the Essex parish of West Ham, which in the first half of the nineteenth century was still mainly a rural parish, although the nearby River Lea had always been the location for water mills and for silk, calico and other trades.

Change came in the 1850s when the Stratford railway works and neighbouring Hudson, later Stratford, New Town was established by that dodgy railway entrepreneur George Hudson. At the same time the Victoria Docks were built by the Thames in the south, to be followed a few decades later by the Albert Docks, transforming the marshy area. Owing to prevailing westerly winds that carry noxious fumes eastwards, London's unpleasant industries have mainly been established on the east side of the city. As London expanded in the nineteenth century, becoming the greatest manufacturing city in Britain, so West Ham, five miles east of the City, became full of chemical and food-processing factories. The smell of the chemical factories is a pungent memory from my early years.

To accommodate the labour needed for these factories, railways and docks, some 40,000 houses were built between 1840 and 1914. They were mainly for letting to working-class tenants, although on a northern fringe, close to the Romford Road, some better-class housing was developed, catering for doctors, lawyers and clerks who worked either locally or in the City. As my great-grandfather Isaac aged, the West Ham he knew thus changed from a rural area into a seaport and a great manufacturing centre. A population of 12,738 in 1841 rose to 289,030 by 1911, helping to earn West Ham the status of a borough in 1886 and a county borough in 1889. The Gays were no longer to be country bumpkins but Cockneys.

One distinctive aspect of this community, differentiating it from similar working-class areas, was that it was a fairly self-contained place with people mainly both living and working within the county borough; this led to a certain pride in being a West Hammer, eventually with its own First Division football team. By all accounts West Ham became a respectable working-class community with only isolated spots of dire poverty and crime, its ethos determined by Victorian morality. Isaac and his wife Elizabeth were typical Victorians with six children. He was a policeman and probably of the same determined character as his heirs. My mother always used to say that the Gays were 'think-me's', that is, they were people who had a fairly high opinion of themselves and liked to get their own way – and especially enjoyed the sound of their own voice!

This love of words was probably the most notable family characteristic. Isaac's eldest child, Walter, became a Nonconformist minister and doubtless enjoyed giving sermons, although my father could tell me little about this uncle of his as he moved away. Isaac's next child, Arthur, born in 1855, was my grandfather. Next to be born, in 1857, was Ernest, who married, became a persuasive insurance agent with his golden tongue and on his death, despite living in a poor street in Stratford, left a large fortune. Isaac's and Elizabeth's one girl was called Henrietta; she married and had five children. Then came Alfred, whose only child was killed in 1917, and finally Albert, born in 1864, who was to become a local teacher, headmaster of Abbey Mills School and a Municipal Reform Party councillor in West Ham. He was known for his philanthropy, donating shoes for barefooted children in his school and endowing a bed at Whipps Cross Hospital. In the 1970s a road near his former school was named after him; he was headmaster there for twenty-nine years.

My father's father, Arthur Gay, whom I never met, was the least successful of Isaac's sons, but as he died comparatively young perhaps it is not fair to judge. According to my father, he, too, was a very good talker. He became a shipping foreman in the London and India Docks, where be spent his hours in huge unheated warehouses guarding stock and accounting for it. Some winter nights, my father said, he came home so cold that his wife had to thaw out his beard; getting warm sometimes took over an hour. Because the ink sometimes froze in the inkwells at his work it was made acceptable in law for indelible pencils to be used for records. Continuous cold finally led to Arthur developing Bright's disease, from which he died, compounded by pneumonia, in 1899 when my father was eleven years old.

Arthur's early death brought the usual problems. He had married in 1879 when he was twenty-four to a Forest Gate girl called Harriet Clark, daughter of a bricklayer who lived in Upton Lane, Forest Gate. His death left his widow with responsibility for bringing up their four children alone, although George, the eldest, born 1881, was eighteen when his father died. The second child, Albert, had been born in 1887 and was twelve, while my father, born in 1888, was eleven. The youngest child, Edith, was born in 1893 and so was only six years old.

I remember my father often telling me of the hard times his mother had after her husband died. To make a home and to earn a living she became a washerwoman, taking in sheets, collars, shirts and other laundry from the more well-to-do local residents, such as the doctor. She worked at home in Hotham Street or neighbouring streets to which they moved, rented accommodation near Stratford Bridge fruit-and-vegetable wholesale market at the western end of Stratford High Road. My father told me he carried washing for his mother from the age of eleven until he was twenty-six. She died when he was thirty-one in 1919. George had begun to work in the Post Office, but after he married and had a family he was not in a position to help very much with money, his first child being born in 1904. Albert, meanwhile, had various jobs, eventually becoming a furniture restorer in nearby Hackney. He was a gambler and a bit of a lad. He was to marry twice but to die at the age of thirty-two, the same year as his mother. Very little was said at home when I was a child about Albert, although occasionally there was a visit by his son, whom I think lived in a home as a result of his uncontrollable epilepsy. These matters were not discussed in front of the children.

My father and his sister, my aunt Edie, grew closer because as the two youngest they were most affected by their father's death. They looked after each other in difficult years. Edie went into domestic service and married William Parrish, a railwayman known to me as Uncle Bill. Aunt Edie used to tower over Uncle Bill as he was rather short. He served in the war, where he was wounded and had, I was told as a boy, a hole in his leg. I was always curious about this but was never shown it. Bill looked after the maintenance of local railway signals and was typically Victorian in his attitude to life, holding a very moral attitude about behaviour.

When my father was fourteen he was able to leave Bridge Road state school and gain employment to help with the family income. He followed his brother into the Post Office and started as a messenger boy at seven shillings a week at Whitechapel. After this he did two years' service as a postman in the City of London, a period in Plaistow and then began his long period of work at Stratford, based at Martin Street sorting office near Angel Lane.

Promotion in the Post Office went by length of service, and it was 1943 before my father was promoted, retiring as an overseer. This was on 11 June 1949 after forty-seven years' service, for which he was given an Imperial Service Medal for his work in Crown service. My father stayed with the Post Office because of the security of employment it offered, especially in the Depression years between the wars. When I was at an impressionable age he urged me to follow his example and to obtain a secure, pensionable job. I must have inherited his desire for security, for I did indeed follow his example and worked for one employer for most of my working life.

For most of his working career my father walked the Stratford streets carrying on his shoulders a heavy canvas sack containing the mail he had to deliver. In consequence he developed strong arm and leg muscles. For a long time my father's patch, called his 'walk', was the Manbey Grove area near Maryland Point. He seems to have got on with the people he encountered and was known as the 'friendly postman', even being featured as such in a local Salvation Army newspaper. No doubt it gave him plenty of opportunities to develop his love of talking.

He was twenty-five when the First World War broke out. Having a widowed mother to support, he did not volunteer, and when conscription was introduced in 1916 he was in a reserved occupation. But this changed, and in 1917 he was finally called up, reaching France early in 1918 at the age of twenty-nine. He served in the Post Office Rifles and was a good shot. But he feared being sent out as a sniper because of the high mortality rate. When the time came for his company to move into the front line he was seriously ill with pneumonia and hospitalised. This probably saved his life, as most of his companions were killed. Occasionally I remind my son and daughter that they, like myself, only exist because their grandfather had pneumonia in the First World War and because their father missed death by German bombs in the Second World War. By such thin threads of chance do lives come into being.

His time in France after the war was over, for demobilisation was not immediate, was one of the best of his life, he told me. His unit was based in Normandy at Doullens, south of Caen, and here he drank red wine, played billiards (at which he was always a good player) and assisted the company barber. Some years later, he had a reunion with this fellow serviceman. In the 1930s we once were on holiday at Gorleston on the east coast when my father took us into Norwich and made us wait outside while he went into a barber's shop. He sat down and asked for a haircut. The barber stopped snipping and turned round. 'You're Eddie Gay, aren't you?' He had recognised what he used to call my father's 'Kraut' or German head with his ginger hair. The man shut up shop and spent the day with us showing us Norwich and introducing to people his wartime friend and his family.

It was while he was delivering mail in Plaistow, in Caistor Park Road, where my mother lived with her family, that her eye was caught by the slim, red-headed postman with a talent for chat, and a romance began. They decided upon marriage in 1918 while my father was in the Army because, so my mother used to say, it enabled the granting of an extra pay allowance that could be used to help my father's mother. My mother told us this in an ambiguous way, making me wonder if she had married largely to help her future mother-in-law.

My father and mother were church-going people. They married, had two sons and remained together – divorce being a shameful thing that was talked about in hushed voices. But, although they were generally loving towards one another, my parents clashed and quarrelled frequently, both being determined people. My father was a sentimental man with old-fashioned ideas about matrimony in which the wife was submissive and the man was in charge. My mother, a quick-witted and intelligent woman, would never fit placidly into this role, being a bit of a tomboy in her upbringing and possessing sturdy common sense and an enquiring mind. So, as I grew up, they argued, and sometimes my father would lose his temper and say strong words. Loving both of them, I was torn between the two of them and hated such situations.

When I look at her photograph, taken in her twenties, my mother seems an attractive woman. Born in 1893, she lived until 1987, her long life due, I think, to the sturdy genes she inherited from her family. Her father, Emmanuel David Adams, was born in May 1865 in Crowborough in Sussex, where the Adams family had been farmers, foresters, carpenters and coachmen in that wooded area. Paul Adams contacted me in the 1990s, and his research into family history traced the Adams family back in a continuous line to the early 1600s. I am no expert in genetics, but perhaps the stock was refined over this long agricultural period to produced a healthy line; my brother and I are now both in our mid-eighties and in good health.

In 1889, when he was twenty-four, my maternal grandfather married Edith Clara Capon, daughter of a cabman in Maidstone. By then he was a railway porter, as he and one of his brothers had decided to make a career on the railways, which in late Victorian times offered a reliable job and respect. He was employed by the London, Tilbury and Southend Railway Company, and he and his wife and four children were to live in different Essex places according to his posting, including Grays, where my mother was born, Little Thurrock, Tilbury Docks, Shoeburyness and finally Plaistow (in West Ham), where he was station-master. My grandfather had ten brothers and a sister, many with biblical names. A local history book about Crowborough has a photo of a Nimrod Adams working on Adams farm. Paul Adams, who contacted me from Bristol, is a grandson of Nimrod.

These sturdy qualities, and a tradition of working with wood, were passed on to Emmanuel's children. Albert and Archibald initially trained as carpenters, and this practical ability and the Adams physical appearance were especially inherited by my brother, always seen in the family as an Adams, although of course his intelligence and talking capacity derived from his father as well as his mother. I, too, feel I am an amalgam of both my parents, taking from him the expression of emotion through writing and speech and from her, perhaps more fortunately, a sense of independence and common sense – the latter, in my view, more important that mere intelligence.

As a child I was often taken to see my mother's parents, who lived at 9 Caistor Park Road, now demolished, a house conveniently close to Plaistow railway station where my grandfather worked. It was a Victorian house, lit by gas, hung with pictures, with the front-room fireplace lined with a curtained top with bobbins along the edge; above it was a large wooden overmantel filled with ornaments. A cover over the round table dropped to the floor hiding the table legs. There was a piano, a Victorian scrapbook in which colourful pictures were carefully pasted, and a glass dome ornament covering a stuffed bird. The beds had brass knobs.

My grandfather was a well-built man who sported a watch and chain across his waistcoat. I remember his wife as a diminutive figure dressed in black, looking like Queen Victoria. We gathered as a family on Boxing Day when Uncle Albert would be there with my three cousins and sometimes Uncle Archie. My grandfather would play the piano, and we would have to join in, usually favourite old songs such as 'Sweet Lass of Richmond Hill' and 'Hearts of Oak'. My grandfather also played a concertina. My Uncle Albert dressed up as Father Christmas for the five children. I always believed in Father Christmas until one year my cousin Vera said she recognised her father's boots. But who could deny that receiving Christmas presents was a pleasure?

In the scullery, beyond the kitchen my grandfather would set up his magic lantern and show huge glass slides, mainly scenes of foreign lands. Radio was then in its infancy and I recall his crystal set on which you tinkered with a wire on the crystal to pick up broadcasts. Later here he had a proper set and I remember Children's Hour and plays by L. Du Garde Peach. My brother and I were taken by my grandfather to the railway station and shown round; we climbed up the signal box outside stairs to see the signalman at work. By then the railway was part of the London Midland and Scottish Railway.

In the summer my grandfather sat outside under his lilac tree, puffing away at his pipe and contemplating the world. Wire runs in the garden contained his chickens, and there was a dog kennel for Flossie, a Manchester terrier we adopted when they passed away. My grandmother died first, in October 1931, and my grandfather in January 1932. Diabetes had taken hold, and although his gangrenous leg was amputated in Whipps Cross Hospital he was to die there.

Emmanuel's four children were Albert, Edith, Clara Jane (my mother) and Archibald. Trained as a carpenter, Albert had been called up in the First World War and stationed in Stoke-on-Trent, where he met his future wife, my Aunt Lizzie. He became a carriage builder for the Underground, and when the works were transferred from Barking in Essex to Acton he moved into an inter-war house in Hounslow. At work he rose to be in charge of a design office. His eldest child, Vera, was about the same age as my brother, his son Donald was about my age and his last, Leah, a few years younger. Practically all my life as a Londoner I have travelled on the Underground (colloquially known as the tube), and I suppose this began as a child when I was taken to visit Uncle Albert. This was made easier when, in 1933, the Piccadilly Line was extended to Hounslow West and later, after the Second World War, all the way to Heathrow. Most of the journey was on the District Line, and as a boy I was fascinated by the hand-operated sliding doors to the carriages; often these were left open and you looked out at the speeding wall of the tunnel with its cables and fixtures. Such indifference to safety would be unthinkable today.

My mother's sister Edith, known as Aunt Cis, lived in Maidstone, and visits were less frequent. Cis had gone into domestic service and would give me advice on the order in which cutlery and china should be washed. Cis's first husband had been killed in the First World War, but she was married again, to Albert Broomfield, my Uncle Bert. He had been brought up in the Medway village of Aylesford and had become a regular cavalry soldier in the Kings Dragoon Guards, serving on the North-West Frontier in India and in an Afghan war. I still have his medals.

Uncle Bert married my aunt on discharge and worked in Maidstone as a builder's labourer. He was proud that, through a mortgage, he had become the owner of a fine semi-detached 1920s' house just off Buckland Lane on the north-east side of Maidstone. His sizeable plot on a corner was almost exclusively used for growing vegetables, with the house bordered by apple trees. In those days the area was hardly built up and we used to walk down the lane, close by Allington Castle, to the nearby River Medway and the Malta, then a small pub. We passed apple and pear orchards and hop kilns and saw wild flowers everywhere.

During the bombing it was a good place to take a break or stay for a short holiday. My Uncle Bert was a quiet man and said little in company but when reprimanded by his wife , had a gift for witty repartee that always amused my father, perhaps more so because of his own verbal battles with my mother.

My Uncle Archie was less often seen, but he sometimes came to our house for family gatherings. Born in 1900 Uncle Archie had trained as a carpenter but was conscripted as a young man into the war. At the end, without a job, his family advised him to stay on in the Army. He married a girl whom everybody liked, but she and her child died in childbirth. He was a handsome, likeable man who seemed to have girlfriends my family did not want to talk about, although he did later get married for a second time to a woman called Billie. He rose to be a captain and was stationed in Egypt and Malta. At the outbreak of the Second World War he went with the Army to France and, as an officer, spent several days with his men on the Dunkirk beaches. When he visited us after the war he told us that when he got back to England he slept without a break for twenty-four hours and his hair turned white. He died of asthma in his fifties.

Apart from visiting relatives our family did little travelling other than for my father's paid fortnight's holiday, usually taken in late August. Southend, Westcliff, Ramsgate, Gorleston and Folkestone were the chosen resorts, often for two years running, always staying in boarding-houses. Sometimes my parents would take us on tram journeys to places like Purley or on the bus into the City or into the West End. One evening we went to Westminster Hall where we queued for a long time before seeing the late George V lying in state, his coffin guarded by soldiers. We also attended his funeral, standing by Green Park in Piccadilly in January 1936 to watch the procession, with the late king's sons walking behind the hearse. I have always been grateful to the policeman who allowed me to slip through the crowd and stand at the front for a better view. Two of those royal sons were to be kings, but I cannot rival my father who boasted of living under six monarchs, Victoria, Edward VII, George V, Edward VIII, George VI and Elizabeth II.

My only time away from home on my own was to Woolacombe in Devon with the cubs. I enjoyed cub activities as an eight-year-old, learning such skills as tying knots or signalling with flags, with the evening rounded off by readings by the cub leader of the *Just So* stories by Kipling. At Woolacombe we stayed in a big rambling house with each room full of beds. One day on the beach the leader asked if I would like to learn to swim. I perplexed him by saying no . Later on I was to learn to swim with the school at West Ham Baths, and it is the one participant sport (apart from rowing) that has really appealed to me. Another memory of the holiday was passing a shop with a tray outside full of the 'William' books by Richmal Crompton, an author I was reading avidly. I longed to buy all the books on display.

My brother had also been away with the cubs, to Swanage, but I did not follow him into the scouts. The meetings were held in Meeson Hall, a gaunt building not far from the church. I remember seeing a long procession of men walking one evening along the Portway. I was told afterwards that they were unemployed, trying like those on the famous march from Jarrow to draw attention to their plight. My brother and I both had piano lessons. Most homes had a piano, popular form of entertainment in the 1920s before the radio became dominant. My father could play and both my parents could sing, but we were not a particularly musical household. Possibly one reason children were given lessons was that music could be a way out of poverty for those with especial talent. For two years we each attended a weekly lesson with a Miss Duckenfield, but I found I had clumsy fingers and no aptitude. My brother and I gave up. My most vivid memory of those lessons is of sitting in Miss Duckenfield's house, aged eight, enjoying the comics and magazines, especially *Film Fun*, which she left there for her youngest students to peruse while waiting for their tuition.

Apart from reading, cinema-going was to become a great enthusiasm of boyhood, extending into adult life. It can be very addictive. I remember sitting on my mother's lap when first taken and bawling aloud at the moving images, but I must have been very young. Regular cinema-going started with Saturday-morning shows. George Green and I would walk down to Plaistow to a 'bug hutch', as we called it, which stood opposite the Jeyes Fluid factory. We paid fourpence. Usherettes would spray us with what must have been Jeyes Fluid, a common practice then. Small boys would crawl under the seats chalking shoes. Oranges were peeled and objects thrown, and the row from the audience as the film proceeded was often tremendous. There were cowboy films with heroes such as Tom Mix and Gene Autry triumphing over the baddies. Serials with cliff-hanger endings were shown, luring us to return next week. Eventually we moved on from children's Saturday-morning films to general shows, and while at secondary school I would go two or three times a week. In those days programmes were continuous so that you could enter halfway through a film and stay until it was shown again and you reached the part where you had come in. There were always two films the B film was often the most enjoyable.

One special occasion was a show for the borough's schoolchildren laid on at cinemas near the schools. This was to mark the Jubilee in 1936 of the incorporation of West Ham as a borough. When we left the cinema, we were each given an orange by none other than George Lansbury, the famous Labour politician and pacifist who held the Labour Party leadership before Clement Attlee. We were also handed a small white envelope, suitably inscribed, containing a sixpenny piece. This I still retain, along with two similar small envelopes, one commemorating the Silver Jubilee of King George V in 1935 and the other the Coronation of King George VI in 1937. Even Labour councils were stalwartly loyalist in those days of the Depression, it would seem.

The Labour council also believed in education, and, although I did not know it at the time, I took an educational step which was to lead me eventually to university. I took a school examination commonly referred to as the 'eleven plus', although I was only ten when I sat it. My parents were as surprised as I when I passed. I think they had written me off as a nice boy who was not as bright as his elder brother. They were right in this, but I think they had not yet appreciated how exceptionally bright my brother Ernie was; he would skip a year at school and gain distinctions in all subjects when he took his final examinations at the age of sixteen. He seemed capable of accomplishing any task, mental or manual, and he overawed with his powerful personality.

I attended West Ham Municipal Secondary School in Tennyson

Road, Stratford, which was the grammar school serving the north of the borough (Plaistow School served the south). It was made possible for my brother and me by bursary payments that covered our uniform and other costs. The varied curriculum included English grammar, English literature, Latin, French, mathematics, physics, chemistry, biology, history, geography, music and woodwork, and there were numerous sessions spent in the school gym. So on a Monday morning in September 1934 I turned right instead of left when I left my White Road house and began what was to be seven years' study at my new school. Although my father was in a manual job paying just three pounds ten shillings a week, out of which he had to pay ten shillings a week rent for our White Road house as well as feed and clothe a family of four, he was able to provide me with a background of literacy as he sat composing his sermons as a lay preacher. My father liked books, although financial restrictions meant he could buy few, but I was able to browse in the next few years, before war broke out, among his Victorian volumes and in particular his collected edition of Charles Dickens, obtained cheaply through an offer by a national newspaper – part of a circulation war. I steadily read through much of Dickens before I was sixteen. Another favourite was Jerome K. Jerome's *Three Men in a Boat*, which my brother and I read with great delight; apart from my beloved 'William' volumes it was the first book that really made me laugh out loud. Commissioned as a Victorian guidebook to the Thames it contained, along with unforgettable humour, a streak of sentimentality to which I found myself sympathetic and which stayed with me in my outlook. Or perhaps I imbibed sentimentality from my father.

The year 1935 brought changes for us in the shape of a Dickensian-type legacy. One Sunday morning in March I was sitting in our armchair in our small living-room looking at *The People* newspaper while my parents and brother finished their breakfast. I pointed out to them that on the front page was a story about an east London insurance agent, living in Albion Street, near Stratford Broadway, who had left a personal estate of £111,167 (equivalent to about £5 million today). My father immediately grabbed the paper out of my hands. The newspaper story was about Uncle Ernie, who had died in January, and the prospect of a considerable fortune suddenly loomed into sight, for he had promised his nephew 'Eddie' that he would be 'all right' after his death.

Uncle Ernie was somewhat of a legend when we were growing up. He had given us a large antique Chinese vase – broken after the war by my mother's cat – and according to my father lived in a house containing antiques, books and coins. He would sometimes call on us when he would be given pride of place and dominate the conversation in the usual Gay manner. My father visited him regularly at his house at 9 Albion Street, calling on him on Sundays and attending with him a men's meeting every Sunday afternoon, then going on to Katherine Road chapel in the evening and back to his house. Ernest's wife died in 1931. There were no children. My father would also call on him on Tuesday and Saturday evenings, and he told me that he had learned much from him, especially about insurance.

After acting as a clerk in the Victoria Docks, Uncle Ernie had gone to work for an insurance agent called Mr Bacchus who, as he grew more elderly, arranged for Ernie to take over his agency. On his death Mr Bacchus left Pearl Assurance shares as part of his estate to his wife and three daughters. Mrs Bacchus took to drinking gin, soon got through the money and offered Ernie a chance to buy the shares, which he accepted. These included what my father called 'Pearl Founder' shares, which were the chief source of Ernie's wealth. My father told me that he was a very good insurance agent, having started in the profession when it was comparatively in its infancy. At that time agents got no wages, just commission. Ernie built up his agency so that when he died his 'industrial' book had to be divided among six men. He was a good talker and could persuade anyone of the need for insurance. 'When you heard him, your fingers itched to find the pen to sign,' my father told me.

Now Uncle Ernie was dead, and the will had been published. The executor was his younger brother, Uncle Albert, the councillor, headmaster and Justice of the Peace, who was left to dispose of the estate, which, according to the will, 'should remain in the Gay family'. There were some specific bequests, including £1,000 each to my father and his sister, Aunt Edie. She persuaded Uncle Albert to give £1,000 to the other surviving nephew, my Uncle George, who had not been mentioned. The two nephews and the niece, my father and his brother and sister, waited expectantly for a further share of Uncle Ernie's fortune, perhaps some of the Pearl shares. But nothing came from Uncle Albert who, quite legitimately, saw himself as the chief legatee, although my father argued that the money had been left to the Gay family in general. Uncle Albert did give his surviving sister Henrietta 185 of the 2,400 shares, as I discovered from a note in my mother's handwriting, but none went to the elder Gay brothers, Walter and Alfred, both of whom might well have been deceased, or to their descendants or those of Albert's other brother, Arthur, my long deceased grandfather.

Albert's only child was his daughter Madeline, who was born in 1897. She had married a Stanley Warren, and they had had two children, Alberta and Frederick. These descendants dutifully changed their name by deed poll from Warren to Gay-Warren to meet the provision in the will that the money remain in the Gay family.

In the 1950s I was persuaded to take informal advice about this clause from the legal department at my workplace, and was told that it would have been the subject of great argument if it had gone to court, but of course nobody could afford that at the time. This nearness to fortune soured family feelings and taught me how dangerous money can be to a person's peace of mind. 'Store not treasure up for thyself on earth.' Was it because of this that I have, for most of my life, held seeking money in disregard and never made its attainment my goal, other than to secure a reasonable standard of living for my family? At the time, talk among my father, mother and his siblings was intense, but it eventually faded away. Perhaps my father was influenced by his reading of Dickens's *Bleak House* and the terrible case of *Jarndyce versus Jarndyce* and knew that it would be the lawyers who would benefit. There was, of course, no legal aid in those days.

Although this engendered considerable ill feeling within the family, I believe my great-uncle Albert was a good man of charitable nature who did many useful things in his pedagogic, Nonconformist, chapelgoing life. Perhaps he thought that large sums of money would be too much for two Stratford postmen and their sister to handle. Or perhaps, like most people, he found it difficult to give money away and thought it best to keep it under his control. Others at the time thought that Albert had simply manipulated his brother into making such a will.

Stan Warren, the son-in-law, used to call on us, and we remained on friendly terms. Not long after the war a party was held in a church hall to celebrate Albert's and his wife Agnes's golden wedding anniversary. Physically he appeared short and stout, was soberly dressed and had an air of self-importance, airing his views decisively. His Municipal Reform Party had changed into Conservative, and I had some pleasure later in putting a Labour Party election leaflet through his letter-box with my name as a speaker at a ward meeting. Uncle Albert died in 1950, and his family passed out of our existence. Somewhere or other they are probably still clutching their Pearl Assurance 'Founder' Shares which my great uncle had bought on the cheap from gin-drinking Mrs Bacchus a century or more ago.

My father had his £1,000 if nothing else and did the sensible thing by buying a house for just over £600. This was in Forest Gate, at 77 Upton Avenue, destined to be our family home from 12 November 1936 until my mother, by then widowed and living on her own, died on 27 January 1987 at the age of ninety-three, having lived there for over fifty years. The house was sold, and I have never been back.

Forest Gate was one of the better parts of the County Borough of West Ham. Situated in the north-east corner of the borough, it was close to the open spaces of Wanstead Flats and Wanstead Park and beyond them Woodford and Epping Forest. It contained some quality houses, among them the Woodgrange Estate, built up from 1877, where Uncle Albert had lived. Upton Avenue was further south and adjacent to West Ham Park. In rural times this area had been occupied by private estates, many of them owned by wealthy Quakers. The Gurneys, for example, lived in Ham House, which in due course became West Ham Park, with a cairn and a plaque indicating where the house had stood. The Gurneys helped finance its acquisition by the Corporation of the City of London in 1874 so that open space was secured for the fast-growing local population.

Another Quaker family, which had an estate opposite the Gurneys, was the Listers. Lord Lister the surgeon, who had pioneered antiseptics, lived here in a Georgian mansion built in 1731. When we moved to Upton Avenue a plaque on the wall outside the house indicated that it had been his birthplace. The mansion still stood, used as a vicarage by St Peter's Church. Upton Avenue had been laid out over part of the former Lister estate. The mansion itself survived until 1968. By chance at school I was assigned to a notional Lister 'house'. (The others were Gurney, Fry and Langthorne, the latter a reference to the former Cistercian abbey of Stratford Langthorne, which had also given its name to Langthorne Street in Stratford, where in 1855 my grandfather had been born.) 'We will try, in spite of cramp and blister, to bring the house trophy home to the house of Lister,' we used to sing zealously.

Another surviving eighteenth-century mansion stood at the other end of Upton Avenue, although its former estate was totally built up. It was called the Red House and was used as a clubhouse by the Catholics. Their huge church, St Anthony's, designed by the firm of Pugin and Pugin and built in 1874, towered over us at the Lister end of Upton Avenue. Next to it was a Franciscan friary and then St Bonaventure's, a Catholic boys' school. I was astonished when I first saw the friars in the street, with their brown cassocks and open-toe sandals.

Older still was the Spotted Dog, a pub in nearby Upton Lane, the oldest West Ham building after the parish church, with a history dating back to the sixteenth century. It took its name supposedly from Henry VIII's hunting dog kennels and was used during the seventeenth-century plague years as a refuge by City merchants.

Upton Avenue houses had once accommodated better-off families, some of them with servants. One near neighbour was a Colonel Luscombe. Next door to us at No. 75 were an elderly gentleman and his wife who had to get used to a cockney postman living next door in place of the army major who had sold us the house.

No. 77 was the end-but-one house in a long brick terrace, each with a substantial square double-height bay and inset porched doorway, built in the late nineteenth century. It had three bedrooms, two reception rooms and a rear extension containing a living-room and small kitchen. My brother Ernie and I each had our own bedroom. At last, too, we had an internal bathroom and piped hot water and a WC but no hand basin. In addition there was an outside toilet, useful during gardening and also as a place to keep gardening tools. My brother and I agreed in later life that we had not liked the house very much. It was not as cosy as our previous home. It was without central heating, and I remember freezing in my bedroom in winter.

My brother was now sixteen and was turning into a dark-haired, good-looking young man, sporting plus-four trousers and going out with girls. I recall that one day he acquired a motor cycle, driven straight from the garage as road licences had not yet then been introduced. He was to progress to a small car, still without having to take a test (he is still driving in his eighties). Despite his academic ability he left school at sixteen to be apprenticed to an electrician, as it was the working-class tradition to leave school as soon as legally possible and to start earning a living to help support the family.

In November 1936 I began my longer walk to school, going in a direct line through the middle of West Ham Park (sometimes difficult on days of great London fogs) to the school buildings in Tennyson Road. I returned home for lunch, back to school after lunch and crossed the park yet again to go home at the end of the day. From those years I remember learning in biology classes about all the workings of the human body, the politics of the nineteenth century, how to write an essay and to savour such works as Thackeray's *Henry Esmond, Don Quixote*, the varied works of W.H. Hudson and *Twelfth Night*, plus something of the Greek classics.

The street companionship I had enjoyed in White Road I experienced again in Upton Avenue, despite it being a better-class area. I soon found a motley collection of boys and girls from surrounding streets who met together in a crowd, often near Upton Lane Board School, which took up a portion of Upton Avenue. By this time I was fifteen, and the games had begun to move into the usual direction, with kiss-chase a popular sport. I caught the eye, as a new boy, of a lively older cockney girl who was a sort of gang leader. She called me 'her little bit of meat' and gave me my first kiss, in order, she said, to show me how to do it. She must have already turned sixteen, worked in the nearby sub-post office and was to get married barely a year or so later.

Do girls mature earlier than boys? I was still very immature but was made a useful recruit by two girls, Lily and Margaret, who decided one evening to spend their time on a prolonged kissing session for which I and another boy were recruited. This meant changing partners, turn and turn about. In the end we all just walked home and remembered it as a happy evening. In those days sex behaviour did not seem as rampant as it appears to be today, although perhaps I was just too innocent to see it. Apart from what I learned in biology, I never received any formal sex education; certainly my parents never addressed the subject.

I never teamed up with one particular girl and still found my main companionship with boys. Gordon lived opposite, and with him I shared a new passion of making model aeroplanes. These were either carved out of balsa wood or constructed out of thin strips of balsa wood and covered with Japanese paper. A rubber band was inserted to power the propeller that we carved out of a block of balsa wood. We would go up to the flat open landscape of Wanstead Flats and attempt to fly them after winding up the rubber band. We would release the plane and hope that the whirring propeller and the lightweight wings would allow it to go up and forward. Most often it did but only to plunge earthwards very quickly. A few seconds of flight would lead to necessary repairs made at home. We were more successful with carved balsawood gliders, which when thrown would often make successful flights.

I developed a fascination with aviation, which was, after all, not much more than thirty years old. My father was in his late teens before the Wright Brothers' successful flight at Kitty Hawk in America. I sent away for Royal Air Force apprenticeship papers, which would have meant my going to Cranwell, but I realised that my short sight would probably prevent me being recruited. I had begun to wear glasses for short sight soon after I began at secondary school. I borrowed a book by Harry Benjamin based on a book by a Dr W.H. Bates, called *Better Sight Without Glasses*. The Bates Method gave exercises designed to improve sight, and I spent hours doing these, including 'palming' my eyes in my hands, swaying to and fro in front of a window or loosening the relevant muscles in my neck. My optician thought the exercises a good idea, but as I began studying steadily at school my short sight worsened rather than improved. In the end I never sent off the application form to the RAF.

Instead I contented myself with a book from the library by Stanley Cramm, called, I think, *How to Fly*. I sat on the edge of my bed practising how to use a joystick to zoom and dive and the ailerons to turn left and right and how to make a three-point landing. Thus I made imaginary flights, reliving the exploits of wartime air aces. I found a newspaper shop that sold American pulp magazines and read avidly the stories of wartime flyers. I joined an aero club that met in Water Lane, Stratford, and listened to talks about flying given by a middle-aged man. There were about half-a-dozen lads in this club, two of them being Graham Nixon and Bob Cash, boys in my class who shared my enthusiasm. Both joined the RAF during the war, and I remember the commissioned Graham Nixon at a school reunion during the war telling me of his flights in bombers over Germany. Neither he nor Cash survived.

Another friend I made at school was Freddie Green. I called on him one Saturday at his home in nearby Stopford Road, Plaistow, to find him with his father, a docker, and friends sitting playing cards.

He was a tall, somewhat *louche*, independent West Hammer with a good heart who led me into scrapes, such as being caught by a policeman climbing over the vicarage wall. But films were our main interest. There were nearly twenty cinemas to choose from in Stratford, Forest Gate, Manor Park and Upton Park and East Ham, ranging from those old and small in the 'fleapit' category to grander buildings such as the Broadway, Stratford, or the Odeon at Forest Gate. As well as the two feature films and the shorts, some also added stage shows. The cinema organist would entertain us with words projected on to the screen. Slides advertising local firms would be also projected, and every programme ended with a picture of the monarch over which the national anthem was played. Many tried to get out before it began; if you did not, you had to stand to attention until the anthem ended. 'Refreshments' mainly consisted of usherettes walking backwards down the aisles bearing trays of ice creams and chocolate, although in the Kinema in West Ham Lane I remember my mother being served with tea on a tray, a practice common in West End live theatres until after the war. If you were in the middle of a row and you ordered ice cream it was passed by hand down the row and the money for it passed back to the usherette.

As well as going to the cinema with Freddie Green, I also went with my parents, especially after moving to Upton Avenue, walking to the Queens Cinema at the junction of Upton Lane and Romford Road. The building was demolished in the Blitz. It was on the ABC circuit, and we saw many films especially pleasing to my father, such as *Les Misérables* and *Mutiny on the Bounty*, featuring Charles Laughton, the Fred Astaire and Ginger Rogers musicals, Shirley Temple films and all the great stars of the time, such as Clark Gable and Edward G. Robinson. In 1937 our choice was extended when an Odeon was opened almost next door to the Queens. If I went to the Odeon on my own after school and an 'A' certificate film was showing, I followed the custom of the time by asking a respectable couple to take me in with them, giving them the money to buy the ticket for me. I saw *Gone with the Wind* at the Carlton in Green Street, Upton Park, and *Sanders of the River* at the Broadway, Stratford, stirred by Paul Robeson's magnificent singing voice.

My mother shared my enthusiasm for film-going but often annoyed my father by insisting on changing her seat for a better view of the screen in the days when cinemas were full and empty seats with a good view were scarce, obtainable only when people left. One was shown to one's position by an usherette with her torch, often disturbing a whole row to be shuttled into four seats by a side wall. My mother's seat-shifting never went down well with my father, who liked to settle down and remain in one place.

My father enjoyed cinema stage acts, often tumblers, magicians and the like, which reminded him of the music halls of his youth. Such entertainment still flourished locally at the Stratford Empire. I never went there but listened in envy at school to a boy describing the acts he had seen. Live theatre was not entirely ignored, for occasionally my father and mother took us to the West End – 'The Smoke' as Freddie Green called it – to see a production. I remember accompanying them to the Coliseum in St Martins Lane to see *The Lambeth Walk* with Lupino Lane and some other musicals. Another pre-war theatre experience was going with my school to the Old Vic to see *Henry IV, Part One* in which Falstaff was played by George Robey, the famous comedian of the day.

Around 1938 I was given a bicycle by my parents. My father already owned one, for after Uncle Ernie died he had taken over part of his Royal Insurance book. This meant collecting quarterly insurance payments from places out in Essex, such as Stapleford Tawney, something he enjoyed doing in his spare time away from regular work. It would have been logical for my father to teach me how to ride, but it was my friend Freddie Green who accompanied me to Wanstead Flats where, on the grass, away from traffic, I learned the art of staying upright. He suggested it would be good for me to go for a long ride with him so that I could get used to road conditions. Foolishly I suggested riding to Maidstone to see my Aunt Cis.

It must have been during the school holidays. One morning we rode to the Woolwich Ferry, crossed over to Kent and pedalled through Sidcup and along the old coaching road, the A2, pushing our way up and over the hills of the North Downs. At about one o'clock we reached my aunt's house. Surprised to see us, she asked if she could get us anything. Freddie said no, and I asked for a glass of water, which she brought out to me at the kerbside. Then we turned and cycled back, a total distance of around seventy-eight miles – not bad for a beginner. My mother was shocked when I told her. Next morning I lay in bed recovering. When I travelled to Maidstone recently I found the road transformed, and I felt nostalgia for earlier, simpler days.

Another family outing was going to see a show-house on one of the new suburban estates being built in Essex, possibly at Goodmayes. The 1930s was a time of expansion for London with building both by local authorities and private developers. It was a decade when the electricity supply companies were fighting to displace gas in people's homes for lighting and cooking and trying to sell domestic appliances such as vacuum cleaners, which would work only if you had electricity laid on to your home. This was a domestic innovation that began to spread rapidly in the 1930s, especially among the working classes.

When our White Road house had been converted to electricity, my mother had to learn how to use an electric oven instead of a gas one. My father had never cooked in his life, but he had read the literature and may well have been with my mother at a cooking demonstration run by the electricity company. The pay-off occurred on our visit to this new estate. We were used to our father going off on his own without warning or walking behind us deep in thought, perhaps brooding over a problem or, more likely, indulging in his acting skills, pretending to be someone else such as a private detective (he confessed this to me). On the housing estate we lost him completely. We finally discovered him in the kitchen of one of the show-houses giving an extended talk to a group of admiring women on how to cook by electricity. My mother never let him forget this, especially when it was time for a meal to be prepared.

Despite family outings, cinema-going and playing in the street, school occupied the bulk of my life. I was taught the basics of carpentry by an ageing Scotsman called Mr Mitchell, introduced to the detailed refinements of English grammar by Miss Bailey, patterns of history by Miss Coverdale, French grammar by Mr Unwin, Latin grammar by Miss Howard, the intricacies of mathematics by young Mr Holmes and chemistry by a Welshman, Mr Evans, plus physics and biology by others and geography by Miss Burness. Sergeant Pritchard made us climb ropes, leap a wooden horse and do drills in the school gym.

There were no playing fields. The playground was divided by a fence, girls on one side and boys on the other, but in the classrooms we sat side by side. I felt physically attracted to some of them by the time I was in the Upper Fifth but was too lacking in self-confidence to follow up incipient friendships, some begun when we were taught to dance.

Shyness and sensitivity develop in the teenage years, but at this time I was altogether lacking in self-confidence and I began to have periods of anxiety, not helped by my parents arguing and the gloomy new house. Moreover several incidents occurred to upset my around this time. One was when I broke my glasses. Another was when the fox terrier we had bought when we moved to Upton Avenue turned ferocious and started barking incessantly; perhaps he was affected by the tension between my parents. One day he jumped up at a towel I was using while drying my face and – inadvertently or otherwise – attached himself by his teeth to my lip instead. Astonishingly, perhaps, a similar attack took place a week or so later, and for a long time I had two small scars near my mouth where he had hung on. In addition, the Upton Avenue house proved to have cockroaches, which would appear in our living-room around ten o'clock at night. The sight of the swarms of black insects filled me with fear and disgust.

A greater anxiety came from my growing political awareness, inescapable perhaps at that time, with the Jewish struggle against the British Union of Fascists manifesting in street fights in the East End but even more through hearing on the radio the terrible voice of Hitler and reading in the newspapers about Mussolini and his territorial claims, the Spanish Civil War, the invasion of Ethiopia and similar world events. I pinned maps up in my room trying to understand what was going on, but I was an idealistic young boy who believed in the church's tenets of love and peace. I had by then been confirmed into the Church of England and received communion.

We all felt relieved when Chamberlain flew back from seeing Hitler in Germany, but it soon dawned on most of us that the 'peace in our time' he had announced on his return was not a realistic option, and from 1938 a sense of impending war began to hang over our lives. It was in September that year that we went down the road to Upton Lane School to try on gas masks. The start of 1939 was as bad, as Hitler invaded Czechoslovakia; war preparations began, with searchlight and anti-aircraft gun sites plotted and trenches dug.

Nobody could tell me in 1938 why my hair slowly began to fall out, but I suppose it was the accumulation of anxiety and stress, teenage *angst*, plus the fear of war. Patches appeared on the top and sides of my head, and by the end of 1939 I was bald – total alopecia they called it. Nobody at school said anything except Sergeant Pritchard, somewhat feared in the school as a disciplinarian, who told me not to worry, acting perhaps as a good NCO looking after his men. My respect for him grew enormously after this kindness. Naturally my mother was upset and tried out on me a variety of folk remedies, including rubbing my head with an onion. We did not know it then, but I was to remain bald for the rest of my life.

Fortunately, despite my diffidence and lack of self-confidence at this time, there was within me another person who was extrovert, loved acting and had a sense of humour. This side of me would develop as I grew older. As I matured I was to discover that I have a fundamentally optimistic nature: I am one who wakes up thinking it will be a good day, sees the funny side of things when situations get too serious and, most importantly, enjoys company. I have been blessed during my life with the advice my parents gave me, especially my mother, a resilient person who would take orders from no one. She advised me always to look forward, not back, for the past cannot be relived and prolonged regret leads nowhere. In my old age I seem to hear the her common-sense voice urging me not to give up when things threaten to get me down.

In the summer of 1939 I sat my General Schools Certificate examinations and learned in due course that I had passed all six subjects except French and had earned some credits. As was the custom, I was expected to leave school at sixteen, and my parents began to look for clerical jobs for which I could apply. My mother took me to Horseferry Road for an interview with the Gas Light and Coke Company, where I joined a line of some twenty other applicants but was not successful. I was interviewed for a job in the local library services but was not chosen.

In mid-August my father began his two-week annual holiday, and we travelled to Folkestone where we had spent our vacation the summer before. The *Daily Express* said there would be no war, but few were convinced. After a few days we cut the holiday short and returned home, thinking that if war broke out our house was likely be bombed soon after. We began to erect an Anderson bomb shelter in our back garden. My father and my brother dug out our central flowerbed and dropped in the sheets of curved corrugated metal that had been delivered and bolted them together. They covered the curved metal hump with excavated earth and put wooden steps down into it. Two tiered bunks were erected on either side. My brother took two tea chests, placed them in front of the entrance and filled them with earth. As additional protection against bombs they were to prove very useful.

We put the shelter in place on 26 August. The elderly couple at No. 75 saw us doing this, shut up their home and, sure that war was imminent, moved out of London. The family at No. 79 erected their Anderson shelter, too.

The government had prepared plans for the evacuation of school-children, young children with mothers and expectant mothers in advance of the outbreak of war, and these they now put into operation. Civil war casualties in Spain had led them to predict a high level of civilian deaths, and they established hospitals and mortuaries around the cities. Starting on 1 September 1939, over three days, one and a half million people were evacuated by the government and another two million evacuated themselves independently. An estimated 47 per cent of the school population moved out.

I was one of the pupils to go. West Ham Municipal Secondary School, under the headmastership of Mr W. Spikes, had joined the scheme, and on that Friday I reported to school with a small case and a badge. I was sixteen years and two weeks old, destined not to become a local clerk but to stay on at school for two more years. And I was leaving home.

2

OFF AND AWAY

I FOUND MYSELF on a steam train leaving Stratford Station and the same compartment as a teacher, Dr Clifford Smith. Over the next two years I was to come strongly under his influence, and it would be he who arranged for me to go to university. The train rumbled on and stopped at Brentwood, a small town in Essex. Dr Smith could not believe it. 'Brentwood,' he says in his Bristol accent that I was to come to know so well. 'Why, that is hardly out of London!'

We disembarked, lined up and shuffled off in long crocodiles of children to different parts of the town. My crocodile wound its way along a footpath beside the railway line until it reached Ingrave Road, where we turned south away from the town. At each house in Ingrave Road one or more children were taken in, the hosts specifying boys or girls and how many. I was one of the last to be given a billet, along with two upper-sixth-formers a year older than me. Tony Simmons and Stanley Cohen were friends and hoped to stay in the same house. But both had younger brothers in the school, and their mothers had said that the brothers must remain together. So Tony Simmons and his younger brother, Monty, and I went into a billet that would take three children, and Stanley Cohen and his younger brother, Duggie, ended up in a house a few doors further along.

The house we moved into was called Rannoch. It was detached and had a long back garden that ended at a field with sheep grazing, a landscape to which we were not accustomed. It was occupied by Chick Searle and his sister Topsy, both single and in their thirties. The weekend we arrived two of their sisters also arrived to stay, because they were anticipating heavy bombing at home. One came with her husband and small boy; the other was unmarried and eagerly anticipating an enjoyable time flirting with service officers. Topsy was easy-going and welcoming, as was Chick. Topsy, with frizzy hair and usually dressed in brown, borrowed books from the Boots Lending Library, and her favourite recreation was to sit in front of the coal fire in the living-room reading. We would join her in the evenings, often listening to the radio in those pre-television days. Jack Warner in *Garrison Theatre* was a popular programme, and listening to Lord Haw-Haw with his dire threats was another diversion.

Chick was a postman and travelled each day on the train to work in a suburb on London's eastern outskirts. The only other family member we met was an uncle, seemingly rather rich, who lived in a large house a few miles out of Brentwood.

We visited the town next day. Together with two boys from the next house who were waiting to return to their boarding-school, we walked up Ingrave Road. Brentwood is some eighteen miles out of London and together with neighbouring Shenfield had become a dormitory town. It was established on a hill in what had been a forested area ('burnt wood') on the road to Colchester and contained some old coaching inns. Our headmaster, Mr Spikes, stayed at one of these in the High Road and rented garage space there to store school supplies. Nearly opposite this inn were the ruins of a medieval chapel and behind them an Odeon cinema. We ended up seeing *The Four Feathers* there, a Korda film set in the Sudan war, based on the novel by A.E.W. Mason, with John Clements and Ralph Richardson in the cast.

Next morning, Sunday, 3 September 1939, we boys went across the road to an open space on what was the Thornton Estate to kick a ball around. Chick came over and told us we were at war with Germany. I think an air-raid siren sounded, but we had no air-raid shelter anyway and nothing happened. There were no immediate air raids, and the two sisters went home again. We began a period known as the 'Phony War', in which not much occurred except that Hitler and Stalin consolidated their hold on Poland, which they had both invaded. We did not know it at the time, but nothing much was to develop until the spring.

School began on Monday. My morning lessons were held in a former private school called Gweedore. This occupied a long wooden hut built for classrooms in the grounds of a large house. The hut was raised above the ground to avoid damp and was heated by a coke stove, with its flue pipe set against a wall. As autumn turned into winter it was damp and cold. It was here that Clifford Smith strode up and down teaching us basic accountancy, economics, shorthand and typing. I had found, not long after arriving in Brentwood, that physics and mathematics were not subjects that suited me, despite getting credits in both in my General Schools examinations, So one day, after assembly, I approached the headmaster and asked to be transferred from the Science Sixth to the Commerce Sixth. I still looked on my time in the sixth form as a temporary reprieve before call-up, and commercial subjects seemed a better qualification for getting a job, perhaps at eighteen. At this time I had no thoughts of university.

Brentwood had a public school founded in 1557. It stood at the junction of Ingrave Road and Brentwood High Street, and we were allowed to use it during the afternoons. Here I was taught English by a Mr R.P. Hewett, who was also to be an influence on my life. Then still in his twenties, and called up into the Army two years later, Hewett treated his pupils in a friendly, informal way, which contrasted with the more disciplinarian approach of Clifford Smith. The two men and their wives shared a house in Brentwood. Calling there one day I found Hewett in the basement, limbering up with a punch ball to keep fit. I was most impressed. Hewett was a minor poet whom I think was published in later years while teaching in the Ipswich area. He was to encourage me to write.

Perhaps my greatest benefit from Brentwood was the company of Tony Simmons and Stanley Cohen. We would gather together in the evenings, and I was introduced to authors such as T.S. Eliot and W.H. Auden and to intellectual interests of a sharper kind than I had previously encountered. Tony in particular was critical of my woollier ideas and attitudes but at the same time encouraged me to write, especially to attempt humour. In the house was a Victorian set of Shakespeare's plays, and Tony embarked on a school production of *Much Ado About Nothing*, offering me a small part. The play was not put on, but this was one of Tony's first steps to his subsequent successful career as a film director.

My time in Brentwood was to spark off another interest. One day the history master, Mr H.R.E. Rudgley, tall, good-looking and impressive, took the sixth-formers out into Brentwood High Street and showed us how to identify the age of a building, for there were plenty of period houses to be seen. This was the beginning of a life-long love of architectural history. Another inspiring teacher was Dr Arnold Burness, son of a previous headmaster, who was to become headmaster himself after Dr Spikes retired after the war. He taught geography, and I was to see more of him in my second year in the sixth form.

Is it at sixteen that you begin to be more aware of yourself and to develop characteristics and interests that are going to make you what you are in later life? If you have a special talent, for music perhaps, this may begin earlier, but for most not knowing what they want to do in life is probably more common. I suppose that it was at this time, living away from home, that I began to develop quirks, characteristics and interests that continued during my adult life. I found I liked sitting at a desk or table, handling notebooks and stationery, making lists. One of the first fruits of this was starting a notebook in January 1940 in which I listed the title and author of each book I read. I have maintained this, in several volumes, until the present time. Writing letters was another desk occupation, a way of using and manipulating words, the sound and balance of them, their order and structure. Over the years I suppose I have bored my friends with my letters. But it was then a world without a telephone (no phone calls home for me because there was no phone at home). My parents replied to my letters while I was evacuated, my father having the same obsession with writing, and no doubt I inherited it from him.

As a result of being taught basic double-entry book-keeping by Clifford Smith, I also began to record income and expenditure, a practice that evolved in adult years to a personal cash book that is not only a control on expenditure (I do like to spend) but also a relaxing hobby. It also keeps in good shape the ability to tot up rows of figures and maintains mental arithmetic, useful when paying at the checkout.

I was also a collector. No letter that I received was thrown away, so that in consequence my cellar contains several shoeboxes with missives dating back to 1940. Similarly with books: I am a collector of books. I have bought them all my life, mostly second-hand or remaindered or at a discounted price. When in the first year of my marriage I tried to give up buying books for the sake of economy, I felt a real pain. Now I own over ten thousand books, a problem my children will have to deal with, avoiding if they can the sharks, for some are first editions and many are in mint condition.

And what will they do with my diaries? In January 1940 I began using a fat one, in which I recorded my feelings and thoughts as much as activities. I did the same in 1941 but gave up the third in March 1942 because I felt diary-keeping made me too introspective: I was beginning to regard events almost solely in terms of how I would write them up in my diary. After a gap I turned to small pocket diaries, recording only facts and often using initials for other people's names. I have kept this practice up ever since, so I can find out what I did on any day from 1943 to the present.

And what will they do with my photo albums? For the past half-century I have taken photos and mounted and captioned them in albums. They cover holidays, local scenes, outings, friends, the house and garden. Some of the prints are fading, so perhaps they will all be thrown away, along with my cash books, boxes of letters, record of books read and all the other impedimenta of my life.

The winter of 1939–40 was cold, and sometimes we trudged to school in quite deep snow. A life evolved but as winter turned into spring it was to change. There was no bombing, so it seemed unnecessary for us to remain there. On top of that, as Brentwood was only about 15 miles from home, many pupils began to go back each weekend, myself included. There was a good bus service, but then I took to cycling, returning early on Monday morning. A major change occurred for me in February 1940 when Tony Simmons and his brother returned home for good. This was possible because Dr Spikes had reopened the school in West Ham; it also catered for children who had not joined the official evacuation. The head was arranging for another evacuation, this time to Cornwall.

I decided to stay on. I had got used to living in Brentwood and wrote an enthusiastic piece about it in the school magazine. I suppose I was glad to have independence away from home. The weather improved, and for the first time in my life I became aware of spring. I had my bike and could travel out into the Essex countryside within minutes. I became aware of the song of the blackbird, undisturbed by my silent approach, and the growth of blossom. My romantic, sentimental heart was overwhelmed, and I promised myself that for every future year of my life I would notice the coming of spring, watch the budding and the blossoming, hear the song and enjoy the sight of fresh, green leaves. This is a promise that I have kept, with much joy.

As spring burst into life I developed a yearning for the company of girls. Other schools had been evacuated to Brentwood, including a Forest Gate girls' school. When I used Brentwood public library to look things up, I would see a group of three girls from this school on some days. In my diary I named them Strawberry Roan, John Bull and Powder Puff, and it was Powder Puff I fancied. One day she was with her friends but crying. That endeared her to me even more. Anotherday I cycled to the common and saw the three girls together by the pond. I longed to speak to them, but I was sixteen and shy. The scene stays in my mind, these many years later, wondering what might have happened if I had been bold enough to speak.

My schooling had been co-educational, so I was used to girls, and early on I learned that they could be cleverer than me. I did for a while have the regular company of a fellow pupil, Elizabeth Smeaton, There were very few sixth-formers left in Brentwood by now, and we two were assigned to do a combined geographical and historical project about Brentwood. She was an attractive girl but not my type. Nevertheless, we got on well, cycling around the area undertaking fieldwork, sometimes making physical contact which gave us pleasure but which was not to develop into a romantic relationship.

I found local history interesting and pursued the subject, looking up Essex historians such as Wright and Morant in West Ham reference library and drawing maps. Finally I typed out the project at school, using a purple typewriter ribbon, which seemed the only kind available at the time. I still have it, in its brown folder, one of my longest-held possessions. It was a little bit of Brentwood and me to store away.

Then our world changed. Hitler moved his armies into Holland, Belgium, Denmark and France early in May, Prime Minister Chamberlain resigned and Winston Churchill took his place. Sunday 26 May was a day of national prayer. I even mentioned some of these events in my self-absorbed personal diary. By then it had been decided that I should return home. On 27 May 1940 my mother visited the school in West Ham; she saw Dr Spikes and Dr Smith who said that I worked well and that I should stay on in the sixth form for the second year. On the same day she took me to a hospital specialist, who advised that I give up the sunray treatment for my baldness, which I had been having at Brentwood Hospital, and to try massage and not yet to think of wearing a wig. I went with my mother to Brentwood, collected my belongings and said goodbye to the Searles. Next day I returned to my old school in Tennyson Road.

June came. Italy entered the war on Hitler's side. The British Army had evacuated from France via Dunkirk. Invasion was feared. Dr Spikes put in place a second evacuation of the school, this time to Helston in west Cornwall. I was to go there eventually, but for the time being I carried on where I was until the end of term. My 1940 diary is almost empty of reference to the war at that time, although I do record a siren alert that kept us in our Anderson shelter until 4 a.m. on 25 June. I think I have a tendency to ignore unpleasant things that do not intrude on me, as many people do. My memory of that fine summer includes sitting on our lawn reading Trevelyan's *History of England* and other school books, as well as volumes by Shaw and Ruskin and other authors. I recall planes going to and fro in the sky but was not really aware of how critical a time it was for the nation.

In fact 10 July 1940 was the start of the Battle of Britain. Air Chief Marshall Sir Hugh Dowding, assisted by Sir Keith Park, deployed six to seven hundred British fighter planes to combat the German Luftwaffe as it crossed the Channel into British air space as a preliminary to staging an invasion. The fighter pilots were no more than a few years older than me. That August, as I sat in my garden, eighty-eight RAF pilots were killed within ten days. In six weeks from mid-July to the end of August, 240 pilots were killed and 130 seriously wounded. The newspapers dealt with it as if it were some kind of sport, matching the numbers of aircraft downed on each side.

Sunday, 18 August was my seventeenth birthday. Alfred Price's book *The Hardest Day* describes how, on 18 August 1940, three major air assaults were launched and 100 German and 136 British aircraft were destroyed or damaged, the greatest numbers of any day of the air battle. This myopic teenager must have been oblivious to it all, for he never bothered to record it in his diary, except to say that two air-raid warnings had interrupted his birthday tea.

That week I started a new term at my Tennyson Road school. War began to have a greater impact on the following Saturday: I had cycled over to Plaistow to collect our weekend meat from our butchers, Goodings, when the air-raid warning sounded and I rushed home. From then on, air-raid warnings and raids became more frequent until eventually Hitler launched the full fury of the Blitz . A raid on Saturday, 7 September was heavy, with the brewery bottling plant close to Upton Avenue hit by a bomb and fires started at Stratford. Shrapnel from anti-aircraft fire littered the streets. My diary records on 8 September: 'Bombs all around on Canning Town, Silvertown, East Ham, Forest Gate and all over the East End. Hitler has launched a grand attack on London. God has preserved us.' This was the start of the Blitz, beginning with attacks on east London, with its docks, factories and railway lines, although destruction of civilian morale was another aim. These air raids were to continue until May 1941, almost without pause. Other cities were attacked but not so continually over such a wide area.

We were among the first Londoners to be bombed out during the Blitz. On Sunday night, 8 September 1940 we went early into the Anderson shelter in the garden and heard bombs falling around us, shaking the earth, with the drone of German planes overhead and the noise of the anti-aircraft fire. One bomb fell very close. In daylight, the all-clear sounded and we inspected the damage. It had fallen in the road in front of our house, and the blast had brought down our front bay and all the ceilings. The front door had been blown in and my father's bicycle, which had stood in the hall, had been blown up the stairs. The house opposite had suffered more, being virtually demolished.

Other bombs had fallen near by, including another in Upton Avenue further down. My brother's handiwork in putting tea chests filled with earth in front of our shelter had paid off, for we found embedded in them a long metal bar that had hung as a counterweight for the wooden sash windows. The chest had prevented the missile hurtling into our Anderson shelter.

Where were we to go? Although coffins had been manufactured and hospitals extended in anticipation of heavy bombing, less thought had been given to the homeless, driven on to the streets by the destruction of their homes. Schools and shelters had to be used to house those with nowhere to live. One solution was to stay with relatives, and this is what we did. Many, like my father, needed to travel to work each day, so moving too far was not an option. He was still based at Stratford, although as he rose up the ranks he would cycle to Hackney. Conveniently, his sister, my Aunt Edie, and Uncle Will lived in Stratford, so that was where we moved. My father would don his steel helmet and pedal off early, often before the all-clear had sounded. Uncle Will similarly set out each morning for the railway yards.

My brother, now working, had gone to live with his girl-friend and her parents in another part of Stratford, and so it was three of us who had to squeeze into my aunt and uncle's Anderson shelter with them. It was at once obvious that it was not large enough for comfort. My mother and aunt had never really got on well together, and such close confinement did not help the situation. So my mother, always a woman of action, arranged for the two of us to stay at her brother's house in Hounslow, leaving my father in Stratford. On Thursday, 12 September we moved out. I could not go to school, as it had been closed to accommodate evacuees from Canning Town, one of the worst-hit parts of West Ham.

My Uncle Albert and Aunt Lizzie's house was not far from Hounslow West tube station and quite close to Hounslow barracks. Their semi-detached house backed on to playing fields of a local school, and a large surface air-raid shelter of brick and concrete, with long wooden benches inside, could easily be reached through a gap in the fence at the end of my uncle's garden. It was in this school shelter that we slept each night, using the benches as beds. No one else joined us.

My cousin Vera was away in North Wales, where the government ministry for which she worked was evacuated, and my cousin Don had been called up and was based in Ulster. My cousin Leah was still at home, attending school, and we used to go about together, sometimes to the cinema before the evening air-raid siren sounded. During the day I cycled around the area, which was far more pleasant than West Ham. I read J.B. Priestley's *Angel Pavement* and wondered what it would be like to work in an office in the city when my career started.

The nightly bombing raids had soon spread from the East End across the whole of London, and every night we would go to the shelter. The Germans began to drop 'land mines' – bombs on parachutes that would be caught up on a tree and hang there unexploded. I think twice we were evacuated, as one of these had landed near us and had to spend the night in a Salvation Army hall. Once the mine was not dismantled until 9 p.m. and we walked back after the night raid had started, throwing ourselves on to the ground when a bomb fell not too far away.

Some days my mother and I would travel back to West Ham to see my father and deal with other matters. During one of these visits my mother encountered a teacher from my school who asked where I was. The teacher recommended that I be sent to Cornwall, where the school had been evacuated, to continue my studies. My diary entry for 26 September reads: 'Indecision as to whether to go to Cornwall. I want to travel, see the country, meet different people, broaden mind if used properly. Ma says, no, don't want to be separated in case of invasion.' It was widely believed at this time that Hitler would invade us and that the bombing was a prelude to this.

A couple of days later the decision was made for me: on the Saturday night we were bombed out for a second time. We were in the shelter when a bomb fell on my uncle's house, some twenty-five yards away. It hit the chimney stack but did not explode. A soldier next door at No. 59 had not taken shelter and was killed, presumably by falling masonry. In the morning we trekked to a centre for bombed-out people, a church hall where they served meals. We stayed that night in Shelter 13, my diary records.

Leaving my uncle and aunt to sort out the problem of a house that could not be inhabited, my mother and I returned to my aunt's home in Stratford. My family was indecisive about what was to be done, but my diary shows that on Monday, 30 September we assembled my belongings, including a new pullover and shoes, and prepared for my second evacuation with the school. By this time the Tennyson Road building had been bombed; rescuers tried to retrieve books and furniture from the girders and debris.

On Tuesday, 1 October I took the 10.30 a.m. train from Paddington. Some other pupils were travelling, and as a prefect I was in charge, but all I remember is looking out of the window and marvelling at how the English landscape changed as we travelled, being particularly struck by the wide spaces of Wiltshire. We changed at Gwinnear Road Halt and arrived at Helston at around six. By 7.30 the local evacuation officer, Mr Roseweare, had installed his new arrivals in billets. I found myself in the fishing village of Porthleven. That night I slept in a bed. Next morning I got up, pulled back the curtains and saw the sea. It was a glorious sunny day. My billet was a small private hotel called Trepolpen. It stood on the cliff road on the east side of Porthleven harbour. The village was about three miles south of Helston, the town in which my evacuated school was based. A bus ran between them, but my diary shows that more often than not I walked, often with friends, making my way through the woods past the legendary Loe Pool, the long lake separated from the sea by Loe Bar.

I did not know it then, but on that morning I was drawing the curtains open on one of the most pleasurable periods of my life. Thinking about it engenders in me a sense of guilt, for while I was studying and enjoying friendships in the most magical of English counties many were dying in Europe, being tortured, imprisoned or suffering or, as we know now, experiencing the horrors of the Holocaust. But what could a seventeen-year-old do other than carry on with what life had set before him? I was due for call-up at eighteen and a half, and that was soon enough to get involved in the war effort. Meanwhile I consoled myself that my experience of the Blitz with its two close escapes from death had already given me some experience of the effect of war.

Trepolpen was run by Mrs Hocking, whose husband was a coast-guard who spent much of his time in a small hut on the edge of the cliff near the hotel. His geniality was not matched by his wife, who seemed upset at losing her rooms and thus her hotel business, although I got on well enough with her. My first lovely bedroom had to be given up, and I was transferred to another at the back of the house, which was set against rock. When you pulled back the window curtain you found yourself facing bare granite a few feet away. In 1998 I returned to Porthleven and found that Trepolpen had been replaced by other buildings.

My fellow evacuees there were to become my friends. There were two sixth-formers, Hector Davis and Ken Stanton, both a year younger than me, and Jocelyn Chesters, a small, pretty infant-school teacher, no more than a few years older. I was to establish a particularly endur-ing friendship with Hector that continued after we returned to London.

Ken, Hector, Jocey and I started going around together, heading out in the winter evenings in the blackout, enjoying the light of the stars and the moon. In wartime you could really appreciate the night sky, a lost pleasure in the over-lit cities of today. We would walk along, our arms linked, chatting away. In time it was Ken Stanton that Josey seemed to favour and began to go out with most often.

The time I spent in Cornwall, among the best years in my life, involved relatively little contact with the Cornish people. It was a sort of village within a village, although of course those who lived in billets with families had greater contacts with the locals. Within the school I was one of the oldest pupils. Masters treated you as equals, and the work set intellectual targets. It was, nevertheless, a time of growing up and extending experience.

My first day I took the bus to Helston, met people, did shopping and acquired an emergency ration book. On the walk back to

Porthleven I was given a lift by Mr and Mrs Davis. He was the local postmaster, and they drove me on into Penzance where we saw the bomb damage; Penzance was a target because it was a port. I kept in touch with Mr and Mrs Davis after I left Cornwall, and we exchanged letters for a while. With petrol rationing and reduced bus services it was common practice to give lifts, especially in country areas, and this had yielded a pleasant acquaintanceship. I was soon to develop hitch-hiking skills, which I continued during the war years and after.

On a Saturday soon after, Hector and I walked around Porthleven harbour trying to hire a boat, but we failed. We caught up with Jocey and the three of us walked westwards. Suddenly a Spitfire came out of the sky and landed in a field. We ran some distance to it, along with other people, to find that the pilot was uninjured and pretty calm, having just shot down a German plane. That evening Hector, Jocey and I visited Helston's small cinema to see Basil Rathbone in the *Hound of the Baskervilles*. We walked both ways, but on the return journey we took turns to carry Jocey, who was tired.

Although I had my own bedroom at Trepolpen, it was not a place in which I could study, and the downstairs lounge, which had a table, had no electricity and you had to study by oil lamp. However, I found I could use a room in the nearby village institute. This was a tall granite building that still stands by Porthleven Harbour and was used as a community centre. It was here that I wrote school essays; I also read as much as I could, using the library. Books borrowed included Osbert Sitwell's *Before the Bombardment* and John Gunther's *Inside Asia*, chosen to extend my knowledge any way I could.

I began to develop a certain discontent with Porthleven, probably because, as a city child, I was not used to village life and missed streets full of shops and passing crowds. The problem was resolved when Ken, Hector, myself and others were temporarily transferred to Helston to help Mrs Hocking with her accommodation problems. The three of us would return to Porthleven to visit Jocey, who had not been moved. When I was offered a room to myself in our Helston billet I chose to accept it, while Hector and Ken went back to Porthleven.

Towards the end of November 1940 I wrote in my diary that 'a dream is realised for me today. I have a room to myself. It is just like home.' I was now at No. 3 Cross Street, a large three-storey house close to the parish church, inhabited by Mr Penfold, an elderly, single, retired civil servant. It was being used as a hostel housing some twenty boys from our school, with local women preparing our meals and attending our domestic arrangements. Mostly of these were parents of children at our school. As the senior boy and a prefect I had responsibility for pupils' behaviour and became accustomed to shouting for order at mealtimes, even clipping a boy round the head to make him shut up. My consolation was the room of my own at the top of the building, probably once a servant's room, where I could work without having to shut myself in a bathroom for peace and quiet. I acquired a desk and a chest of drawers and slept on a government-issue canvas bed with blankets like those I had been issued with in Brentwood; there was no carpet. I put my paperbacks on the mantleshelf. I had very few clothes, and storage was not a problem.

One contact I made with local life came when the school was invited to the election of a new Helston mayor and to submit a descriptive essay about the ceremony. I am not sure how many entries were sent in, but I won the prize. This was a book of my choice, and Hewett, my English master, was astonished at my apparently pretentious purchase of the Everyman volume *Religio Medici and Other Writings* by Sir Thomas Browne. Why I bought it at the local bookshop I cannot recall, but I must have read it, for inside are my notes on it, although these may have been made later during my college days. Pasted on the inside cover is my ticket admitting the bearer to the Guildhall on Saturday, 9 November 1940 at 11.30 a.m. for the election of the mayor. On another page is the inscription 'This Book was presented to Kenneth Gay as a Prize for an Essay on Helston's Mayor Choosing Ceremony 1940'. It is signed by Leonard W. Oliver, Mayor of Helston.

My journalistic ambitions were clearly developing at that time, because I posted a version of my essay to a local Cornish newspaper called *The Western Briton*. It was not used. But when the paper came out, its report on the ceremony was so close to my own that I was convinced that a lazy local reporter had made use of my article. I tried to obtain redress but without success.

My writing was carried out in my single room. I had placed my writing table next to the window, and I sat with the window on my right-hand side, with my back to the wall, looking into the room. As winter came, heat was supplied by a portable oil stove, the fuel for which I bought after approaching the deputy head, Joe Rigby, for the cash. One luxury I had through the generosity of Mr Penfold was a wind-up gramophone with an enormous horn. He lent me some of his records, most of them operas. Each evening after school I got down to work at my table, now and then posting up mottoes on the wall. Once, in a particularly serious mood, I wrote out the word EFFI-CIENCY and pinned it where I could view it from my desk. It was a day or two before I noticed – or maybe someone else did – that I had spelt it EFICIENCY!

Teaching in Helston took place in different buildings. In the morning we occupied Epworth Church, where different classes assembled in separate groups around the circumference of the interior, with the teachers speaking *sotto voce* as much as possible. The church was in Coinagehall Street, in the centre of the town, with the bus stop for Porthleven and other buses outside it. Not far away was the Angel Hotel, all very much the same today – or at least it was in 1998 when I visited it. My diary also records meeting in the Masonic Hall, but I have no memory of this.

At midday we went to our billets for meals and then in the afternoon we would walk up past St Michael's Anglican church to Helston County School, a modern building on the edge of the town. The local school used it in the mornings and let us have it for the afternoons. It had a new well-stocked memorial library where we often met for lessons.

Living in a hostel filled with West Ham boys I still had little contact with Cornish people – apart for Mr Penfold, the elderly owner (who, because he was bent with age, the boys cruelly called Quasimodo, after the deformed bell-ringer played by Charles Laughton in the 1939 film *The Hunchback of Notre Dame*). Others did, however. Alan Smith, a fellow sixth-former who lived with a family, was years later to deposit an article with the Institute of Cornish Studies called *Devil on the Blackberries: The Reminiscences of a Schoolboy in Wartime Helston*. He considers that the greatest impact of the war on Helston was the loss of its younger people to join the services and the arrival of evacuee hordes.

Another published account of life in Helston as an evacuee is given by film-maker Bryan Forbes in his first autobiography, *Notes for a Life*. Johnny Clark, as he then was before changing his name for career reasons, was in the fourth form, three years younger than me. My memory of him from that time is of a boy of irrepressible energy, famous for his imitations of Hitler. It was in school plays that he first demonstrated his acting talent.

My studies were for the Higher Schools Certificate (to be replaced in later years by 'A' levels). The subjects I took were English History (two papers), Economics (three papers), Physical Geography (one paper), Human, Historical and Economic Geography (one or two papers), Statistics (one paper) and Accountancy (one paper). I studied a different subject each evening of the week, sitting at my desk with notebooks and textbooks to hand, usually for two or three hours. Dr Clifford Smith had advocated studying Statistics: his long-term intention was that I should apply to the London School of Economics and Political Science, a college of the University of London, for a degree specialising in Statistics. He had the same aim for my lower-sixth-form friend Stanley Bloom, and to concentrate our attention he arranged for Stanley and me to take an examination in this subject in the spring of 1941. This was the London Chamber of Commerce examination in Business Statistics (Higher). I must have liked the subject for I gained a distinction, and when I took the subject for Higher Schools I gained a 69 per cent pass mark, my second best subject mark after Accounting.

In Helston I still held strongly to my Christian beliefs and had thoughts of entering the ministry and becoming an Anglican vicar in a country parish, with time to write in my parsonage. I have always loved walking, and that November I began the routine of setting off from Helston each Sunday morning to attend Breage church, an hour's walk away. I am not sure how this came about, but it reintroduced me to the surrounding countryside, which even in winter offered a kind of magic world. I shall never forget how in later months I found the hedgerows full of flowers in bloom, wild and beautiful – and free to pick. The vicar was probably nonplussed by the appearance of a schoolboy evacuee at his Sunday morning services, and in due course he invited me to tea. I don't think we knew what to make of each other. I continued with these Breage visits until the following summer, when I took the easy option and attended St Michael's Church in Helston instead.

The English teacher, Mr Hewett, also came with us to Helston and was given some responsibility for the Cross Street Hostel, helping to set up a small committee of boys to deal with problems such as good behaviour. I did my best to impose discipline, but boys of fourteen or thereabouts can be a wild bunch, and, as is common at that age, they would steal if they could, both within the hostel and in local shops.

For one boy this led to a Juvenile Court case, which was not good for the school's reputation.

Eventually it was decided that a member of staff should reside at the hostel, and Miss Howard, the Latin teacher, who was a disciplinarian, moved in, although not until March 1941. I felt somewhat disappointed at losing my role as senior boy in charge of maintaining order in the hostel but relieved that I could spend the months before my examinations concentrating on my studies rather than on disciplinary responsibilities.

Hewett thought I had writing ability – I suppose this was from reading my school essays, but I was also writing stories for my own pleasure at this time. One evening, he came with a journalist friend and we discussed writing as a career. This was the time that John Lehmann was editing *New Writing*. This monthly Penguin publication, first issued in December 1940 and sold at sixpence, became almost compulsory reading for many, keeping readers in touch with the current literary and arts scene. Hewett got me to write a description of life in the hostel, which I sent off but which was never published.

Thoughts of girls and longing for their company, despite immersion in study, were another aspect of my life as a seventeen-year-old. One of the women looking after us was Mrs Jeffery, who was a great help to all the boys. She had a daughter in the school called Katherine, a few years younger than myself, and now and again we went on walks together; perhaps her mother urged to do so. I don't think we had a great deal in common, but she was pleasant company, 'refreshing comradeship' as my diary put it. Another of the hostel ladies was Mrs Godwin; she, too, had a daughter in our school but who was far too young for me. Mrs Godwin and I developed a friendship, which continued after my return to London, as she lived near by. I remain grateful to her memory because of our discussions did much to help me become more mature in terms of my outlook on the world.

One girl in the school I fancied was Katherine Carpenter, also a few years younger than me. I knew where she lived, and one evening I sat on my bed for over an hour debating whether to call on her, full of indecision and lack of courage. When I did finally did pay her a visit Katherine quietly turned me down.

Throughout that winter in Helston, which was often wet, the school offered a good social life. I liked the arrangement whereby I worked by myself undisturbed in my room but knew that at any time I could go downstairs and associate with others. School activities included debates, dancing lessons and amateur theatricals, and I would still go to Porthleven to visit my friends there. In Coinagehall Street there was another school hostel inhabited mainly by lower-sixth-formers, including Stanley Bloom, until he moved into a billet. I was offered one myself by the evacuation officer Mr Rosewarne, but after considering the matter I decided to stay in the hostel.

Smith kept us on our toes in lessons and called on us at other times. At Christmas 1940, for which return home was inadvisable because of the intense bombing, he invited Stanley and me to join him and his wife in their bungalow. He also invited two soldiers from the East Yorkshire Regiment stationed near by. The conversation tended to be intellectual.

I was at this time full of intense Christian belief, and my father would sometimes send me Bible notes or the like in his letters or family parcels (I used to send my washing home, and when it was posted back letters or goodies might be enclosed). This attitude to life seems to have made an impression on Mrs Godwin, who in March returned home to live in London and wrote on the 24th:

Dear Kenneth,

Tonight I felt the urge to write to you to tell you how much your Faith must have impressed me. Through the dreadful raid of last Wednesday our conversations whilst we were taking our walks together kept passing through my mind and I was truly grateful to you because of the comfort and trust in the Lord which you so strongly possess. You told me once of the inner happiness which you felt in your Belief and now I understand perfectly what it means to you.

The Trust which I now have is saddened by the great destruction and loss of life this way. Tomorrow is a special day of prayer and we shall go to St Peter's in Upton Lane. If it had been at all possible I should have liked to have had your company as well, but you will be in my prayers. If you can help me you can help others, maybe thousands of them, so if you have doubts about your ability to preach the gospel put them completely out of your mind. Goodnight Ken.

Yours Sincerely,

Winifred Godwin

PS Your keepsake I always wear.

Perhaps this letter encouraged me to think of visiting home. I had been in Cornwall for six months, and end of term and the Easter break of three weeks would give me time to stay in Forest Gate for a while and see my parents. By now the attacks on London by the German Air Force were more sporadic and life was quieter. Our family home, No. 77 Upton Avenue, had been spared from demolition but had yet to be restored. My mother had secured an upstairs flat at No. 15 Upton Avenue, a 1930s' house at the other end of our road, She had achieved this by pestering the borough housing officer, and the flat was in his home. I wrote, and my parents sent a money order for my fare to London. Air raids would be little problem, as they had an Anderson shelter in the back garden that they used when the siren sounded. Anticipating my return made me very happy.

My diary entries before my journey back on 4 April 1941 record my round of activities in Cornwall:

I go to a Ministry of Information film show and walking home from a fish shop supper (6d) with Lionel Kenner we agreed it had the effect of pacifist propaganda . . . the talk with Kenner upon the significance of man in the universe has been a tonic. I buy three books, *Three Men in a Boat* (2s. 6d.), *The Century's Poetry* (2s. 6d.) and *Penguin New Writing 3* (6d.). Air Training Corps. Next day I go to the school drama production of Barrie's *Quality Street* in which I think Johnny Clark [later to become Bryan Forbes] acted with aplomb. The following day a Saturday Sixth Form ramble was put off because of the rain and on Sunday I walked to Breage church where I met Hector, Ken and Jocey in a still surviving alliance. On Thursday there is an end of term school concert and much hilarity in the air. I pack my bag and go to the fish shop with Blunkell, one of the older boys in the hostel, strolling back beneath the moon.

My long train journey back was uneventful, and in my returning days in Forest Gate I found the war atmosphere of September 1940 with its fierce air raids had dissipated. I got measured for a suit and went to Charing Cross Road with Kenner to buy books in Foyles and take tea in Lyons tea shop. I travelled to Hounslow where my uncle and aunt were ensconced in a new house. I visited Mrs Godwin on Good Friday, and she continued to give me good advice on growing up. I met my friends Stanley Bloom and Freddy Green and went with my parents to Maidstone, where we stayed four or five days with Aunt Cis and Uncle Bert. During this stay we missed a significant air raid on London by five hundred German planes. We enjoyed country walks and cinema visits and appreciated the break.

We had been sleeping in the Anderson shelter in the garden in Upton Avenue, and on my penultimate night there was another massive raid. My mother's main fear was that rats might be driven into the shelter, but fortunately this did not happen. No other night raid occurred before I returned to Paddington and took the 10.30 train back to Cornwall on the morning of Monday, 21 April 1941.

My diary records that I was soon plunged back into work under the remorseless direction of Clifford Smith but still found time for a walk on the moors and a hitch-hiking trip with a hostel boy, Johnny Miners, to Falmouth to see the film *The Thief of Baghdad* and to read the anti-fascist Italian novel *Fontamara*, as well as a book on literature by Stephen Spender. But the main change in my Helston life was a new friendship that was to mean much to me.

When I returned to the hostel after my Easter holiday I discovered that there was a new helper, Mrs Stubbs. Physical attraction can be instantaneous, and when I saw her face I knew that I wanted to be with her. I was discreet in my diary entries, but my friendship with her, which was soon to become one of kisses and cuddles, was the nicest thing that happened to me in my Cornwall year. We developed a friendship which, for the few months it endured, we both enjoyed. Before I sat my examinations in July she returned to Essex; her husband, who was in a reserved engineering occupation (and whom I liked on his visit to Helston), said that things were quieter there now and she would be safe at home. I recall that her son, about my age, had been trapped in the Channel Islands when the Germans invaded.

After my return to London I was to cycle out to see her a few times, but the conditions in which our friendship had bloomed had irrevocably changed, and I was not to see her after that. Still, a memory can remain with you all your life. Perhaps most of all I remember the long country walks in that wonderful Cornish spring of 1941. 'Hedges, walls, ditches, stiles, gates, cows, sheep, grass crops, bluebells, cliffs, landscapes and direction – one great playground – how grand is the country ramble and what lack of initiative to go by road' is how I described one outing with her in my diary. Perhaps that was the day that as we sat to have our picnic we slid into each other's arms for the first time and began to kiss, alone in a green unobtrusive spot.

After her return, my dear friend, who used to call me by my middle name David, rather than Ken or Kenneth, wrote me a letter:

Dear Chum

I am keeping my promise to write to you, but first of all I want to thank all those dear boys who contributed to that lovely present. I suspect you had some say in its choice. I was too upset at leaving you all even to go into the dining room and bid them adieu . . .

I don't know quite whether I am glad to be back or sorry. It was my duty to come back and so I am here. I should like to thank you, however, for how much I enjoyed your companionship and how much it meant to me. I found expression in your company for my love of the country (jumping ditches, climbing hedges, etc included) . . . so much so that I found myself making excuses to go out with you and arranging my half-days to suit you – a ridiculous attitude, as you would be the first person to admit. I hope you are settling down for the final spurt and if good wishes will help you at all you have them. Do you remember my talks to you about *Young Woodley*? There is a moral in the book, David – I want you to read it if possible – it will help you to understand yourself, from fits of depression to your desire for sympathetic companionship . . . The planes are very busy here, going to Germany, I presume. Thirty-six went out today at 12 a.m. Two squadrons went out last evening; they almost take the roof off. Just as I am writing this letter twelve more planes have gone over . . .

I have some collars to send you as soon as I can get a laundry to do them up for me . . .

I am sending you a rose out of my garden for remembrance. Keep it as a bookmark, dear, and have faith.

Your sincere friend

What warmth this letter inspired. I kept it and reread it for comfort. *Young Woodley* was a play by John Van Druten about a schoolboy who falls in love with his teacher's wife. It was staged in London in 1928 and released as a film the following year, starring Madeline Carroll. Mrs Stubbs told me I would be in the same position if I was not careful. But one cannot predict one's own future.

Spring and early summer in Cornwall were to be wonderful, despite knowing that I had my examinations looming up ahead of me, determining my future plans. 'How can I describe the whims of a warm, empty Helston afternoon,' I wrote of one Saturday in May in my diary, 'or the quietness of the Moor, the crowds in town and the fun of the Hostel?' 'The country reminds me of that in *The Wind in the Willows*,' I wrote next day when I walked north of Sithney with Mrs Stubbs. 'I see rabbits and a water rat. That impression of Cornwall made in the dreary, wet winter days is wiped out by the sun. The granite remains, but red ragwort grows beside it.'

Despite the war, Helston turned out on 8 May 1941 for the traditional Furry Day musical dance and parade through the town. As I stood on the corner of Meneage Street and Coinagehall Street I spotted a schoolfriend named Dyke among the dancers. He was well-grown boy, and his two equally tall parents had come down to watch him. He was often to call on me in my hostel room and to accompany me on walks around the town. I was unaware, until informed by a letter in the following year from Mrs Davis, the Helston postmaster's wife, that he had died of a goitre operation in Truro Hospital; a boy lost far too young.

It was in these days that I hitch-hiked across the county with different friends or on my own, encountering the world of the lorry driver. Often these were to the nearest town, Falmouth. 'Three miles on foot, ten miles by lorry and car and once more I am in Falmouth for the day . . . I meet Kathleen Jeffery and Stanley and see the film *The Prime Minister*, John Gielgud's Disraeli being excellent . . . I buy a book on Titian and *Penguin New Writing No. 5*.'

My longest trip was with young Johnny Miners: 'Hayle, St Ives, Penzance, Marazion . . . Forty miles all told, twenty-three of them walked, the rest by five cars and two lorries . . . We enjoy a half-pint of cider at Cripples Ease, eat on the beach at St Ives, buy ice cream in Marazion, have a glass of water at Breage; at no expense and no cares, who can grumble?' Other trips included one to Newquay with Cyril Cohen, whose brother was stationed there in the RAF, and another on my own to Truro to see the great cathedral by Victorian architect John Loughborough Pearson.

It was at this time, too, that my friendship with Stanley Bloom developed which would last a lifetime. We went one Saturday to Gunwalloe to paddle and continued on to Mullion where we drank cider and got sunburnt. During such excursions he expounded his ideas on Liberalism and other matters. I also took regular walks around Loe Pool with Lionel Kenner who had bought many of the Everyman volumes on philosophy, and Lionel would talk about Nietzsche and other writers. (Later in life he was to make a career overseas as a university lecturer in philosophy.)

All this time I was being encouraged in my school studies by Clifford Smith, who had an insatiable appetite for work and made sure I kept going. On 9 July the examinationss began with a paper on Public Affairs and ended on 21 July with a paper on Physical Geography, followed by one on Economics. 'I am free, free,' I wrote in my diary. Thursday, 24 July was my last day at school.

Next day many people went off by train on their return journey to London. I felt I wanted to stay in Helston a while, free of study pressures. Mr Roseweare said that this was possible, as evacuees could stay on 'looking for work', so I remained at Cross Street Hostel enjoying my room for a little longer. With many of my friends still down in Cornwall, as well as Clifford Smith and other members of the staff, this proved a good idea, and I continued to explore the county. Smith gave me an application form for the London School of Economics, and I began to study Algebra in preparation for a career in statistics and also German, as I had to take a paper in German and French for the degree. In August I received a letter from the County Borough of West Ham education department awarding me a Professional Training Scholarship. This consisted of payment of my tuition fees for the three-year course and a grant of £70 per annum, payable in instalments, to help cover expenses: 'maintenance, travelling, books and stationery, examination and incidental expenses'. I was to discover that £70 was not enough. However, in the event the London School of Economics gave me a means-tested extra £78, on which I just got by, living in lodgings with board for 35s. a week (£1.75 in today's money). I was lucky to get the West Ham award, as just six were granted a year. The time when students were to be adequately financed did not come until the 1960s.

Eventually I felt the need to move on and return home. My last talks with teachers and friends over and gifts exchanged, on Tuesday, 12 August I took the eight-hour journey back to London. In my diary I wrote: 'I felt that I was leaving a sheltered but limited valley.' Back at Upton Avenue I regretted the loss of my private room but enjoyed being reunited with the friends I had made in Cornwall – Stanley

Bloom, Johnny Miners, Mrs Godwin and others. Among these was Peter Colverd, who had lodged at the Coinagehall Street hostel and with whom I developed a firm friendship. He lived across Wanstead Flats in Dover Road and had a clerical job at the electricity offices in Romford Road, Stratford, not far from my birthplace. I found that he was writing poetry and that we shared literary interests. Soon we began to go on Saturday afternoons to Charing Cross Road, exploring the bookshops. We were to keep in touch until his untimely death in 1945 in Holland in a road accident while serving with the Army. He had landed on the continent on D-Day plus six. I missed his friendship very much.

Soon after my return I took myself off to Maidstone to spend ten days on holiday staying with my uncle and aunt and exploring the town and surrounding countryside, mostly on long walks. It was while I was there that I received a telegram from Clifford Smith in which he congratulated me on passing everything in Higher Schools. Thus the way was clear for the next stage, joining the London School of Economics to study for a BSc (Economics) degree, specialising in Statistics. The college had moved from its premises in Houghton Street, Aldwych, and was now in Cambridge for the war period. My next three years were to see me alternating between Cambridge and Forest Gate.

3

CAMBRIDGE

O<small>N</small> T<small>HURSDAY</small> 2 October 1941, together with my mother and father and accompanied by luggage and my bicycle, I made my first journey to Cambridge by train. We had our midday meal – called dinner – with my mother's friend Mrs Cook, and I was then inducted into my new lodging at 105 Coleridge Road. This is a turning off Cherry Hinton Road, on the south-east side of Cambridge, running into Mill Road, then a relatively poor area of the town. Mrs Cook lived near by and had found me lodging at my mother's request, spotting a card in a shop window. In due course I saw my parents off at the station and returned to take up residence in Coleridge Road, where I was to live for three terms.

Mr Reed, my host, was a slightly built Cambridgeshire man who cycled to work each day as a carpenter. His wife looked after the home, and Margaret, their only child, in her twenties, worked in a chemist's. I gained the impression that she used her face as a kind of palette on which to try out the various beauty products the shop sold. But she was an attractive girl, whose heart seemed to have been given to an airman who had been posted by the RAF to Texas for flying training, and she eagerly awaited his letters.

The family took me in as a lodger to help make ends meet. It was a semi-detached house with no inside toilet. My bedroom did not have a desk, was not a bedsit and was not as pleasant as my room in Helston. For study they provided me with a gate-legged table in the front room, which they kept for best. Working here was all right, especially when Mrs Reed kindly lit a fire as the weather grew colder. But I always had a faint discontent with my circumstances, wishing I had made use of the college's accommodation bureau and had rented a conventional Cambridge student bedsit. Against this, the Reeds were hospitable; they were a working-class family with whom I felt comfortable and it was a bonus to live in a house with an attractive young girl, even though we did not share many interests. Mrs Reed served traditional working-class meals, and I was fed well enough considering wartime rationing.

Settling into Cambridge was not all that easy. It was my first experience of an essentially middle-class world, and my working-class hackles rose at some of the public-school accents I heard all about me. I still had a London accent, and it would be a long time before it was modified into a less class-identifying speech. I soon came to appreciate the different social habits and attitudes of the middle classes. For instance, at home I had been used to the sequence of daily meals being known as breakfast, dinner and tea. Here the upper classes partook breakfast, lunch, tea and dinner. When I was first invited to tea at an academic house I was disappointed to discover that all it meant was a cup of tea and a piece of cake, not a full meal.

Peterhouse College played host to the evacuated London School of Economics, with some academics, such as Professor R.H. Tawney, lodging in their historic premises. LSE administration was based in a modern brick Peterhouse building almost opposite in Trumpington Street. (On a recent visit I saw that a plaque recording LSE's tenure had been erected on the wall.) The college base used by students was Grove Lodge, an early villa set in its own grounds across the road just past the Fitzwilliam Museum (which today occupies it). The upstairs room was used for seminars and teaching and to house the Shaw Library for cultural study. Downstairs was a lending library for students and a canteen, with the two main reception rooms, opened up into one, used for the social life of the college. This hosted events such as Director's receptions (I remember Sir Alexander Carr-Saunders extending a limp hand to me as he met each fresher for the first time), a visit by Sir William Beveridge, talks by visiting speakers and meetings of social clubs, but in the main it was the place where students gathered and relaxed. It had a grand piano and large armchairs. On one wall was a set of pigeon-holes for student correspondence and next to it a wall newspaper, called *Beaver* after the college emblem and mascot, run by Ken Sykora and Hugh Burnett.

Adjacent was the office of the influential Student Union Executive Council. It contained typewriters, which I was able to use after being elected to the council. The entrance hall to Grove Lodge was plastered with notices of all kinds, mainly political, representing unceasing student activity. Crowds of students came and went, and suddenly you found the building almost empty. In summer there were deckchairs on the lawn where many a discussion went on. Bicycles were stacked round the main door.

Cambridge University also showed wartime hospitality in allowing London University students to use its lecture rooms in Mill Lane and to attend Cambridge University lectures. We had free access to all timetabled lectures. For our part Cambridge students were welcome at LSE lectures at Mill Lane and could help pack out a lecture, for example, on Saturday mornings when Professor Harold Laski gave his popular, awe-inspiring hour of talk. I remember attending economics lectures at Mill Lane by Cambridge University's Marxist academic Maurice Dobbs. In the audience one sometimes saw King Peter of Yugoslavia, his kingdom having been occupied by Germany in 1941.

Peterhouse College allowed us the use of its boats, and I joined the LSE rowing club and learned how to row in an eight on the River Cam, one of my most pleasant memories. When I first turned up for training I discovered that this was being given by none other than Tony Simmons, of my Brentwood days, who had gone up to LSE a year before me. He had matured, lost his London accent and proved a good instructor.

Other societies and clubs that I joined included Dem. Soc., a Labour Party-orientated political club. Its rival was Soc. Soc., Marxist-dominated and to the left of Dem. Soc. In those days political division in the student world was not between Conservative and Socialist (although a Conservative club existed for a minority) but between Left and Far Left, with an active Communist group organised among students. It was not publicised, but some of its members were well known for their views. It must be hard, sixty years on, with the long history of anti-Communism that has dominated politics in the West, to appreciate the esteem in which the Far Left was held by many thinking people in the 1930s. Fascist forces in Spain, Italy, Germany and elsewhere ruled the peoples of those countries and threatened others. The Communists and the Soviet Union were, at one time, seen by many as the only effective force opposing them. No wonder that so many idealistic young people, in later life to be respectable names, joined the party as a matter of course. The civil war in Spain was the key event for many in deciding their allegiance to the Far Left; the poignant photograph on display in a Rose Crescent bookshop of John Cornforth, who had died in Spain, was testimony of the feelings of many in those 1930s years. It was only later with the unmasking of the Cambridge men Burgess, McLean, Philby and Blunt that the divided loyalties were revealed, with the empowering of Soviet Russia through spying seen as more important than British nationalism by young idealists when they gained influential positions in the British establishment.

College music and drama societies drew me in. The music society put on gramophone record programmes on Sunday evenings. The drama society invited theatre people down to speak, men such as Walter Hudd and Andre van Gyseghem, and also ran play readings in which I was soon taking a pleasurable part, my first being the role of Firs in *The Cherry Orchard*. I was to continue with amateur drama my whole time at college, ending with a stage production put on at Cambridge's famous ADC theatre.

I brought my Christian beliefs with me to Cambridge, although I did not bring them back when my university life ended three years later. In my first year I joined the LSE branch of the Student Christian Movement and heard speakers such as William Temple, Archbishop of York, and Father Grosser, the famous East End priest. I usually attended St Paul's Church in Hills Road although sometimes I went to the university church of St Mary.

I was not very happy in my first year at Cambridge. The war laid a gloomy pall over everything, Britain not being in a good position in 1941–2, even though Pearl Harbor in December 1941 brought the United States into the war and some military successes were at last achieved in North Africa. People were supposed to carry with them everywhere a small brown cardboard box containing a gas mask, a daily reminder of possible war horrors. Aerial attacks were always a threat, although the bombing of London had more or less finished by the time I went to Cambridge and was not really resumed until 1944 with the attacks by V1s and V2s. Bombing of ports and other military targets across the country nevertheless continued. Cambridge was not bombed while I was there, although a raid did take place in August 1942 during the vacation, and bombs had previously fallen on the city in 1940 and 1941.

My uneasiness was due more to the change in the way my life was structured. In Cornwall I had been an integral part of a school with a set timetable, my career closely watched by staff, and I enjoyed a host of friends. At Cambridge I had to adjust to a new way of life, structured and organised largely by myself, and to make new friends. One mostly had a choice regarding the lectures to be attended, and there were no teaching staff looming over one's life. Although I had been assigned a personal tutor I saw little of her. The way I interpreted it, I could do no work and nobody would care.

In addition I did not have the clear-cut objective of the Higher Schools examination which had shaped my life in Cornwall. The Bachelor of Science (Economics) course I was taking meant the first year was spent studying for an intermediate examination, followed by two years studying a specialist subject, plus economics and history, before taking Finals. But my Higher Schools results had exempted me from much of the intermediate examination subjects, leaving me with little to do compared with other students. However, to gain the degree you had to pass translation papers in French and German and these two language courses were to become an important part of my first year, as students were encouraged to take them ahead of Finals proper. I also had to undertake a paper in Economic History in my first year, but all this did not add up to very much compared with my Higher Schools work.

A more important troubling matter was that I had to do a paper in Pure Mathematics so that I could make Statistics my specialist subject. As that first term wore on, it began to dawn on me that Pure Mathematics was beyond me. This view was shared by my tutor for this subject, Dr Rhodes. I always remember the first time I encountered him. He slowly walked all round me as I sat in a hard chair in front of his desk, then sat down and said, 'You have no hair at all.' This was a fact with which I could only agree.

I was to write in my diary for Monday, 1 December 1941:

A Maths lesson after which Dr Rhodes advises me to drop the subject. Claus says Stats is OK if you are fond of figures. A talk with Tony decides me to talk to Geoffrey Beck. I do so, walking round and round the garden with him. He advises me to study Logic instead, and then either Government, Sociology or Economic History. The vision of the church attracts but he is not enthusiastic. Are you sure?

With hindsight I was lucky to have sensible fellow students with good advice to give. Claus was Claus Moser who was to become head of the government's Central Statistical Office and later ennobled, and

Geoffrey Beck became a clergyman. Tony was Tony Simmons from my school.

So Clifford Smith's recommendation that I should do a degree in Statistics faltered, despite his letters urging me to do three hours of mathematics every day. I enjoy figures in a modest, elementary way, but I am not a mathematician; calculus and other advanced mathematics do not come easily to me. The right decision was taken and I said farewell to Dr Rhodes.

Making my choice for my specialist subject for the final two years led to interviews with the three LSE professors in charge of alternatives. First I went to Professor Morris Ginsberg, who ran Sociology. This was a comparatively new academic subject, and it seemed to have no finite end, with students studying for five years. Next I saw Professor H.L. Beales, who was in charge of Economic History, and then Professor Harold Laski, who ran the Political Science Department. I had already heard Laski lecture and knew his personal charisma. His kindliness and charm led me to choose Government as a subject, although sometimes I have regretted not choosing Economic History. In due course the transfer was arranged, and in October 1942 I was to become one of Laski's students.

As well as the gloom of war, minor dissatisfaction with my studying and living conditions, loss of school supporting structure and uncertainty about my choice of academic subjects, I also experienced the need for friends, especially a woman's companionship. There was no shortage of women about. Because of the war the majority of the students were female. Men such as Tony, for example, were able to study only for a year or so before being called up into the services, usually at eighteen and a half. Most of the male students were either young eighteen-year-olds awaiting conscription, men with low medical classification or exiles such as Poles, Czechs and French, some in the uniform of their country, as well as some Asians, Africans and Indians. Women predominated, many of them attending the popular two-year Social Sciences course. Of course it was not long into the war before women students also began to be conscripted for war work. In these war years the college was small and residential, with close contacts between students and academic staff. No authoritarianism or set rules existed as in Cambridge University, and students were free to develop relationships between the sexes. Inevitably marriages took place between students after graduation. I began to be aware of this as I developed friendships within student societies, many with female students. But when I began to express any romantic interest I was not encouraged. Nor did I meet anybody through St Paul's Church. My attendance there led to an afternoon at the vicarage for young people with tea and a talk. The vicar began to expound on his social work in the impoverished East End, and with rising horror I realised that this had taken place in Stratford. I did not divulge that he was talking about my home town.

I was not without male friends. Tony Simmons shared lodgings with others at No. 8 Roundchurch Street in the heart of Cambridge, and I was to call there and to join in its left-wing discussions, but we did not share our lives. Roy Simpson, who had been in the form above me at school, was also up, studying for a Bachelor of Commerce degree and, as he had had tuberculosis, was exempt from the services. I was to get to know him better the following year when we played chess together. In due course he was to help me get a job that determined my career path. Sadly he was to die in the 1950s as the result of a car accident.

A third boy from my school at LSE was Danny Cohen, who took the intermediate examination at the same time as me. Our paths did not cross often, and in due course he was conscripted into the Army and commissioned as an officer. He was to die in February 1944 of wounds sustained during the Allied invasion of Italy. A new friend was Tom Umpleby, a short, sturdy Yorkshireman. We began to take country walks together, go to the Cosmo and Rex cinemas and the Arts Theatre and to meet for tea. After a year he was called up, commissioned and spent most of the war in India. A weekend with me in Forest Gate while he had an army posting in southern England coincided with a bombing raid in which we sheltered in our Anderson. Happily our friendship has continued since, sustained mainly by correspondence.

There were a host of other male students with whom I had pleasurable but casual acquaintance. These included Ivro Jarosy, who was to marry fellow student Joan Grant and to run the Academy art cinema in Oxford Street; Les Presnell, who was to become a history professor; Ralph Miliband, a left-wing voice who was to become a well-respected academic and whose sons now serve in the Gordon Brown cabinet; Peter Richards, with whom I shared tutorials in Government, who became a close friend and was to become Professor of Government at Southampton University; Kenneth Glynne, also to become an academic; Arnold Weinstock, later to be head of the General Electric Company and ennobled; Ken Sykora, to become famous as a musician and broadcaster; Hugh Burnett, who later achieved fame through his cartoons depicting monks; Jack Mendelson, a powerful figure in the student union whose Hungarian accent did not prevent him delivering impressive speeches and who was to become an MP; Chris Freeman, also an academic; Eprime Eshag, an Iranian who was to perform important liberating politics in his own country; Susan Strange, to become an international journalist; Stanley Benn, from my own school, also to go into academia and to settle in New York; Roy Heilbuth, to become an educational pundit; Jo Yagchi, a student with more interest in Newmarket than examinations; and Steve Wheatcroft, who was to become an authority on aviation.

One of the dominant students of my time, until he graduated in 1943 with a First, was Norman Mackenzie, a figure of the left, whose enormous energy and self-confidence made him a natural leader. He, too, was a student specialising in Government and was to be offered, through Harold Laski's friendship with the editor Kingsley Martin, a journalist's post with the *New Statesman and Nation*. He was to write books, some with Jean Sampson, the student he married, and later was to be a professor at Sussex University. While at college I found some of these students quite overpowering, but they were all good people, and gradually I adjusted to my new life.

One of the great pleasures of Cambridge for me was its bookshops. The Economist Bookshop had relocated from London and established itself in Trumpington Street, close to Grove Lodge. This was my first port of call before I would walk down to visit Bowes and Bowes, Deighton and Bell and David's stalls in the marketplace before walking to Heffer's in Petty Curry. Holding a book in my hands gives me enormous pleasure. It is not just the contents; it is the book as an object in its own right, with its design, weight and especially the smell of the paper. I love nothing more than being in a bookshop, a second-hand one as much as any other, often impoverishing myself through unrestrained desire.

In Cambridge I encountered for the first time the social habit of drinking coffee and tea with friends in establishments designed for that purpose. Tulliver's was the nearest to Grove Lodge. Beyond that was the Copper Kettle in King's Parade and then the Whim and

Matthew's in Trinity Street, the latter a favourite with Laski. Pubs I visited less frequently, never having found alcohol that crucial to my well-being.

Another factor that impeded my enjoyment of Cambridge was the coldness of its winter. The icy winds seemed to hit it from across flat land stretching as far as the Urals in Russia. Having no hair, my head was often cold, despite my trilby hat. I did not have a large number of clothes and usually wore a tweed jacket and flannels. A list I made in 1941 shows that I had two blue suits, one overcoat, one mac, nine shirts (three with detachable collars so that I could wear a shirt all week with just one change of collar), eight cotton handker-chiefs, two pairs of underpants and three vests, four pairs of socks and two pairs of pyjamas, three pullovers, seven ties and two scarves, one of them being the college scarf – a small-sized, wartime version bought at an outfitters in King's Parade. My list also shows that in September 1941 I was 5 feet 8 inches, weighed 10 stone 9 pounds, had a 28-inch waist and a 35-inch chest and wore 8½ size shoes. Today I am 5 feet 9 inches with a 45-inch waist. Such is the progress of man.

A bicycle was essential for getting into town from Coleridge Road, and I was soon to sport the usual wicker basket on the handlebars in which to thrust my books and notes. I would often make my way directly from my lodgings to the Cambridge University Library, which LSE students were allowed to use. This gave me a base in which to study during the day and allowed me to work regular hours, as in Helston. I came to enjoy using the large catalogue, ordering books that were brought to my seat in the reading room. The quietness of the figures sitting at the tables in this large, high-ceilinged room made it seem to me like a knowledge factory. One went downstairs to a café bar for small cups of black coffee, no milk being available in wartime. Shared study in a library is always something I have enjoyed.

On Monday, 8 December 1941 a small somewhat bewildered figure travelled home to Forest Gate at the end of his first university term. It was the day of Pearl Harbor, the attack by the Japanese which was to change the war, bringing Britain and its Empire into alliance with the previously isolationist United States. No bombing of London was occurring when I returned, and so life continued with more mundane concerns.

On 16 December 1941 I began work as a Christmas casual at the

Stratford Post Office where my father was employed. This was the first paid work of my life. It was a ten-hour day, most of it spent on the back of a lorry, jumping up and down from it to deliver parcels. I had been assigned to a hired van manned by two others and myself. Doing this work led to my losing confidence in statistics because the postman in charge, an ebullient Cockney, cheerfully entered his own figures for the number of parcels we delivered, usually doubling the real number. I was paid a shilling and sixpence an hour (7.5p), and I was to do the job again the following Christmas.

Our family Christmas was spent at No. 15 Upton Avenue, the flat my mother had secured, but on 2 January 1942 we were able to move back into our house at No. 77. This was because my mother, with her usual determination, had collaborated with the owner of No. 79 to prevent the demolition of our two bombed houses at the end of the terrace. Our square double-bay window, damaged by bombing, was replaced by a new round one. My parents had worked hard to restore the interior.

Romantic thoughts rose in my mind when, alone in the house, the electricity meter was read by an attractive, uniformed woman, but they were not expressed. Uniformed women doing jobs previously the preserve of men were now common, such as on the buses and at railway stations, a step towards the changing society that emerged from the war. Many women in uniform were to be seen on the streets, in the Army, Navy, Air Force and the Land Army. Around the corner in a primary school playground a barrage balloon was stationed, staffed mostly by Women's Auxiliary Air Force personnel or WAAFs. The blackout prevailed, with masked lights for vehicles, netting on Underground train windows, white rings around trees so that you could see them in the dark and of course shutters and curtains to exclude light put into place in every house each night. Brick air-raid shelters with concrete roofs were to visible in streets and parks, and bomb sites were occupied by emergency water tanks. Signs indicated where shelter might be taken during an air raid. All these things became the accepted way of life. The war and what it might bring hung like a cloud over our lives.

My return to Cambridge in January 1942 saw me developing a new friendship with fellow student Ronald Godfrey. He lived in Hobart Road, off Mill Road, and I nicknamed him Hobart. A reserved, handsome young man, he wrote poetry, and we took walks together, discussing common literary interests. He used to tell me about Chichester, where he had been evacuated, and gave me his address there. He was called up into the Army and was to be another of my generation lost in war. His father worked for the Rank Organisation, and his family published a volume of his poems after the war, a copy of which I treasure. The dedication reads: 'In memory of Ronald Godfrey, Lieutenant in the Hampshire Regiment, who fell in July 1944 in Normandy at the age of 22.'

Whether I was to follow in my friend's path and join the Army was put to the test when I had my medical examination for the services in Cambridge in May 1942. I found this a traumatic experience, walking naked from doctor to doctor in a bare hall while I was punched, examined and questioned. They seemed concerned about my thyroid and the intense nervous reaction of my leg when they tapped my knee. They tested my sight and asked about my alopecia. They gave me a buff-coloured card and sent me back to the cubicles to dress. The man in the next cubicle asked me how I had got on. 'It's on your card,' he said. Unaware, I looked at it to find I had been put into Grade III. I was then taken to a small office where an elderly army officer covered in red tape commiserated with me. 'I am very sorry to have to tell you that you have been judged as not the right material for active service.' I cannot say I was upset. My short experience in the Blitz, missing German bombs by yards, had, I thought, been my war service. The grading, however, was no guarantee that I would not be called up later as the war continued, and I waited rather anxiously on the post each day to see if it included a buff envelope with my call-up papers, but none came. The irony is that I have since never been ill and lived into my eighties. I suppose they did not want a bald, short-sighted, nervous teenager in the ranks.

In this new term, which began in January 1942, I added Logic to my study subjects of Economic History, French and German and dropped Mathematics. The joy of Logic was sitting in on lectures given by Professor Susan Stebbing. This formidable woman, whose textbook I studied, was a dowdy, middle-aged person with a first-class brain. I listened with awe to her clarity of expression. The lectures were held in Newnham, one of the two women's colleges in Cambridge (although I think that female students were not awarded proper Cambridge degrees at that time). I used to enjoy cycling to the Newnham brick pile, designed in the nineteenth century by Basil

Champneys, as I was to discover later. I felt a touch of Cambridge's academic glory in the ambience and delivery.

Witty, caustic and enjoyable William Pickles struggled to deal with our inadequacies in LSE seminars in French. I always remember him saying to me, 'I hope I never have to teach you how to speak French', after I had read aloud to him; sadly I never did master the accent and nuances of that glorious language. Fortunately the examination paper was a written one, not oral, which I was to pass in due course. The economist George Schwarz was another forthright character I remember from this time, a man of wit. Two other LSE economists I encountered, both young, were Nikki Kaldor and Eugene Grebenik, who were to develop brilliant careers.

It was in this second term that I discovered LSE's Shaw Library, set up a few years before by Charlotte Shaw, George Bernard Shaw's wife, to encourage students to study arts subjects as well as their college curriculum. Located in the bow-windowed upper room above the Grove Lodge entrance porch, it had walls lined with books, comfortable armchairs and a fire. In charge was a young, copper-haired woman, hampered by a limp, whose name I do not remember, although her kindnesses were several. It was here I encountered the French Symbolists, Robert Frost, Russian writers and more Thomas Hardy. At this time I read Henry Fielding's *Joseph Andrews*, which made me laugh aloud. I was captivated by David Cecil's *The Stricken Deer*, his study of the poet William Cowper, and I went on to read his *Early Victorian Novelists* and *The English Poets*. E.M. Forster's *Aspects of the Novel* was another favourite at this time, and I was to seize the chance to hear the great man himself in 1943 when he gave the Rede Lecture on Max Beerbohm, Forster being resident at King's College.

Most of all I remember reading John Keats, who is still my favourite English poet. I sat on Grove Lodge lawn with J.M. Murray's *Keats and Shakespeare* and took my copy of the Oxford edition of Keats's poems (bought new for five shillings) on to that most beautiful of places, the Cambridge Backs. It was not the first copy of Keats that I had owned. When Mrs Stubbs left Helston she gave me a tiny edition of some of his verse as a gift, writing on the flyleaf, 'I slept and dreamt life was beauty; I awoke and found that life was duty.'

Like many young people, I wrote poetry at this stage of my life. I do not remember doing so in Cornwall, so I suppose I began now. When I returned from Cambridge at the end of June 1942 and again in later vacations, I sat in my Upton Avenue bedroomscribbling away. I filled a notebook with a play written in Shakespearian-style verse, although without much plot and never finished. I filled other notebooks with stories and essays.

I found no paid work in that first long vacation of 1942 but that summer kept in touch with Stanley Bloom, Roy Simpson, Michael Heppenstall and Hector Davis, all of whom lived near by. Hector's family seemed better off than mine (Hector had to collect rents for the family business), and he invited me to stay with him in West Mersea for a few days, where an aunt and uncle had a house. Hector and I cycled the fifty miles or so through Essex to the coast. A rowing boat was available, and Hector suggested we went out in it for a swim in the Blackwater estuary. Unfortunately the water was full of currents, and try as I might I could not swim against the pull of the water back to the boat. Hector saw my plight and promptly life-saved me, using the orthodox method with his hand under my chin. I might have drowned that day without his swift action. I was always grateful to him. This personal adventure coincided with an attempt by Canadian forces to make a landing at Dieppe, on 19 August 1942, the day after my nineteenth birthday. The raid was a failure, and many lives were lost.

Stanley Bloom had taken his Higher Schools examination in July 1942 and had secured a place at LSE. He invited me to share digs with him in Cambridge, and this seemed a good idea. We found a room at No. 22 St Andrew's Road where Miss Saggers took in lodgers. At the end of this road, which was close to the river Cam and in the Chesterton area, stood Pye's factory, once a place where the famous Pye radios were made but now devoted to the war effort. Every morning at about eight o'clock a stream of workers, mostly women, would move down the road to the factory, watched by us from the front upstairs room which we shared. Stanley had a bed on one side and I had one on the other, and we were to live there for a full academic year.

Meals were taken downstairs (we were on half-board) using an indoor Morrison shelter as a table. Other residents included an Irishman who worked at Pye's – who maintained that Sidney Chaplin was a better actor than his brother Charlie – and the mysterious Mr Slipper, who never said anything if he could help it, thus exciting his landlady's intense curiosity. Miss Saggers came from Ware and had a distinctive Hertfordshire accent, pronouncing Pye's as 'Poye's'. Food rationing was getting more stringent, and meals were only just about adequate.

From St Andrew's Road we cycled across Midsummer Common to our lectures, seminars and student meetings, or we went to the libraries. As well as using the University Library I now began to use the Seeley Historical Library near the Senate House and the Marshall Library of Economics in Downing Street. My reading now was not only in history and economics but, for my specialised subject, in systems of government and in the history of political thought. The books I sat reading in the university library included a set of the writings of Thomas Paine, whom I thought one of the greatest writers of prose in the eighteenth century, some of which greatly influenced the birth of the United States of America. Hobbes, Locke and Burke led to the outstanding range of French thought, with Pascal, Voltaire, Diderot and Rousseau to be read for the eighteenth century and Proudhon, Jaurès and many others for the nineteenth, as well as the Germans Kant, Hegel and Marx, although I found these difficult. Then of course there were the Ancient Greeks.

Was it under these intellectual influences that I moved away from metaphysical beliefs and grew lukewarm in my Christianity? There was no dramatic moment when I rejected my adherence to the Church, but a diminution of attendance occurred and I probably stopped going during 1942. My approach to problems became centred more in reason and logic and less in desperate hope and seeking divine guidance. My ability to consider a problem intellectually and deal with it accordingly gradually became my guiding way in life. I wanted to be dependent upon myself. My thoughts of becoming a vicar dropped out of sight. This was not to say that I no longer acted in accordance with Christian precepts; these had marked me for life. But I began to fear that too much prayer and devotion made me introverted and basically selfish; loving your God could become an excuse for loving yourself and asking Him to do things for you.

Of the precepts 'Love Thy God' and 'Love Thy Neighbour', it was the latter that meant most to me. In other words, try to do well and help others when you can. Make your own mind the judge of this. Forget metaphysical beliefs. Find inner strength.

Weekly seminars with Harold Laski now began. These were held in his room in King's Parade, opposite King's College Chapel, which

I used to stare at out of his window during our discussions. Usually I shared a tutorial session with fellow student Peter Richards. Brought up in Worthing – where he would invite me for weekends later on – he had been graded IV in his services medical examination. He was a precise individual, very good on constitutions and detail and with a somewhat sceptical attitude to life. We were to take Finals together. He then became a librarian in Surrey, lectured for the Workers' Educational Association, was taken on by Southampton and ended up as a Professor of Government there. He published books on political subjects, served on government committees and tragically dropped dead in a Westminster street when his body gave out in his fifties.

Laski, lecturing in an Americanised Manchester accent without notes, was, in those war years, the central figure of LSE life. A Labour Party *éminence grise*, his conversations were peppered with references to talks with Roosevelt, Churchill and other leading political figures, giving the impression that he was at the heart of events. His audiences were always slightly suspicious of the stories he told, but he was a figure no one could ignore. He was a superb teacher, encouraging his students in any way he could. I always remember the plaintive story he told of being unable to get a girl student to discuss a subject and resorting to buying cream cakes as an inducement. I have seen him stop and give a porter's child a coin and know he helped students in many ways. Laski's own books on government lacked the fire of his lectures but were required reading. He was a short man, usually clothed in a respectable black suit, and he walked slowly along the Cambridge streets on the days he came up from London, his health never having been good. He was to die in March 1950 at the age of fifty-six.

Life was much better for me in those last two years at college. I had a solid two years of study to deal with, and I had the daily companionship of my room-mate Stanley. There were other West Ham boys now in Cambridge. Some of these had gained special wartime government places at Cambridge University to study engineering subjects, seen as potentially valuable in a long war. These included Denis Dickinson, Michael Heppenstall and Denis Jackson. Harold Noah also came up with Stanley. After graduating Harold was to teach in the United States and make a home in New York. The new intake of LSE students allowed me to make new friends, and I felt more integrated into the community than in my first desolate year. I was active in the Dramatic Society, where play readings continued, and was to appear on stage in Cambridge in Dodie Smith's *Call It a Day*. My modest part gained a favourable mention by the reviewer for the *Cambridge Daily News*. Harold Noah was in the cast. The producer was Frederic Rapoch. A note in the programme said: 'Throughout the performance a coloured light on the side of the stage will indicate All Clear (green) or Alert (red). Nearest shelter the Union.' Fortunately no interruption occurred.

The war was, of course, always a factor, hovering over what we did. Stanley was recruited into the Senior Training Corps and was issued with an army uniform and compelled to undertake army activities, such as night manoeuvres. His boots and uniform clogged up the bottom of his cupboard. The Student Union decided that all students should give up four hours a week to war work. In consequence, in January 1943 I became a porter on Wednesday afternoons at Addenbrooke's Hospital, which stood opposite Grove Lodge. I would report to the head porter at two in the afternoon and join a motley collection of men who, for some reason or other, had ended up there as porters. One was a ballet dancer, who I think was a conscientious objector. Stanley also worked there, and we made some friendships among our fellow workers. Our duties most often consisted of fetching and carrying, often wheeling a patient from his bed to an operating theatre or elsewhere and even sometimes to the basement mortuary, although this was usually the job of one particular porter.

Sometimes I was assigned to controlling the visitors. There was no policy in those days of unrestricted visiting. There were set hours, and no more than two people could visit a patient at any one time. We would wheel out a large wooden frame on which were hung metal discs, each numbered according to ward beds. We would then issue the two discs to the two visitors. Others would have to wait until the discs were returned before they in their turn could go to the wards. I quite enjoyed portering and was to continue with it up to taking my Finals in June 1944.

Another piece of war work that I shared in was helping to make camouflage nets. This took place in a hall somewhere in the middle of Cambridge in the evenings. Some twenty or so people, mostly women, circled a huge net and leaned over and tied on to it pieces of rag coloured either green or brown. It was fairly simple work and allowed conversation to take place. One night I came out of the hall about ten o'clock and found that my bicycle had been taken. Fortunately I recovered it next day with the help of the police. Borrowing bikes was not uncommon. But I never came across any real crime while I was in Cambridge and had no fear of walking about, even in the blackout.

The Student Union played an important part in the role of the college, its weekly meetings being the focal point of discussion. These were chaired by the elected Union President, and a succession of the brightest students held this post. Tony Simmons was among these, as well as Steve Wheatcroft, Joy Reed, Jennifer Forsyth, later an MP, and my friend Elwyn Jones. There was an elected Student Council, and in November 1943 I gained a place on this.

The Wednesday evening meeting of the Union, with guest speaker, took place in the Junior Common Room of Trinity College. I remember those evening walks, usually in a crowd of students, making our way down to the Great Gate of Trinity and walking through that large forecourt to the Junior Common Room on the far side. One of my heroes then was G.M. Trevelyan, who was Master of Trinity, but I never saw him there. Usually every chair was taken for animated discussions, usually on political subjects. Then the guest speaker would talk, having previously been dined at the University Arms Hotel where he may have been given a room for the night.

In this way we encountered men of distinction: George Orwell, Arthur Koestler, Kingsley Martin, Olaf Stapledon, Paul Rotha, the actor Lewis Casson, F.R. Leavis and others. The willingness of busy, well-known people to speak to undergraduates is one of the best features of university education. I suppose it could be called elitism of the intellect, but if you have got to university, it is likely that some of those there as undergraduates will reach positions of importance themselves in later years.

My role on the Student Executive Council included responsibility for the production of the college magazine, *Clare Market Review*. I worked on the Michaelmas 1943 issue, which was edited by Elwyn Jones, with Claus Moser and Oliver Marston as sub-editors, and I had a short story called 'The Cliffs' published in it. I became editor of the summer 1944 issue, which came out just before I took my Finals. Sub-editors were Pauline Rackham and Kathleen Prince. My contribution to this issue was a review of the recently published *The Road to Serfdom* by Professor Hayek, whose lectures I attended, trying to understand both his Viennese accent and the complexity of his ideas in the field of economics. I thought, immodestly, that in my review I had demolished his arguments. Readership of his book continues to this day. In this issue Claus Moser reviewed a book by Jacob Burckhardt, and there was an article by Jennifer Forsyth.

Friendship with Elwyn Jones was one of the benefits I gained from being at LSE. He was one of the 1942–3 intake and rapidly established a dominant position, becoming the president of the Union through his brilliance and strength of personality. He came from a family of coal miners in Aberdare, South Wales, and was tall, dark and attractive to women, with a persuasive voice and a certainty of manner. He was well aware of the way working people had suffered during the Depression years and saw no wrong in taking sums of money from neglected handbags if he was short, believing that their middle-class owners could afford the loss. When this was discovered in 1944 it meant the end of his university career.

I always found Elwyn's personal magnetism compelling and considered that he had one of the best brains I had ever encountered. We served on the Student Council together, and he helped me with *Clare Market Review*, on which we worked together, and he seemed to think I had an acceptable writing style. His downfall was devastating, with many students turning against him. It was at this point in life that I think I learned that you stand by your friends, whatever they may have done, and that personal loyalty should be a matter of pride.

Elwyn went on to make a successful career. Starting with a lowly job in a London second-hand bookshop, he wrote and talked himself into a job with a magazine, worked for Odhams, the great publishing conglomerate based in Long Acre, secured a job on the *Radio Times* editorial staff, after passing a competitive examination, and was to stay at the BBC for many years before becoming a freelance. He wrote the first television *Z Cars* scripts, and his musical interests led him to write an opera libretto. Throughout his life he suffered from a weak heart, with threats from his doctor he would only live six months if he did not change his lifestyle; he was to die in his forties. My friendship with him in London in the years immediately after college was a great pleasure.

Another friend I made was George Brand, a law student. He came from Bishop Auckland and worked with the Cambridge town Labour Party rather than in the university. He had gone through a bad birth, which had left him with a twisted arm and leg. But he had a good brain and a generous nature. We were to remain friends until his death in his sixties. By then he had married three times. After service with the War Crimes Commission, he landed a job with the United Nations, working first in New York and then in Geneva. In the 1940s we went youth-hostelling together and I always thought we made an odd pair, he with his twisted limbs and me with my bald head.

Dances were a regular feature of college life. The first I attended was the Freshers' Ball at the prestigious Dorothy Café, known as the Dot. In time my most regular partner was Daphne Brook from Huddersfield. I am not a great dancer, but I used to enjoy the waltz, foxtrot and quickstep with a girl in my arms and music with a good beat. The best was when a US Army band played in Glen Miller style. Daphne and I seemed to make a good couple, and we danced together regularly. She was a Quaker who took me to a Friend's Meeting. I admired her character and enjoyed going for walks with her. She told me she had a boyfriend in Yorkshire, which inhibited me from attempting to take our relationship further. We continued to be good friends after the war, meeting in London and exchanging letters. Eventually she married a man she met while rock-climbing in North Wales.

Kari Polyani was another girl I had the pleasure of taking to a dance, but she and I were less compatible on the dance floor. In my view she was the most beautiful girl in Cambridge, and I liked her enormously. She was the niece of Michael Polyani, a famous political writer, and Kari also held Far Left views. In my final term we worked in the Marshall Library, and when we went out for coffee together her wooden sandals clacked loudly as she walked down the street. Later, taking her degree post-war after call-up, she was to meet and marry a man from Canada and emigrated there.

Kate Prince was a friend whose company I also enjoyed, working with her on *Clare Market Review*, and in the Dramatic Society and sharing a friend in George Brand. Her associates were Pauline Rackham and Dorothea Baker, among others. This is a friendship that has endured through writing letters to each other regularly, although now we both have grown-up grandchildren. An element of nostalgia runs through her letters when she reminisces about our lives in Cambridge.

Ruth Neufield, of German parentage, caught my eye, cycling by on King's Parade in a white mackintosh, an image that I still retain. An attractive, down-to-earth girl, she and I used to share coffees and we were to meet for a while in the years after the war. Sadly she died in 2006. Margaret Chalken was in the cast of *Call It a Day*, and a friendship of a kind developed, continued by correspondence and meetings after we left university. Other names I remember are Gwen Barnes, Bridget Sutton (who was to marry the historian Christopher Hill), Ann Firth, Susan Jacobs, Joan Mercer (who married the poet Dannie Abse) and Mary Bromley, a friend of my last year whom I was to continue to see for a year or so and who stayed in Forest Gate with my family on a weekend visit.

Joyce Swale was someone I met in my first year and she married Frank Cummins, a fellow student, just before he was called up. Frank wrote me witty letters while he was in the Army and I was to visit Frank and Joyce in their married home before they moved to Birmingham. Male acquaintances included Max Reinhardt, who was to take charge of The Bodley Head publishing company, John Rees, a left-wing Welshman who died early from a weak heart, and Eric Bicknell, who was to specialise in antiques.

The scene in Cambridge changed during 1943 as the US military established itself in East Anglia from where it flew bomber raids on Germany. It opened a social centre for services personnel in a former hotel in King's Parade, and the traffic began to include Jeeps and other army vehicles marked with a white star. Black US soldiers were frequently to be seen on the streets; one told me it was the best time of his life. It was uncanny to hear American accents. I had been brought up on Hollywood films, and it almost seemed as though the United States had invaded Britain.

Like other students I used the long vacation in the summer of 1943 to search for casual work to augment my income: of course I also spent time studying. Laski, through his contacts, secured me an interview with the editor of the *Daily Herald*; this was in Long Acre at Odhams Press. During the course of the interview the well-known columnist Hannen Swaffer slipped silently into the room; his penthouse overlooked the Nurse Cavell monument in St Martin's Place. Next I had an interview with Gerald Barry, the editor of the *News Chronicle*, the Liberal newspaper later taken over by the *Daily Mail*. Sadly I did not strike either editor as suitable for temporary employment. The *Daily Herald* has since disappeared.

I next initiated off-the-cuff visits to offices in the huge Edwardian blocks around Kingsway and Lancaster Place, offering myself as casual labour. This was not an unreasonable hope, given the wartime shortage of labour. But I did not find an opening. Fortunately the LSE provided me with work. The college had been asked by the British Institute of Public Opinion, which had offices in Aldwych, to provide students to meet a government contract. BIPO ran the Gallup Poll, the American pioneer of opinion-polling. The project was for the Ministry of Food and was designed to provide a check on the effect of rationing on the working population. Its details must be buried somewhere in the National Archives at Kew in a government file, but I have never heard it mentioned or described.

Reporting to BIPO's office on 19 July 1943, I was asked to travel the next day to Luton and to Bedford the following week. My task was to find small firms and persuade their managers to send their employees to be weighed and to have their height measured at pharmacies on a regular basis. For this I had to secure the agreement of local chemists. Armed with a bundle of forms I took a train to Luton, the first hurdle being finding somewhere to stay. All the regular hotels were full. Eventually I found a landlady who assigned to me a bed in a large upstairs front room. When I returned late that night I found about six American servicemen occupying other beds in the room.

I went first to Luton Library where I obtained a list of local firms, and I bought a map of the area. Then I began to walk around the town finding firms and chemists. The traditional industry in Luton was the manufacture of straw hats, and I found several of these craft firms still at work. Most employers and chemists agreed to my proposals, accepting them as part of the war effort, I suppose. Daily reports were sent by me to BIPO. The following Tuesday I took a similar train journey to Bedford and carried out the same exercise there. It was a very hot week, and I took the opportunity to row on the River Ouse. Here I stayed in a conventional hotel, but it had once been a medieval religious building, and my room was rather like a monk's cell; I cannot recall a window. I still have a book I bought in Bedford, *The Death of a Moth and Other Essays* by Virginia Woolf, who had committed suicide not long before. The assignment was well paid in terms of both fees and expenses. Whether it was all worth while I have no idea.

My father was now in his final Post Office years, working as a supervisor in Hackney. My mother was now also working, as she was still only in her forties. She travelled each day to Aldgate and sorted clothing coupons at the headquarters of the Co-operative Wholesale

Society. Eater she transferred to a better job in a bank headquarters, sorting cheques. I had the house to myself during the day while I was at home on vacation. When back from my travels I joined Stanley, who lived close by, on hitch-hiking journeys, using the skills we had developed in Cornwall. We visited war-devastated Coventry, Ipswich and Guildford on day outings. We also played chess.

Peter Colverd was at work during the week but on Saturdays we would travel on the 25 bus to the top of Charing Cross Road. We made our way down, our favourite shops including Better Books and Zwemmer's, both of which had good stocks of contemporary literature. In Zwemmer's there was a tall assistant who had the habit of making sure that every dust-jacket was tapped down into place after someone had handled a book. There was also a shorter assistant who I believe was a writer. After a great deal of browsing we would end with tea at the Express Dairy tea rooms at the Leicester Square end of Charing Cross Road. We began to augment these outings by theatre visits, since shows would start about four in the afternoon during wartime, allowing people to get home before the nightly air-raid sirens began to blare. We saw Ibsen's *Ghosts* in St Martin's Lane, with a powerful performance by Beatrix Lehmann as Mrs Alving. Soon after we saw Chekhov's *A Month in the Country*. For me it was the beginning of a life devoted to the West End Theatre, one of the great glories of London.

Peter and I began to build up collections of books and talked about what we were reading. For me I most vividly recall Christopher Isherwood's *Lions and Shadows,* his autobiographical volume of 1938, followed by *Goodbye to Berlin* of 1940 and *Mr Norris Changes Trains.* We read Dylan Thomas, James Joyce, Stephen Spender, C. Day Lewis, W.H. Auden, T.S. Eliot, Virginia Woolf and Franz Kafka in translation. These outings and meetings came to an end in September 1943 when he was called up into the Army. He thus embarked on a course of life that was to end with his death in Holland in a traffic accident while he was serving as a dispatch rider. In his will he left me his books; his parents, agonised at the loss of their only child, offered me his bookcase as well. Upset at the thought of gaining from his death I refused both books and bookcase. His collection included the first editions of Dylan Thomas that Peter had bought early on and other good volumes. Where they ended up I do not know.

A week after Peter's call-up came my brother's, who had, until then, beeen working in a reserved occupation as a Post Office engineer. He was to be a cadet in the Royal Air Force and went to Rhodesia to learn to fly. As a boy he had often been physically sick while travelling on Underground trains, and motion sickness prevented him passing his medical in the final stages of training. He thus avoided becoming a pilot, which probably saved his life.

In the summer of 1943 I went to see Will Thorne, once a powerful figure in the labour movement and then still a Member of Parliament (there were no elections during the war, so elderly men carried on working in government). Thorne lived near by and I sat in his front room while he recalled his days of 'talking on the stump' when he addressed huge crowds of workers in the docks in the early days of the Labour Party. A few days later he showed me round the Houses of Parliament. This may have been my first visit and could have been the occasion when I saw Winston Churchill telling the chamber that General Sikorski, the Polish leader, had been killed in an aircraft accident at Gibraltar. At that time the Commons was meeting in the House of Lords' chamber, the Commons' chamber having been bombed.

In October Stanley and I returned to Cambridge. Our room in St Andrews Road had served us well enough during the 1942–3 year, but Stanley, who had built up his own group of friends, wanted to find other lodgings, preferably near the centre of Cambridge. At first we settled on a house in Kimberley Road in Chesterton, providing half-board. The landlady had never got over the loss of her husband in the First World War but was amenable enough to us. But Stanley was not happy here as it was still too far out, and he found a place near central Downing Street in January 1944. I moved to a room at No. 4 Chesterton Hall Crescent, which I discovered was next door to where the famous Cambridge literary critic F.R. Leavis lived. I used to see him cycle away from his home occasionally. This was not a very good lodging for me, as I do not recall any meals being provided, and every evening I had to go out to eat, often to the well-known restaurant called the Blue Barn. I remember once, trying to avoid this, sitting in my room attempting to make a meal out of a tin of condensed milk, spooning the sickly-sweet substance into my mouth and still feeling hungry afterwards.

I stayed in Chesterton Hall Crescent for the Lent term but decided I must move for my final one, if only to get meals provided. I found lodgings by knocking at random doors in the Chesterton area and finally getting a favourable reception at No. 16 Holland Street, a turning off Victoria Road. This was a Cambridge University lodging run by three very elderly ladies, and I enjoyed living there immensely. It was a smallish terraced house where I had a bedroom and the full use of the front downstairs room, in which I studied and to which the ladies brought meals. A small bell was provided on the table so that I could ring for my next course when I was ready. On Friday evenings a hip bath was placed on the linoleum in my bedroom and three cans of hot water provided. I would pour these in, sit upright against the back of the bath and wash myself. I felt like a Victorian. But houses without hot water were still common. The old ladies seemed to belong to a golden age of Cambridge of the well-to-do with servants. Holland Street proved to be my fifth and final Cambridge address. When I went down I arranged for the accommodation to be taken by a fellow LSE student called R.B. Cant, who in due course became a Member of Parliament.

Living next door to me was Cecil Pickavance, an LSE law student with whom I was already friendly. We were to call on each other in Holland Street, and our friendship has lasted and we still keep in touch. After qualifying in law Cecil returned to his native Lancashire and became a town clerk. On his visits to London for meetings we would meet in the White Horse restaurant which was located so conveniently within the underground passages of Piccadilly tube station. At these lunches I used to enjoy Cecil's gift for making puns.

Like me, Cecil was a friend of George Brand and also of Betty Yates, a charming legal student whom we called the Dormouse because of her short stature. I managed in due course to get the three of them to come to my house in Forest Gate for a meal.

Although living in different lodgings, Stanley and I remained close friends. He had always been a great traveller, and we cycled together to St Ives, Huntingdon, Saffron Walden, Ely and Newmarket. Other places further afield, such as Peterborough and Bedford, we visited by bus. In September 1944 Stanley was called up and became a Bevin Boy, working in Nottinghamshire coal mines and, in Nottingham city, meeting his future wife. This did not stop his travelling, and in his holidays in the summers of 1945 and 1946 we hitch-hiked to Wales and to Scotland. It was not until 1947 that he was able to return to LSE, obtaining his degree in 1949.

About this time I attended a lecture given by the famous economic historian R.H. Tawney, and I wrote to him afterwards expressing differing views on liberty for minorities in a democracy. He wrote back to say it was gratifying to learn that anyone had actually listened to what he had said and invited me to his rooms in Peterhouse to discuss the subject. He gave me an interesting hour of his time. Tawney was a pioneering thinker and greatly respected. Clothes did not seem to concern him; Harold Laski maintained that Tawney always bought his suits in Petticoat Lane and did not own more than one. He was a lovable man.

Part of my vacation was spent in preparing *Clare Market Review* for publication, which was achieved through a Fleet Street contact that arranged a printer and supplied proofs which I had to paste up. I returned to Cambridge on 17 April 1944, and the copies of the magazine arrived on 27 April. As it was my last term at college I surrendered the editorship.

Waiting for a feared event is, as we all know, often worse than the event itself. For me, waiting for the war in 1938 was worse than 1939 when war itself actually came. I found it the same now with my Finals. I feared failing and so letting everybody down. I lost concentration and went to see Harold Laski about it. 'You need a holiday,' he said. 'Here, I have just won a £5 bet on the result of an election in America. Go and take a holiday.' He then gave me £5. 'But where should I go?' He recommended the George Inn in Winchcombe, Gloucestershire (I later learned that a famous literary US academic had dropped dead on its doorstep while staying there). Overcome by his generosity I made my thanks and, as he recommended, sent a telegram to book a room, using the grand-sounding Grove Lodge as my address.

I travelled by train to Cheltenham and took the bus up Cleeve Hill to Winchcombe. Each day the hotel gave me a packed lunch, which I ate as soon as I left each morning, wartime breakfast not being particularly adequate. It was spring, and the countryside was wonderful. Stanton and Stanway were two fine villages within walking distance. But solitary country walks became monotonous, and I hitch-hiked to more distant places such as Tewkesbury and, most memorably, Stratford-upon-Avon, my first visit. I joined a small party looking over Shakespeare's birthplace, which included two American servicewomen), and remember hearing the woman curator praise the virtues not of the playwright but of the great actor David Garrick.

I returned to Cambridge in great spirits and set about studying previous examination papers, especially in Economics, so as to develop the technique of answering set questions within time parameters. This I mostly did in the Marshall Library, having coffee with Kari Polyani whenever I could. Social life went on as before. On the Sunday before Finals I met up with my friend Daphne Brook and enjoyed a an enjoyable eight-mile walk with her along the River Cam, mainly discussing religious belief.

On Monday, 12 June 1944 I went to the Senate House and began the first of ten examination papers which would take up the week and beyond. Nervousness beset me; as an antidote I prepared a tiny bottle of gin from which I sipped to steady my nerves. I have never been a big drinker, but alcohol has a role to play at times! My other strategy for controlling anxiety had been a steady reading of Plato's *The Republic*, which taught me a system of intellectual enquiry that has always stood me in good stead. So I began my Finals, with papers in the Principles of Economics and in Banking. On 19 June I dealt with the last of the examinations, and on 21 June 1944 I left Cambridge for good.

A month later I went to South Kensington where London University examination results were posted and I found that I had gained an Upper Second. Of the forty-one students who had sat the examinations, two got Firsts, one of them Oliver McGregor, later to be Lord McGregor. Fourteen obtained Upper Seconds, seventeen had Lower Seconds and eight gained Passes. So the long three years were over and I had not let anyone down. I was twenty years old, and now it was time to look for a job. War of course still filled our minds. On 6 June 1944 the long-awaited Second Front opened with the Allied invasion of Europe supplementing the campaign against the Germans in Italy. News came through that there had been unexplained explosions in London, soon to be recognised as the result of the first of Hitler's secret weapons, the V1, known as the 'doodle-bug' – a pilotless bomb launched by rocket power. This was to be followed by the V2 explosive missiles that descended from a great height. I was to return to Forest Gate to this new form of bombing.

What were my thoughts about Cambridge as said my farewells? The place where you live your young, impressionable years cannot help but become part of you. So the occasions I have visited that venerable university city again have been nostalgic ones. A street is not just a route lined with buildings. It is a place where you met people, experienced emotions, passed your time. So if you go back after a gap of years you find yourself clinging to your memories of what you did there. When someone demolishes a building they delete part of your past life. Perhaps that is why the old are conservative; they have more emotion invested in the past than the young.

So what did the education I received in Cambridge mean to me? I especially enjoyed discovering a new world of political thought, realising that ideas thought up by individuals turn into great political movements and change history. I had endured, rather than enjoyed, economics, which got more mathematical the more I studied. I had appreciated extending my historical knowledge, social, economic and diplomatic. I had discovered the power of the mind to tackle problems logically and the importance of knowledge in liberating the mind from narrow, limited views of existence. My innate sense of curiosity was enhanced, and I saw beyond narrow parameters.

Despite the intellectual stimulus to the mind of my degree course, part of me had always been drawn to creative literature. I was torn between the ordering of knowledge to assess our existence both now and in the past and a different world of novels, poetry and essays in which human emotions are examined and interpreted. With my pleasure from reading good writing, both prose and poetry, and with my modest facility to write fluently, I yearned to escape from the world of economics. Literature offered a greater allure.

My nature, I think, is on the whole modest and self-deprecating, and I never saw myself as possessing dominant leadership qualities or being in one of the top brains of my generation at university. I was never to achieve a position of power and influence, as many of my fellow undergraduates went on to do. I think I had common sense, inherited from my mother, and in time I came to realise that this was a quality separate from intelligence. What I did have as an abiding ambition, as the years passed, was to make my name as a writer.

4

INTO THE WORLD OF WORK

I TRAVELLED HOME to Forest Gate aware that London was now under-going a new form of bombing and that my parents had been among those who first had experienced it. My father had written to me on 11 June describing what had happened but did not post it until 19 June, when my last examination paper had been taken, presumably not to disturb me. He wrote:

No doubt you have read something of the new form of air terror and how Jerry sends over a plane without any crew which at a given time comes down etc and of course causes much damage. Well, at 11.20 p.m. Thursday we had the warning and had to stay up all night as we did not get the all clear. Without going into details, at 5.30 a.m. one of these planes fell at about No. 49 Upton Avenue and of course caused much damage and loss of life. Our house is damaged, chiefly at the back, but fortunately we can still live here. Neither Ma nor I are hurt although we had a shaking. Ma was by the cellar door and I was in the front bedroom. You know how damage looks so I need not try to describe it. ARP workers and first aid repairs were commenced immediately [sic], and I did not go to work. Yesterday I went to the Doctor's and he has given me a week off. On Friday we worked all day to clear the debris.

We are still in a mess as the workmen are repairing the roof etc. Still we do not mind as it is getting our house put right. Next door Mrs Phillips and family had a marvellous escape. Mr Heppenstall and family had injuries. Colonel Luscombe's injuries were fatal, also some others. We have slept in the shelter since then and if you come home on Wednesday you will have to do the same . . . Well, son, you say you are coming Wednesday, Ma says do not rush and if you want to stay a few days longer do so, Ma will send you some money if required, please yourself. We will of course be pleased to see you but it is not so pleasant as anticipated a week ago. Everybody has cleared

Arthur Gay (1855–99), my
paternal grandfather

Arthur's wife Harriet
Clark (1855–1919)
with whom he had
four children

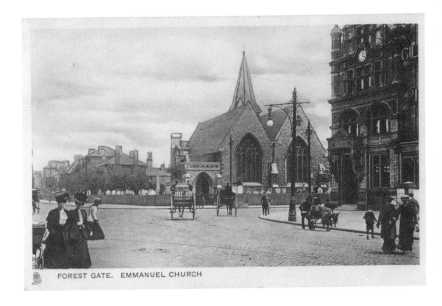

FOREST GATE. EMMANUEL CHURCH

Top: Emmanuel Church,
built in 1852 on the corner
of Romford Road and
Upton Lane, Forest Gate,
where my grandparents
were married in 1879

Left: Arthur's and
Harriet's third child,my
father, Edgar Charles Gay
(1888–1967)

Top left: My
father in uniform
during the First
World War

Top right: My
father's elder
brother, George
Gay (1881–1969),
in army uniform

Right: My father's
sister, Edith Gay
(1893–1986),
with her husband
Will Parrish
(1888–1962), who
was also in the
Army in the war

Above: The Adams family, with my mother on the right, taken in 1904 in their house in Morley Road, Plaistow

Below: The Adams family in a 1913 studio portrait with my mother on the right

Grandfather Adams (1865–1933), my mother's father, who also had four children

My mother, Clara Jane Adams (1893–1987)

Left: My mother's elder brother, Albert Adams (1890–1970), in First World War uniform, with his wife Lizzie (1890–1967)

Below: My mother's younger brother, Archibald Adams (1900–1957), who became an army captain and later served at Dunkirk; photograph probably taken in Malta, *c.* 1936

My mother's sister,
Edith Adams (1891–1960),
known as Aunt Cis

Albert Broomfield (d. 1958),
Aunt Cis's second husband, as a
young cavalryman in the King's
Dragoon Guards

Above left: My parents, who married on 15 May 1918 while my father was in the Army, as he wasn't discharged until 1919

Above right: My father and mother, taken on their honeymoon in Eastbourne, 1919

No. 12 Glenavon Road, Stratford, the home of Auntie Edie and Uncle Will; the design was identical to No. 12 White Road, where we lived

Above: The classroom at Park Elementary, where my education began in 1928; I am in the second row on the right with a toy lorry.

Below: Class 4; I am in the front row, nearest the camera. Some fifty boys fill the room; the girls must have been photographed separately.

Above: My father in the 1930s, sorting letters for his delivery round in Stratford

Below: My father playing Christian in a church production of *Pilgrim's Progress,*
c. 1932

Above: On holiday in the 1930s in Ramsgate; my brother Ernest (b. 1920) is in plus-fours next to Aunt Cis with my father, mother and me.

Below: This magnificent 1898 building, known from 1921 as the West Ham Municipal College, was a few minutes' walk from my home. The public library within it (on the left) helped shape my life.

West Ham Institute, Stratford.

West Ham Municipal
Secondary School
Sixth Formers
outside Helston
Girls' School in
July 1941

Below left: Me aged seventeen, in Helston, Cornwall; a 1941 photograph to send to
my parents in London

Below right: Schoolfriend Peter Colverd who was to die in uniform in Holland
in 1945, aged twenty-one

Above: Me with my Cambridge landlady's daughter, Margaret Reed (left), together with a friend of hers, 1944

Below: Damage caused by a V1 flying bomb on Upton Avenue on 16 June 1944
Courtesy of the London Borough of Newham Heritage and Archives

Miners' Welfare
Commission
staff at Ashley
Court, Ashtead,
Surrey, 1945

Miners' Welfare weekend conference at Barry, near Cardiff, in 1948; Will Owen is sixth from left, and I am second from left, front row. From here I went AWOL.

Above: National Coal Board Public Relations Branch at their 1949 Christmas party; the first NCB Films Officer, Kurt Lewenhak (1920–2005), stands behind grey-suited Lambton Wilkinson on the right.

Above: Hobart House, Grosvenor Place, in 1950s' London. My office for over thirty years, it was demolished and rebuilt in the 1990s.

Above: With Elwyn Jones in August 1950

Below: Walking in Lower Regent Street in 1950 with the Coughlan sisters, Agnes (left of me) and my future wife Teresa (right)

from Upton Avenue excepting our neighbours and us as the houses cannot be lived in. We are keeping cheerful and hope this new air warfare will soon be mastered. Love from us both. Ma and Pa.

The damaged houses in Upton Avenue and the road behind were cleared away. This large bomb site was to remain empty until prefabs were built on it and later a primary school. More bomb sites and damaged houses appeared as the V1 attacks continued. From June to September 1944 nearly fifty V1s landed in the borough of West Ham, twelve of these in Forest Gate, two of them close to Upton Avenue. Then on its heels came the V2, the more deadly of the two weapons. A rocket descending from the sky, it gave no warning of its coming. A heavy explosion, followed by damage and death, told you of its arrival.

I spent the next two months at home, searching for employment, writing to friends and making what visits I could. I spent each day on my own, as both my father and mother were out at work and my brother was away in the Royal Air Force. The siren would go, and I would amble out to the garden and the Anderson shelter and lounge by it. If the sound of a V1's spluttering engine was to be heard I gently lowered myself into the shelter, to be on the safe side. If you were out when one approached you looked for the nearest street shelter. Stanley and I were in Stratford Broadway together soon after our return from Cambridge, and we watched one of the doodle-bugs go across the sky then suddenly fall and explode, sending up a plume of smoke. Fortunately in north London the impact was not nearly so bad as in south London or in southern counties. Allied advances in Europe, with the capture of launching sites, eventually led to the end of this menace, although V2s were still falling in 1945.

It was a time of powdered egg and dried milk, and I would concoct strange midday meals, sometimes frying rice. No. 77 Upton Avenue was without a telephone, not unusual at that time, although later, perhaps in 1945, we acquired GRANGEWOOD 1064 as our number and a big black telephone. So I kept in touch with friends, some of them now in the services, by letter writing. 'Here in France,' wrote Peter Colverd on 8 July 1944 (about a month after D-Day when the Allies landed), 'life is all but intolerable. First night a hole dug with my own hands in the earth, now a ground sheet hung tent-like on a tree. My sudden death likely though. Can hardly think so will write a letter to you later on.'

Peter's letters were censored, and his next letter, of 8 August 1944, related a conversation with his officer who complained about what he said in his letters about the miseries of his life. Peter then went on for a further twelve sides about the role of the artist in society, quoting Rilke and others he had been reading. From time to time Peter sent me poems he had written. I did not know then that I would never see him again.

Freddy Green, my pre-war schoolfriend, served with the Eighth Army in North Africa, and I was delighted when one of the familiar Active Service brown envelopes, stamped 'Passed by the censor', came from him. He was not fond of army life. I don't know what I had written, but he replied once: 'If I were you I wouldn't talk drivel about the Army. You can call it a blessing that you're out. Get your degree while you can. That will help you to get a job and keep it. You'll probably wait a long time before you hear any of my adventures. I was sorry to hear that Danny Cohen had got his ticket . . .'

My women friends at college also had their war problems to deal with. Kate Prince wroter from Hampstead:

I am in London, staying with Ruth [Neufeld]. We are both working for the WVS (Women's Voluntary Service) helping with the London County Council evacuation business [this would have been the result of the V1 attacks]. We were in London till Wednesday morning, despite the pilotless planes. Neither Ruth nor self is yet employed. Comes August 11th and we shall be called upon by one Ernie Bevin to go out and infiltrate industry for the sake of King, Country and what have you. We both send our love and best wishes re your own career. Try and get in touch with us this weekend.

A letter came from Mrs Stubbs in Rainham in Essex:

I am sorry I have not answered your letter before, but I've been busy this last three weeks and what with being chivvied all over the place by doodle-bugs I feel very much in need of a rest. All I can suggest is that if it is at all possible to visit Mrs Jeffery at Sidcup I can make my visit simultaneously, thus killing two birds with one stone. Kathleen Jeffery is going to college in September, somewhere in Wales . . . I don't think that you have chosen a very good time to come back to London.

This meeting did not take place, although I did go to Maidstone to stay with my aunt. The coach was stopped halfway and everyone's identity card was scrutinised.

My mother was still concerned about my alopecia. She had lived in hope that my hair would grow again, but five years had passed and even her old-fashioned folk remedies, such as rubbing an onion on my bald head, had not proved successful. She thought that to get a job I must wear a wig. I set about compiling a list of London wig makers and getting quotations from them. Of the ten firms I contacted, the cheapest – and just about affordable – were the wigs of the firm of J.H. Spaans in Lisle Street, Soho, which quoted me five guineas each. This was a back-street shop catering mainly for the theatrical trade. Mr Spaans was an elderly Dutchman, assisted in his small premises by his son and his daughter. I had not foreseen that I would have to choose the colour of the hair when I went to be measured or else I might have taken someone with me. I chose badly, a sort of blond, which seemed to match the coloured school photograph I had. When it was made I did not think the shade suited me, and I did not feel comfortable wearing it, although I was to try it out when I went for the first job but only for a day.

In the event I was to continue bald and wigless until 1949 when the new National Health Service overcame my financial difficulties. It provided me with a voucher for a pair of human hair wigs (one on, one off for a month, being cleaned). I took this to Spaans and this time chose a more suitable brown colour, which I was to wear for most of the rest of my life. By 1949 old man Spaans had died and his two children were running the business. I was to remain with them until Miss Spaans, by then working at home in Harrow, retired in the 1990s and I transferred to a Paddington-based firm.

The search for employment was my main occupation after I returned to London in June 1944. I registered with the University of London Appointments Board, which began to send me typed slips from their Gordon Square offices describing vacancies notified to them. One of these was to lead to my first job. This was at the *Bournemouth Times*, which sought a candidate not eligible for military service, preferably a young college-leaver who was medically unfit. 'The successful candidate would be given a good training for a career and would start at a salary of £5 5s. a week with the customary rise after a few months if he proves satisfactory.' A letter to me said:

The job now going is to take over the newspaper circulation department of the *Poole Herald* and the *Bournemouth Times*. This means delivering the papers on Wednesdays and Fridays to the newsagents, collecting the monies once a month, contacting the agents and keeping their goodwill. If you consider this you would have to learn to drive (this can be done here) and we would suggest you come to us for a month's trial.

Independently of the Appointments Board I tried other avenues, including applying for a trainee sub-editor job at the BBC. But my interview with a board in the depths of Broadcasting House was unsuccessful. I wrote to three publishers to see if they had any vacancies: Oxford University Press, Macmillan and George Allen and Unwin. For the latter application I sent a letter of introduction from Harold Laski, whose books were published by Allen and Unwin, and this was the only firm that granted me an interview. I was cross-examined by Stanley Unwin himself, after which he wrote from Museum Street, EC1 to offer me a post at £3 10s. a week. It was routine work, he warned, but would give me experience of the publishing business.

By now I had received a firm offer of the job at Bournemouth and I had to choose between them. Bournemouth offered the higher salary and gave me the chance to get away from home again and provided greater independence. With the V1s and the V2s falling, it seemed to be a safer place to live. Involvement with the college magazine and a love of writing led me to believe there would be more writing opportunities on a local newspaper than as a dogsbody in a publishing house. Sometimes I wondered if I had made the right choice. If I had accepted Stanley Unwin's offer I would have got into publishing, a career many sought. But it was not to be.

My financial state at this time was rock bottom. I had no savings and had been living at home with my parents on virtually nothing. My mother had tried to help me as far as she could. All the time I was in Cambridge I had posted a brown paper parcel home with my laundry, which my mother had washed and mailed back, and this maternal care continued now as I set off for Bournemouth:

I am writing from Maidstone . . . I got your toothbrush ready to post and left it on the mantelpiece, so I will send it with the washing next Tuesday, I hope. I washed it out on Saturday morning and will iron it tomorrow evening. I will also send a tie which I have bought you. I will send you some money for the shoes if you can't manage it. I should think you would get a better pair there. I don't suppose the money goes far with having to board out. It has been very nice to stay here for a change. The doodle-bugs have been very active, but one doesn't feel as nervous as they go overhead as we know they are travelling further on. We saw an aeroplane shoot one down last night, and heard several bangs around. It was nice to sleep in a bed again. Aunt Cis and Uncle Bert sleep in their Morrison shelter . . . Did I give you Ernest's address: Hut 127, Carr Site, RAF Station, Melbourne near York. We haven't forgotten your 21st birthday. Will celebrate one day soon.

So on 10 August 1944 I caught the 8.30 train from Waterloo to meet my new employer, Mr Putnum, the director of the firm, for the first time. One week later, on 18 August, my birthday, I was to receive my first regular, weekly pay cheque. A different aspect of the war impinged upon me as I made my way down from Bournemouth railway station to the offices of the *Bournemouth Times*, located near the sea front at No. 60 Commercial Road. I had to make my way through a seething mass of people – not holiday-makers but mostly US servicemen. It was only a few weeks since the bridgehead had been established in Normandy, and more and more Allied forces were being transported across the Channel from the South Coast. It was mid-August, so there must have been some holiday-makers, although the pier had been breached in 1940 to prevent it being used by possible invasion forces. Most beaches still had barbed wire and other defences, but holiday beaches such as Bournemouth had been cleared by 1944 when the boot was on the other foot. American voices sounded around me, as they had in Cambridge. But we were all glad that they were there, although many of the men I saw on that hot August afternoon could only be on their way to death.

My employer turned out to be an ex-naval man, invalided out. He was an affable, middle-class young man, but I always felt slightly wary when with him. After all he was my first boss, and one had to be careful. I don't think his war experiences had helped him to develop an equable temperament, but I had no cause to complain. He was the first of a group of people with whom I was to work. I was sent off to his young secretary, a tall good-looking woman, who was to sort out accommodation for me in the town.

I stood before her in my yellow wig (which made me feel like Harpo

Marx), uncomfortable in the heat. In a sudden burst of confidence I enquired, 'Do you like this wig?'

'I think you would be better off without it,' she replied.

So apart from that first day travelling down to Bournemouth I never wore it, reverting to covering my bald pate with a trilby, as I had previously done when necessary. She then recommended me to take lunch at the 'five and dime store' across the street, by which I think she meant the snack bar in the branch of British Home Stores. I suppose she had a US soldier as a boyfriend.

Getting accommodation at that time of the year in Bournemouth proved a problem and had delayed my arrival when a lodging found for me fell through at the last moment. By the kindness of the works manager, Mr Boyd, I was invited to stay that night with him and his wife at a pleasant home in Iddleston Road. Finding a place thereafter was not easy. I took one in Grosvenor Gardens, but having spent one night under the roof I found it too hot and stuffy to remain there. Mr Boyd kindly took me back in again until it was arranged that I become a lodger with the head printer and his family in Alma Road. I was delighted that the printer's name was Baskerville, and so I hoped that I had as landlord a scion of the great printer of the same name who had designed the famous type. I stayed happily with them, going with Mrs Baskerville and one of her several daughters to the cinema to see films such as *This Happy Breed* and *To Have and Have Not*.

I was assigned to work with the existing circulation manager and began to go round with him in his car, visiting newsagents and other newspaper retailers all over the Bournemouth area and sometimes further afield. This man's home life did not sound a very happy one. His ambition was to write a 'best-seller', for which he claimed he had the plot, but his home was cramped and his mother-in-law made his life difficult, and he could find no place or time in which to write. He consoled himself in pubs during the working day, leaving me outside in the car while he had a 'quick one'.

The firm wanted me to drive in order to take over these duties, and someone took me out in the firm's van in order to teach me. Even though wartime traffic was not heavy, I found myself feeling highly nervous struggling with clutch, gear stick, accelerator and steering wheel simultaneously. Lessons ended when the van stopped working and it was agreed that the 'big end' had gone, whatever that was. It was then decided to send me to a driving school, but no vacant places were available. In the event I was not to learn to drive until I was in my mid-forties.

I was taught the fundamentals of newspaper production and printing. I learned about typesetting and proofs and stood by the large printing machine in the basement on the day that the paper was run off. The firm had a contract to print the popular advertisement weekly *Exchange and Mart*, and now and again I had to help the woman proofreader as she toiled through multitudinous columns of small ads. Absorbed for the first time into a working life, turning up day after day, a new experience for me, I discovered that joining a small firm or organisation is what living in a small village must be like. Human groups such as these run on gossip, people play for position, friendships are made which extend outside working hours, and morale is either up or down.

Master figure in the firm was works manager Mr Boyd. He explained to me that in the Depression years he was the only one who knew how to do certain tasks; because of this he was able to keep his job and those of other employees. The editor was a busy man, and I made no contact with him. More approachable was the advertising manager, a burly extrovert whom I liked. It was the rule for firms to have fire watchers ready at night to put out any incendiary bombs that fell. I did my turn here, sleeping on the premises by rota and usually sharing my shift with an amiable talkative Irishman with whom I drank cocoa. I was still a nervous young man who took more than average time to find his bearings. With the experience gained by old age I know I could have handled the job better than I did.

I was, of course, fresh out of university and still moulded by reading and a desire to write and wondering where my life was going. I was a fairly free agent in my job and out of the office a good deal. So I found spare hours during the day which I would spend in Bournemouth public library, where I would try to maintain my ambition to write through composing essays and stories. With hindsight I wish I had tried writing a newspaper column on aspects of local life, short enough to get into a publication hampered by wartime paper shortages and meagre in pages. I don't think I could have persuaded the *Bournemouth Times* editor to employ me, but I might have stood a chance with the much more affluent, large and dominant rival paper, the *Bournemouth Echo*. Thus I might have started a career as a journalist.

Despite my lack of self-confidence I am at heart a social person who is happy mixing with other people, so instinctively I sought to make contacts outside work. I joined the local Fabian Society and Labour Party branch, but companionship here did not take wing. I started going on Sunday afternoons to the Bournemouth Symphony Orchestra concerts in the Pavilion. Here I met Eileen, whom I took to the theatre, but our relationship did not develop. At the weekend I explored the countryside, visiting Salisbury, Dorchester and Weymouth. The man who gave me a lift in his lorry to Weymouth graphically described how, just before D-Day, the harbour could not be seen, as it was totally filled with invasion craft. One weekend I went to Worthing to stay with my college friend Peter Richards.

Another college friend I saw was Daphne Brook, with whom I had danced so often. She had begun a career in social work and was on a fortnight's assignment in Boscombe, working in a residential home. We carried on our discussions from where we had left off in Cambridge. Perhaps I confided in her my ambition to become a published writer. In Bournemouth I came under the influence of Cyril Connolly's *Enemies of Promise*, which gave guidance on the pitfalls a would-be writer should avoid. His message seemed to be that if you wanted to become a writer, but had to earn a living, it was better that you got a steady job and wrote in your spare time rather than waste your creative talent through living by journalism.

This was a factor I had to consider when deciding whether to continue with the *Bournemouth Times* in a job delivering papers to local newsagents and collecting the monies. In taking a job, security was the keyword, according to my father. Suddenly security was offered, in a quite different occupation suggested to me by Roy Simpson, with whom I had corresponded regularly. Roy, my West Ham school companion in Cambridge, had graduated in 1943 with a First. He had got work as a translator of French books for a publisher but wanted more secure employment. He had been frustrated in the hope of getting a good Civil Service job by his record of tuberculosis – still an infectious, fatal disease for some. He found a suitable job with the Miners' Welfare Commission. A post had become vacant there and, responding to my letters of uncertainty about my work, he suggested I applied. 'You'll never find a better opportunity for permanency and prospects, I can assure you.' 'Try hard for it,' he wrote again. 'Get out of your present job anyway – but don't get out until you've got in.'

The Miners' Welfare Commission, which had been evacuated from its Westminster offices, was securely ensconced in a detached house with grounds called Ashley Court in the village of Ashtead, Surrey, just south of Epsom. 'Doodle-bugs pass over,' Roy had written, 'with a few exceptions which drop around but so far not in.' Roy's description of the job sounded attractive. I could go on living away from home but get back easily to Forest Gate whenever I wanted. It offered the security that my father had recommended and seemed to meet Cyril Connolly's criteria. Dissatisfied with my work in Bournemouth and my lack of a good bedsit, I decided to apply.

After a weekend at home I attended an interview on Monday, 25 September and wa s offered a job at the Miners' Welfare Commission as an administrative assistant. The salary was £197 10s. a year plus a war bonus of £49 11s. or £250 a year in total, a little less than the five guineas a week I was getting in Bournemouth. The job was offered on condition I was not liable for National Service 'of some kind or other'. My appointment letter reached me in Bournemouth on Friday, 29 September, and next day I handed in my notice. Mr Putnum was not pleased that his recruit had stayed for only six weeks and asked for a month's notice. But as I was weekly paid we compromised on a fortnight's notice.

That Saturday I had planned to visit Dorchester, but of course giving notice had taken precedence. Thus it was I made a new acquaintance. Near the office was a branch of Lyons, and I went there for lunch. I noticed a WAAF at a nearby table reading the *New Statesman* and was bold enough to join her. Her name was Evelyn Hitchcock, and she was based at an RAF camp some miles out of Bournemouth. We walked along the cliffs together, sat on a bench, and when I complained my fingers were sticky from eating the blackberries we had picked, she rolled up her skirt and insisted that I wipe my hands on the top of her stocking. I thought Hitch was pretty, and we got on well together. It was ironic that I met her on the day that I had given in my notice and was leaving the area.

We parted at six so that she could get her RAF lorry back to her camp, and I went along to the Pavilion where I had seen that an actor in *Flare Path*, the current theatre production, was Bryan Forbes, or Johnny Clark as I had known him at West Ham Municipal Secondary School. Like me he had gained a local authority scholarship, which enabled him to study at the Royal Academy of Dramatic Arts. We had been in correspondence, and in his last letter he had written, 'Must stop – am very tired – dash up to London everyday doing bloody BBC recordings which nobody listens to. I shall be called up very soon. See you soon, I hope.'

I gained entrance to his dressing-room and found him busy, between stage appearances, typing a story. This was probably included in his first published title, a collection of short stories called *Truth Lies Sleeping*. Bryan has subsequently signed my copy, which is now a rare book. Bryan soon went into the Army, as he describes in the first volume of his autobiography called *Notes for a Life*.

The following week, while working out my notice, I managed to get a lift by lorry to Hitch's camp, but she was away. Through exchanging letters we met again on the day before I left Bournemouth for good. This was a romantic day, with parting a sweet sorrow. Correspondence was exchanged, mine sent from Surrey, hers from Southwold, where she had been transferred, all full of kisses. But soon the letters were more infrequent, probably because she had become romantically involved with someone else, and my wartime encounter was just a memory.

On 16 October 1944, aged twenty-one, I took a Southern Railway electric train from Waterloo to Ashtead, a half-hour journey. I was to start work next day. The wartime practice of billeting, which accompanied evacuation, applied to firms as well: they had the power to billet their staff in private homes for a flat payment by the lodger of 10s. a week. The small, old village of Ashtead had been extended with properties for commuters to London in the interwar years, and I had been assigned one of these semi-detached 1930s houses not far from Ashtead station, No. 8 Broadhurst. I was given a bedroom and supplied with breakfast and an evening meal from Monday evening to Saturday morning each week. For most office workers, the working day included Saturday mornings at that time. This was to last until well into the 1950s.

My hostess was a middle-aged widow called Mrs Stratford, with an attractive daughter, Joan, who was a little older than me. Joan held a responsible committee clerk job with Middlesex County Council at its offices in Westminster. As she tended to work late and I went home at weekends, social life between us did not particularly develop. In 1945 a middle-aged relative of theirs arrived as a fellow lodger. He had been working so hard during the war years as a civil servant that he had had a nervous breakdown and had been sent on sick leave to recuperate. This provided mother and daughter with a new source of companionship and made the lounge full in the evenings and militated against a relationship developing between me and Joan.

Ashley Court, where the Miners' Welfare Commission was based, was an attractive Edwardian house set in its own grounds and backing on to the woods of Ashtead Common. It was reached from Ashtead railway station, near where I lived, by a fifteen-minute walk uphill through open country. Petrol was rationed and private vehicles were scarce, so cars were not used by the staff. Most walked from the station, hurrying to sign in before the red line was drawn above latecomers in an attendance book kept in the front hall. At 6 p.m. a great crowd of staff walked back to the station to travel to their part of suburbia. Normal hours of duty were forty-eight a week, my appointment letter had said, with the salary based on a 42-hour week 'You will receive payment for the six extra hours worked at two shillings and three pence per hour.' 'The annual leave allowance for the post is 13 working days . . . general rules applicable for the staff of the Ministry of Fuel and Power have been adopted for the staff of the Miners' Welfare Commission.' Thus I found that the Commission, supervised by the Ministry, bore the weight of a Civil Service ethos and put methodical procedures as its standard of approach rather than incisive entrepreneurial action. I was to find office life leisurely.

The Miners' Welfare Commission had been created under a 1920 Mining Industry Act to improve the lot of coal mineworkers and their families. A Miners' Welfare Fund had been set up, its income coming from a penny per ton levy (later a halfpenny) on all coal output. With it were established Miners' Welfare Institutes, bowling greens and sports grounds, as well as educational scholarships. Later an additional coal royalty was brought in so that pithead baths could be built, in the provision of which Britain lagged far behind Germany. Pithead baths replaced the practice of a miner going home in dirty pit clothes to wash in a tub in his kitchen. Now he could put his dirty pit clothes in a locker, shower and change into clean clothes before he went home. The new baths buildings were designed by the Commission's in-house architects and were to become a new feature on Britain's industrial landscape. By 1945 some 348 had been built but only forty-one of these during the war. The Commission also created convalescent homes and developed medical rehabilitation centres for injured miners. During the war, canteens were provided to help ensure miners were well fed.

The Commission can be seen as another example of government intervention to ensure good conditions for workers, in the tradition of Shaftesbury. Other developments in the inter-war period, such as the creation of the London Passenger Transport Board, the Central Electricity Board and the British Broadcasting Corporation, anticipated the changes in post-war Britain, when nationalisation provided much greater government control of industries, especially those, such as the coal industry, that lacked the investment needed to bring them up to date.

I encountered Ashley Court and its community life at impressionable age and remember it well. You entered the front door and signed in under the shadow of the staircase. To the left was the office of Mr A.J. Steadman, the secretary who reported directly to the Commission. Opposite his door was that of the Finance Department, consisting of six people. My own office door was directly ahead. I had been assigned to a post in the General Department, which dealt with local applications for grant aid made by Miners' Institutes for their halls, bowling greens and sports grounds. They asked for building work, or furniture or books for their libraries, which we bought from the wholesaler, Simpkin and Marshall. At my wooden Civil Service desk I was asked to deal with a flow of applications from South Wales. This introduced me for the first time to those wonderful Welsh village names which I found difficult to pronounce. Schemes across the country were run by trustees from each side of the industry. Mineworkers were represented on local committees by Mining Federation nominees and the coal owners by Mining Association nominees. It had proved a successful example of democratic local management.

Behind my desk was that of Miss Griffin, who dealt with Yorkshire and Lancashire, and to my left was Ken Dodd, who dealt with Scotland and other areas. Directly opposite me was the desk of Winnie, our demure young clerk. In the bay window sat R.J. Walter, a middle-aged man in charge of our team. The other half of the room (which had formerly been two reception rooms, divided by sliding partitions) was occupied by Aubrey Pullen, who dealt with educational grants for university applicants from mining families. Miss Pitt, his assistant, impressed me by reading novels in French during break times.

Soon after I settled in there was a visit by Jack Reading, who had joined the Commission from university before the war and had worked in its Westminster offices. Jack wore the uniform of an army captain and was on leave. When he was demobbed, he rejoined the Commission and worked with Aubrey Pullen. I discovered that we shared mutual interests in theatre, art and literature, and we were to become lifelong friends until his death in his late eighties.

Turning right out of the Ashley Court hall you passed the office of T.A. Bennett, one of two deputy secretaries, then the typing pool headed by the formidable Miss Warrener, who guarded her girls strenuously, then the registry where the files were kept. These were handled by two local Ashtead girls of about eighteen, each of great charm, called Claire Freeman and Daphne Mann, often to be seen cycling to and from work together from the old village. The next room housed Arthur White, a slim, well-meaning, young establishments officer who dealt with appointments and similar tasks; he was a good cricketer and a Quaker, and later he went to work full time at the Society of Friends headquarters. Another office housed two women assistants, one married to an absent RAF officer and the other a free spirit who found it difficult to arrive on time, and who soon left.

Then came the kitchen, tea bar and canteen where most of the staff ate lunch on a shift system. After that was a courtyard leading to a single-storey annexe built for sporting activities by a previous house occupant. This now housed the Pithead Baths administrative staff, which included Roy Simpson, who had told me about the job, his superior, George Manewell, and a good-looking young local girl called Margaret Stemp, who was their clerk. Head of Pithead Baths section as well as of medical and rehabilitation services was Tony Freston, the other deputy secretary, an ex-civil servant with a reputation for innovation. He was to be joined by a short, balding barrister with a loquacious tongue called Skilton, who vetted the legal documents. Freston also oversaw Arthur White and was a later appointment than Bennett, who saw himself as the natural successor to Steadman – despite Freston's arrival.

Upstairs at Ashley Court were the architectural and technical staff with a large drawing office. Chief architect was John Wood, assisted by Jimmy Dempster and a bearded and arty man called Saise. A quantity surveyors' section was headed by a man called Bowra. Among leading lights of the architectural staff was handsome and personable Kenneth Campbell, of left-wing views, who was to become one of the chief housing architects for London County Council after the war. He was to play a key role when tower blocks began to be built in the 1960s. Another office was occupied by an expert on bowling greens, who travelled the country giving technical advice on choice of grasses and other matters.

In another set of upstairs rooms was the Districts Department, responsible for the Commission's district officers, established in each coalfield to help local schemes with activities and maintenance, and liaison with local authorities. This was headed by an archetypal middle-class Civil Service type called Whitfield Parker, assisted by the handsome, well-built, rather raffish John Herd, whose main interest in life was golf.

The total staff at Ashley Court must have numbered about fifty, and of course I became acquainted with them all to varying degrees, especially after I began, on my own initiative, to organise social activities, such as dinner-dances, theatre visits and the like. I made good friendships, but it was at Ashley Court I began to realise the difference between academic and office culture. At university one could make forthright statements in debate in search of truth, but in a workplace I found that forthright statements could be received as personal criticism. I had not at that time learned the minor courtesies of office life. My various gaucheries made me think I was not a social success, but these feelings were probably rooted in lack of self-confidence and inexperience, and after all I made friends there.

After the novelty of the job wore off, I found myself dissatisfied. When a grant application came in from Wales, it was put on the scheme file in registry and delivered to my desk by Bill Rowe, the uniformed messenger, an ex-army man with a great deal of common sense. I read the file, summarised the previous history, recommended a course of action and then passed the file to my boss. To my annoyance he took my handwritten memo off the file, rewrote it in his own hand and then passed it to Bennett for a decision. For this, or to modify the application, Bennett might travel to see the site and applicants. It was all rather detached and boring and did not occupy a whole day.

The office was pleasant enough, set in the countryside, with no external noise and a leisurely atmosphere. There was only one phone in the room, and it was not often used. To discuss a case with the technical staff, you just walked upstairs and hoped you would find somebody free to see you. All work was done in longhand, with letters given to the typing pool. As a would-be writer I found I could compose things of my own at my desk, using the office notepaper. But I never considered outlets for publication and just wrote for self-expression. This was a wasted opportunity. I had feelings of guilt, with my natural instinct to work hard for the Commission and bring something to fruition, but I gradually became aware that this would never be.

I began to realise that life after hours could be more productive and enjoyable than life at work. I was still driven to read as much as I could, switching from social studies to literature, although my reading included William Morris's *News from Nowhere*, Bernard Shaw's plays and prefaces, George Gissing and other works of social interest, such as B.L. Coombes's *Those Clouded Hills*. But I began to learn about Yeats, T.S. Eliot, James Joyce and Louis McNeice and went through George Moore's *Avowals* and Humphrey Hare's *Sketch for a Portrait of Rimbaud*. I read avidly without any particular plan.

Within a few days of joining the Commission I went one evening with Margaret Court, another member of the staff not much older than myself, to a meeting of the Epsom branch of the Workers' Educational Association and was recruited as an acting member of the WEA drama group. I was to appear in a production of *Distant Point* by Afinogenev, 'the famous Soviet play', as the BBC's Third Programme was to describe it. We staged it in February 1945 in a hall in Epsom and again soon after at Toynbee Hall, Aldgate, as an entry in an annual amateur drama competition. The leading light was an interesting bearded young man, looking a bit like D.H. Lawrence, called Edward Thompson, who acted as producer.

I found drama as enjoyable as ever and still pondered whether I should have entered the profession; in wartime there would have been no difficulty in getting a start with a repertory company. So at the Commission I began to run a drama society, becoming its secretary and concentrating on regular play readings, for which I hired sets of plays from French's. In a year or so I extended this activity by arranging for group tickets for West End plays. Half a dozen or so of us would go up to town by train after work for an evening together. Among these were Janet Perry, Sheila Luckhoo, Claire Freeman, Margaret Court, Doren Knock and Ken Dodd, all of whom I looked on as my friends.

Ken Dodd, aided by his brother, who worked in a Strand book-shop, began to rehearse us for a production of Robert Ardrey's *Thunder Rock*, which was to be staged by the 'MWC Dramatic Society' in halls in Ashtead and Epsom during 1945. I was cast as Dr Kurtz, and thoroughly enjoyed the role, playing opposite Claire Freeman as my daughter. Dodd and I became friends, meeting in the evenings or over Saturday lunch after work. He was an enigmatic, self-contained character, shorter than me and older, and he had served in the Merchant Navy before being invalided out. His brother used to talk jocularly about Ken landing again at the docks with a parrot and another dose of clap. Their home was in Richmond Road, Hackney.

Ken could be abrasive, with his quick brain, and was rather feared by our boss, R.J. Walter, who never had the courage to alter Ken's minutes on file. I think Ken saw me as a raw young man needing advice, and he certainly helped me learn how to make a decision, saying it was a matter of choosing an option and then resolutely sticking to it. Roy Simpson was more likely to make a subtle joke than offer me advice, and I was pleased to go along with him when he suggested we enro at Epsom Technical College for evening classes in German. We continued with these for six months, but, although the German woman lecturer worked hard, I don't think my basic knowledge of German improved very much; I certainly never learned to speak the language with confidence.

Spring in 1945 brought to me once again that sudden appreciation of nature I had first experienced in Brentwood in 1940. This part of Surrey still contained beautiful countryside, accessible by footpaths. On evening walks I would enjoy the birdsong and the bright new leaves. A small rambling club was started at the Commission, but attendance was never particularly good and when only Margaret Court and I turned up for the last walk we ended the programme. I explored by myself, taking a day's leave to go the Derby in 1946 in nearby Epsom but unsuccessfully backed leading jockey Gordon Richards on Edward Tudor, who came nowhere. On Saturdays, before returning to London for the weekend, I would travel to Box Hill, Dorking, Reigate and Leith Hill. Out on this hilly landscape I would sit reading, getting through Eric Gill's *Autobiography*, Louis MacNeice's *Autumn Journal*, Hazlitt's *Lectures on the English Poets*, Katherine Mansfield's *Bliss*, Auden's *The Ascent of F6*, Herbert Read's *Poetry and Anarchism* and James Joyce's *Stephen Hero*, as a surviving notebook reminds me. Ernest Hemingway's powerful prose I first encountered in a lunch break in the grounds of Ashley Court, a place much enjoyed by the staff on sunny days, some playing tennis in the grounds. In summer we had occasional Saturday garden parties, and there were enough men to form a cricket team, in which I played once or twice on a pitch near the village.

Carried away by an inner compulsion to organise things and to work at something with an end result, I ran some Brains Trusts, then popular on the wireless, and organised a coach outing to Eastbourne. I began to set up dinner-dances, hiring a local hall, a band and issuing printed invitation cards to those who paid to come. They were fairly well attended, as wartime did not offer the profusion of entertainments available later.

In all these ways Ashley Court offered a social life, but the other half of it occurred in London at the weekends. On Saturdays, after lunch at an Ashtead café, I would travel up to Waterloo, leave my case at a station deposit somewhere (there was even one at Leicester Square Underground in those days – and a public toilet, so convenient), visit the bookshops and the museums and then quite often go to see Elwyn Jones. He had a room in Stanley Gardens, Notting Hill, then in Leinster Square and in Peterborough Place in Bayswater, before settling in Addison Road, Holland Park, where he shared with Arthur Jacobs, the author of music books. It was there I remember seeing my first long-playing record, which replaced the old shellac 78, before it was itself replaced by the compact disc. Finally, on Elwyn's marriage in 1953, by which time he had a good job at the BBC, he moved into No. 6 Chelsea Embankment. My Saturdays or Sundays with Elwyn in those early days were always interesting, for he would take me to club theatres such as the Chantecleer, for which he often had tickets to review plays for the magazine *What's On*, and introduce me to his various girl-friends, with one of whom at least he developed a passionate relationship. He was astonished at my own lack of similar involvement, but we were different people.

Other college friends I continued to meet included Kate Prince and Ruth Neufeld, Daphne Brook and Mary Bromley, with whom I punted down the Cam to Grantchester (or was it a canoe?) on a nostalgic weekend visit to Cambridge. George Brand was in London, having become warden of an International Youth Club in Pont Street, and I visited him there regularly, especially on Saturday evenings when there were dances or literary meetings, at one of which Tambimuttu held forth. He was then a well-known Ceylonese literary figure and guru of sorts.

Stanley was still working in the Nottinghamshire coal mines, but we continued hitch-hiking together when we could. In August we went to Wales. Catching the tube out to Hounslow West we took to the road, making our way through Reading, Marlborough, Calne and Chippenham to spend our first night at Batheaston Youth Hostel, just outside Bath. Next day we went on to Bristol, then took the Aust ferry across to Newport, staying at a small hotel in Cardiff at the end of the day. I had made contact with William Daniel, who was the Commission's district officer for Wales, and he drove us to Mountain Ash colliery – for me the first sight of a coal mine. We were not allowed down the pit. Leaving Daniel we travelled via Aberdare to Brecon to stay at the Black Bull hotel. The earthly beauty of this place quite overcame me. The two of us went homewards via Abergavenny, Monmouth, Ross and Gloucester and stayed in a flea-ridden hotel in Cheltenham. We visited a cinema where the only seats free were on a side bench near the screen, which gave a distorted view. Stanley then went home via Oxford, but I still remembered the beauty of the Black Mountains and felt a compulsion to return for another look, hitch-hiking back for another night at the Black Bull. I returned to London by train.

The war in Europe had ended and on 8 May 1945, VE-day, I had taken the four o'clock afternoon train to Waterloo and joined the vast crowds of people celebrating in the West End. I spent some time with a Wren, then with a WAAF, then another, walking with the second one along the Embankment while she expressed her fears for a boyfriend who had been posted to the Far East for the continuing war with Japan. Eventually we parted, and I took one of the last District Line trains to Plaistow. The carriages were packed. At each stop we peered through the safety netting pasted over the train windows to see which station it was. Was the blackout still in force as I walked the fifteen minutes home? Probably not: after six years we could have lights in the streets and not have to put black-out shutters over our windows. The general feeling, I think, was one of exhaustion. On 9 May 1945 we dismantled the Anderson shelter in our garden.

VJ Night and the end of the war came on 15 August 1945 after the dropping of the atomic bombs on Japan. This time I did not go up to join the West End crowds but just went home. It was on this day that my brother was demobilised from the RAF, probably getting an early release because of the telecommunications job to which he now returned. Although, after six years, the war was over, general demobilisation still had to take place and evacuated people had to return home, while in Europe great numbers of people sought to get back to their native lands.

The Commission sought a return to London, at least for some of its staff. Roy Simpson and I teamed up as a pair looking for office accommodation when the staff were asked to search for suitable places in Westminster. We were given a floor-size specification to give to estate agents but did not meet success. Eventually offices were found just off Storey's Gate in Old Queen Street, but I was to continue to work in Ashtead for another year. I had decided by July 1945 that my lodgings were too crowded, so I returned to my home in Forest Gate and travelled up and down each day. Although it meant getting up early, the trains out of London were not full and I had the chance of a half-hour's reading. My notebooks show that I got through a good deal of Aldous Huxley, Oscar Wilde, George Moore and Dostoevsky.

By October 1945 I was finding the travelling tiring, especially as I was staying late at Ashley Court for *Thunder Rock* rehearsals. I made speculative calls looking for accommodation and in November 1945 moved into 98 Manor Green Road, Epsom. Mr Goddard was a bank manager, and he interviewed me in a professional way before accepting me as a lodger. His good-looking wife – with whom he had a teenage daughter and younger son – would cheer herself up by serving in the evening in a pub, where sometimes I joined her.

In the spring and summer of 1946 I had a period of drinking in an Ashtead pub called the Woodman with new friends I had made in the architects' department, recruited after the war. This usually meant a beery evening on an empty stomach, and one of my more persistent memories of Manor Green Road is coming home late, distinctly the worse for wear. I remember lying on my bed while the room revolved topsy-turvy round me. Lying there with the curtains open and the light on, the bedroom would be targeted by gorgeous large moths, fluttering around the electric bulb. It is one of my fond memories of Epsom.

The town had changed with the electrification of the railway from a country town to a dormitory suburb for London but with horse-racing still a major activity. Its High Street had been partially rebuilt in the 1930s with new shopping parades and Capitol and Odeon cinemas. I have fond memories of these two cinemas. I queued in the rain to see *Brief Encounter*, the British film with Trevor Howard and Celia Johnson depicting frustrated love. I also recall visiting a lovely old inn near the town centre where I enjoyed a country ambience and good beer. Some cheap cafés near the Clock Tower provided tasty meals. My life in Epsom formed a pattern, walking from Manor Green Road each morning to Epsom station for a train south to Ashtead, buying a copy of *The Times* and the *Daily Worker*. In those days the USSR was regarded as our ally in winning the war, and pro-Communist feeling was still common among intellectuals and others; the days of McCarthy and the Cold War were yet to come, and the defeat of the Germans at Stalingrad at a great cost in Russian lives was vividly remembered. At the end of the day I returned the same way back to Manor Green Road, often to try to write stories in the evening, my thoughts on literature, not politics.

Towards the end of 1945 I felt wretchedly bored with my work. I wrote a memo to Bennett pointing out that, at the end of the year's employment that I had completed, I had gained very little knowledge or experience in administrative procedure. Bennett transferred me to the Pithead Baths Department, starting on 14 January 1946. With the war ended, the Commission was taking on more staff and Ashley Court was proving too small, so within a few weeks my office was relocated to a house the Commission had taken over called Caen Wood. This was not far from Ashley Court, at a bend in the road, and was nearer to the station. I shared an upstairs room with Eric Day, Stan Perrin and Eric Ross, with A.S.V. Skilton, my immediate superior, in an adjacent chamber. It was a pleasant location, backing on to woods. Kath Chick, another staff member, lived near by, and Roy Simpson and I would sometimes spend our lunch-hour splicing logs for her with an axe.

It would be edifying to report that my transfer to the Baths Department gave me more satisfactory employment, but this was not to be. I was assigned to legal work, checking documents down to the last comma, and I found this did not suit my temperament. I worked hard, but I do not think that Skilton gave Freston positive reports about me.

In September 1946, after living in Epsom during the week for about a year, the Baths Department was transferred to London to the Old Queen Street offices. Here I did not have much of a job, as qualified lawyers had been taken on to handle the legal side. I felt I was at the nadir of my career. In December I was called into Freston's office and told I was being transferred to Districts Department. They were still located at Ashtead, so I would be working there again. As I was now living at home in Forest Gate I decided to stay there and travel up and down every day. After months of this I found it physically tiring, catching the District Line at Plaistow, changing on to the City to Waterloo tube and rushing to catch the scheduled train from a distant platform. So in September 1947 I took lodgings in Surrey, first in Mickleham and then, in December, in Leatherhead, where I was to stay until my final return to London offices in February 1948.

My spell in Districts Department proved to be the most pleasant of my time with the Miners' Welfare Commission, mainly because I had been assigned to work with a Mr R.D.V. Roberts, a man with a strong North Wales accent who displayed reserve and intelligence. Perhaps he understood what a wreck of a worker he had inherited and set about training me to do useful tasks. Like me he was an economics graduate, and I came to admire him. In due course he was to join the Electricity Council, and here his talent led him to being made a Board member. Fortunately our friendship continued when we went to work in London; he invited me to lunch regularly, about once a month, and I always found him encouraging. Having an intelligent boss one could admire was, I was to discover over the years, a great benefit in one's working life.

Lack of success while working in the Baths Department in 1946 was compounded by a simultaneous lack of success in love. Jean Henderson joined the Commission in April and was assigned to work for Freston on miners' rehabilitation schemes and other matters. She was petite and blonde with a round face, and she made an immediate impression on me. It was a relief to find someone else not long graduated from London University, where she had read History. She lived in Roehampton with her parents and a younger brother, was keen on tennis and was a member of the Federal Union, a post-war movement campaigning for a united Europe. Like me she enjoyed the theatre, and much of our socialising consisted of excursions to West End plays. Their titles bring back memories: *The Eagle Has Two Heads*,

Family Reunion, Caste, A Phoenix Too Frequent, The Master Builder, The Alchemist, The White Devil, Murder in the Cathedral, Oak Leaves and Lavender and *Othello*, among others. On one occasion at the Arts Theatre in Newport Street where the great actor Alec Clunes (father of Martin) held sway we sat through a weekend production of Shaw's *Back to Methuselah*, holding hands through the Saturday and Sunday.

Although I fell for her, Jean did not seem able to reciprocate, however willing she was to come out with me on a regular basis, once putting me up in Roehampton when it was too late for me to get home. When I was transferred to the London office in September 1946 it meant that we no longer saw each other every day at the Ashtead office, and I felt this might allow me to escape from an unfulfilled relationship. When Freston called me into his office and told me he was sending me back to Ashley Court to work, I almost felt like saying, 'No, I don't want to be too near Jean. I am trying to escape a hopeless infatuation with her.' But I was given no choice. Our daily encounters resumed, and we continued to visit the theatre together.

By the spring of 1947 it was apparent that I was not getting anywhere with her, and I began to experience the despair of thwarted love and sexual frustration.

'There are plenty of other fish in the sea,' her mother said on the phone once when I rang and she was not there. So our meetings ended, even though I have letters written to her later, in 1947, but never posted. It took a long time for me to forget her. After our return to London Jean began going out with Bill Gaskin, who joined the Commission at that time. A short, gentle man, he was a pianist with a great knowledge of music. They were married in July 1950 and had a daughter. Sadly the asthma that had always plagued Jean led to her death within ten years of marriage.

Being in love with Jean put me off friendships with other girls. I was still in touch with college friends, particularly Mary Bromley, who in the last stages of my affair with Jean came to stay at Forest Gate with us for a weekend. She had a good job as a sales representative, dressed well, was liked by my family and seemed quite happy with our friendship. Unfortunately I could not throw off my infatuation with Jean. Mary lived in Birmingham, so it was not easy to see her frequently, and nothing developed.

I found another female friend in Janet Whitelegg, who had given up being a librarian to join the Commission in Ashtead in the spring of 1947. We used to meet over lunch in the canteen, and then I went with her to meet her family in Sutton. We explored the countryside, which Janet always loved. We would walk together at weekends in Surrey and Sussex, talking about the meaning of life. But Janet was not happy in an office job and within a few months left to become an agricultural trainee, at first in Essex and later in Kent. We kept in touch, but when I went to see her in 1948 in Tenterden, while I was staying with my Maidstone aunt and uncle on holiday, she told me that she had become engaged to a fellow trainee called Ken, an ex-RAF pilot. They married and moves to the Wrekin in Shropshire and later to the Forest of Dean where they raised a family. I have a fond memory of staying with them and their first baby in the Wrekin. I kept in touch with Janet by correspondence until her death in 2007.

During 1946 when I was still working in the Baths Department I made the first of several attempts to find more satisfying employment. I was keen to become a tutor-organiser for the Workers' Educational Association, an adult education movement founded in 1901 by Albert Mansbridge to improve educational facilities for working people. Education had transformed my own life, and I always believed in its importance. I applied for a job with the Cambridgeshire WEA and ended up on a residential selection course based at Westminster College, Cambridge. This was in July 1946, and we spent our time demonstrating our various abilities in seminars and practice lectures. I was impressed by my tutor, J. Hampden Jackson, and shut myself in my college room to write an essay on the meaning of life. He said it was well written but that there was nothing particularly original in my ideas.

I was not selected by Cambridgeshire WEA but was successful in obtaining a weekly evening lectureship in Crawley, Sussex. This I had secured through the help of my college friend Peter G. Richards, who had given up being a librarian to become a WEA tutor in Sussex. I began these lectures on 19 September and was to give them every Thursday evening for two terms until 20 March 1947. My syllabus was over-ambitious, covering politics and economics in the twentieth century in different countries, and I had to use annual leave days to swot up subjects the day before. I used to reach home about midnight, the end of a long working day.

I will always remember one incident. Changing trains at Three

Bridges I made my way to London Bridge station with a plump elderly man who told me he was an entertainer. 'My crowning trick is to take off my hat and to show them I am completely bald,' he said.

'Snap,' I replied, removing my own trilby.

I have fond memories of the Crawley class, who were keen to learn. This was of course before Crawley New Town was built, transforming the historic area. The WEA seems to have been more successful with middle-class than working-class people, but it has always played an important educational role – and it still does, whether running courses for trade unions or putting an extra-mural lecturer to work in a village hall, sustaining classes year after year.

5

WORKING AND WRITING

BESIDES MY BATTLE to gain satisfying daily work, I also had the idea of becoming a published author, mainly just because I liked writing. So when Stanley whisked me off on another hitch-hiking holiday, this time to Scotland, in the summer of 1946, I took with me a notebook By this time I had come under the influence of D.H. Lawrence, whose travel writing and superb prose I admired greatly.

I took the train to Nottingham, where Stanley, still a Bevin Boy, was living and spent a Sunday afternoon rowing on the Trent with him and his fiancée, Salome. My trilby fell into the water, and we had to spend some time manoeuvring with the oars to retrieve it before it sank. Stanley took my hat back to his Bulwell lodgings and his landlord, a miner, dried it in the oven so I could wear it once more.

We set off on Monday morning, travelling through Doncaster, Darlington, Bishop Auckland, Durham, Gateshead and Newcastle until we stopped in Alnwick. It took us three days on the thumb to reach Edinburgh. Later we went to Stirling, where I got my first glimpse of Highland scenery, and then down to Glasgow where we took the train back to London. Ironically, putting my head out of the carriage window as the train left Leeds station, my trilby flew off and I lost it for good. It was a favourite hat in blue, made by a firm called Christie. Perhaps it ended up on a tramp's head. I wrote of our holiday:

Feeling of height in Durham and Northumberland, The lost county of the edge. On our right hand a glistening white streak: the North Sea. On our left a chequered row of green and black crests: the Cheviots. Sheep, sheep, sheep. Crows which fly with their wing tips flapping like black hands. Gorse. The white streak grows into a broader, blue streak. Lorries do not stop. Then a modern vehicle carrying a load of white, corrugated sheets. We ride behind the cabin, our feet on the spare tyre and our backs to the load. As in some open landau we roll across the hills. The sea gets nearer and nearer on our right hand. Sheep on every pasture. Big fields of green over which you want to run a giant hand to touch the great greenness. Light and dark blue sky.

Two men are to deliver two new Bedford lorries to Dundee. Yes, we are going to Edinburgh. The land rises and seems to be plucked by invisible hands as it does so with fewer trees, fewer hedges, broader fields, then no fields at all, but sweeps of sheep pasture studded with gorse. We get nearer to the sea. Stop at a transport café and eat scrambled eggs and tea. Community. Single interest in the road: speed, time, type of vehicle, places to sleep, places to eat. Duggie Jessup says it gets into the blood. 'When you see a road you just want to keep on and on.' RASC signs, signposts, white lines, studs. Once the tradition of the coach and horse. Now the tradition of the lorry. The great age of the lorry.

Out of Northumberland and we pass a Miners' Welfare Institute, a pit head, a miner with a lamp cycling past, an urban area. Trams. 'Which way to Princes Street?' 'Straight on.' Into the Royal Mile. Edinburgh. Predominant colour: black. Cobbles and heavy stone. A railway running through the centre of the city. No blatant commercialism. Behind the high square buildings more cobbles, high tenements with narrow streets and eddies of swirling objects in the cold evening wind, not leaves but children, small, hard, round and tough with poor clothes and dirty flesh.

In January 1947, while living at Forest Gate and commuting to Ashtead to work, I began my first attempt at writing a novel. I called it *Peter Barbican* after my main character. The name was not common then, as the City structures so named had not yet been built. When I visited it, the city site to be transformed into residential blocks with an arts centre was just a vast empty space, covered with wild flowers – the impressive change to London's topography made by German bombs. I sat in our living room at my father's bureau, acquired by him before the war to write his sermons, and began this great writing adventure. It was a Sunday and it had begun to snow.

It were better I think if we begin with Barbican as a young man, lying alone in his bed one January morning, very late. The white snow made the ceiling brighter than its normal colour and the whole room was brightened to a glitter which Barbican found extraordinary . . .

Barbican was twenty-eight, an as yet undistinguished young man who had succeeded no way at all in getting into the public eye and whose gifts and talents were limited by the bounds of his economic circumstances . . .

There are plenty of precedents for this type of novel, charting the social progress of a young man. I suppose that I based the character to some extent on my friend Elwyn, who always had panache. In the novel, Barbican dispenses with a mature mistress and sweeps up a young woman he bumps into in the Strand. I introduced a Radical Party to give the book a political flavour. Rereading it many years later I find the style reflects a variety of reading. Moreover I can see now that when, in the spring of 1947, it became apparent that my relationship with Jean was ending in frustration I expressed myself through the medium of fiction, with the theme of frustration linked to violence.

Nothing gives me greater pleasure than the physical act of writing, pen on paper, and at the end of a day I feel much happier if I have written something. Hence, I suppose, my weakness for writing to friends. But was I cut out to be a novelist? To be one you must be a story-teller, and I was more a writer of essays and non-fiction, despite all the novels I have read in my time. Most would agree that the secret of fiction is to create the narrative drive that keeps the reader turning the page to find out what happens next. When writing a second novel later on I enjoyed using the text as a ragbag for my thoughts and experiences, but I was not sure where I was going. Fiction-writing demands craft and patience and a compelling desire to tell a story, using it perhaps to convey messages about human existence and character. A puritan element in me sometimes considers that a factual book is a more serious endeavour than a novel.

In order to finish the novel I overcame my scruples about writing my own stuff in office time. Working in Districts Department I had been placed in a small attic office which I shared with Harold Slade, an ex-wartime lieutenant colonel who had been made responsible for welfare in the Kent coalfield and who was frequently away from the office. I used to reach my desk by nine in the morning and write my novel in longhand before Slade arrived, usually at ten o'clock; or if he was away in Kent I would go on writing longer.

In October 1947 I submitted my first chapters to Harold Laski for judgement. Why he should be a good judge of a draft novel I do not know, but I thought the political aspect would interest him. He was a widely read man whom I revered, and I knew his kindness meant he would spend some time reading it. Alas, was not enthusiastic – no doubt showing good judgement – and he did not particularly encourage me to continue. Despite this I persisted with it, and a year or so later I was able to type it up, but I never submitted it to a publisher.

When a writer has completed his work he must turn himself into a salesman for his product and show persistence in the face of refusals. A diffidence in my nature made me shirk this. I have always found a rejection slip painful. Perhaps there are many manuscripts that never see the light of day owing to the reluctance of the authors to face rejection. Still, I always produce on time an article or a text if it has been commissioned, for then I feel an overwhelming obligation to deliver the goods.

Meanwhile, I continued with writing letters. I remember writing regularly from my room at Mickleham to Margaret Chalken, my fellow actor from LSE, and being very pleased when she wrote back. I lived then in a house called Swallow Court, a large detached property into which I had moved in September 1947 after becoming too tired to continue to commute each day to Forest Gate. The house belonged to a woman called Hope-Johnson and was situated off the old road through Mickleham, with a new main road south to Dorking behind it. During the war years this main road was closed to traffic while it was taken over by units of the Canadian Army.

The Hope-Johnsons and I lived separate lives, and I missed an opportunity to develop acquaintanceship, as they seemed a cultured family of some wealth with a penchant for classical music, which was played constantly on the gramophone or radio. I think they grew tired of me quickly, for one day when I returned they had taken the paintings down in the hall and told me that they were moving, making me look for other accommodation. With hindsight I think it was just a tactful ploy.

Mickleham is set in beautiful countryside with Box Hill near by. Keats had stayed at Burford Bridge Hotel, and George Meredith had had a house in the area. Lord Beaverbrook entertained Winston Churchill at his mansion. Despite the rural attractions I was a city child who yearned for a built environment. So when I left Swallow Court I sought lodgings in the small town of Leatherhead and found them in Woodville Road on the north side. This was to be the most attractive of the four homes I had in Surrey between 1944 and 1948. My landlady, Mary Lerwill, was a sympathetic woman with whom I was to have some enjoyable conversations. She would light a fire for me in my bed-sitting room, which was much appreciated in the cold winter of 1947–8. I used to try to write after my evening meal but more often than not gave up and read by the fire. In the evenings I would sometimes wander round the town, which had retained its character more than Epsom. I used its small public library, shops and cinema.

I was particularly fascinated by short stories, a form I was trying to write. I read tales by Guy de Maupassant, Frank O'Connor, Anton Chekhov, A.E. Coppard, Turgenev, Poe and other masters. Meanwhile I continued with works by Aldous Huxley. During 1947 I read Forster's *Howard's End*, Koestler's *Darkness at Noon*, Defoe's *Jonathan Wild*, Fielding's *Tom Jones*, James's *Turn of the Screw* and books by Siegfried Sassoon and Sean O'Casey. Daniel Defoe's *Moll Flanders* excited me, I enjoyed my first Evelyn Waugh with *Put Out More Flags*, admired the work of O. Henry and read one of the popular books of the time: Nigel Balchin's *Mine Own Executioner*.

I began 1948 with James Joyce's *Ulysses*, read some American novels such as Sinclair Lewis's *Cass Timberlane* and Steinbeck's *Of Mice and Men*, then Gertrude Stein's *The Autobiography of Alice B. Toklas*. I felt I had to read Sigmund Freud's *Totem and Taboo* before going on to Graham Greene's *Brighton Rock* and *Stamboul Train*, Virginia Woolf's *Jacob's Room* and Christopher Cauldwell's left-wing *Studies in a Dying Culture*. My friend Jack Reading enthused over Thomas Burke, a now almost-forgotten writer, whom I accordingly read before continuing with Koestler's *Arrival and Departure*, John O'Hara's *Appointment in Samarra* and Percy Lubbock's *The Craft of Fiction*. Most of the books I had bought second-hand, sometimes from the sixpenny tray that Foyles had on the pavement outside their shop. Buying used books was the norm for me, as new books were much dearer and most of the classics could be found second-hand. This was in an era before the paperback began to be the most common form of binding.

I read as much as I could, but there is a limit to how many bookd you can handle. This was remarked upon by Somerset Maugham at a talk given for the National Book League that I attended at Central Hall, Westminster. He pointed out that one person can only read a small portion of the vast corpus of literature that exists. He did a calculation of how many one person can read to demonstrate how small the number could be in an average lifetime. I am not a particularly quick reader, and my notebooks containing the titles of the books I have read each year show that I do not average more than seventy. This is about one and a half books a week. In my life so far I cannot have read more than about five thousand, although I own about eleven thousand, each an individual purchase. I dip into one when I buy it, checking the index for subjects covered, rifle through, 'gut it', as I call it, so I know what the book contains. But this is not recommended for the great works, especially fiction. My friend Jack Reading had a larger collection of books than me, and when he was asked if he had read them all would reply, 'Books are like women: some are acquaintances, some are friends and a few are to be slept with.'

Another Central Hall meeting I went to was in May 1947 about a united Europe. The speakers were Winston Churchill, the Archbishop of Canterbury and the publisher Victor Gollancz. Churchill's oratory was outstanding that night, but I thought that Gollancz outshone him. My mind went back to those pink-covered Left Book Club volumes which Gollancz had published and which we all read, and I was pleased to see the publisher in the flesh; so, too, when I had my only glimpse of T.S. Eliot and Dylan Thomas, both of whom read their poems at an evening meeting held at the Academy in Oxford Street. I owned a few gramophone records of Dylan Thomas reading, and my father was always moved by his voice when I played them at home.

Evacuation in one form or another – school, college, work – finally ended for me on 24 February 1948, my last working day in Ashtead. I returned to Forest Gate to live, destined to work in Old Queen Street, travelling between Plaistow and Westminster on the District Line, some of it through the poorer parts of London; I can never forget the overwhelming smell of the chemical works as the train passed through the Bromley, Bow, West Ham section of the line. But, as a Londoner, I felt more at home than in the Surrey suburbia in which I had lived for over three years. As if to signify the end of an era, Ashley Court was ravaged by fire soon after the Miners' Welfare Commission left it. It was later restored and converted into apartments.

Our return to London coincided with the absorption of the Miners' Welfare Commission by the newly created National Coal Board. The terms on which this was done did not please. 'Unfortunately the final settlement of salary scales and conditions of employment for the Board's staff presents difficulties which are not easy to surmount,' read the letter from E.L. Turnbull, Director of Establishments. 'Your salary position will not be worsened by the transfer . . . on the credit side I think I should make special mention of the wider field for promotion which is open to you by reason of your becoming a member of a much larger organisation.' At the Commission I was being paid £405 a year in monthly instalments. My personal letter of appointment, when it came, was for the same salary in total, but I was appointed as a Grade II clerk, whereas I had joined the Commission as an administrative officer. I would be top of this grade at £338 a year and receive a London Location Allowance of £25 a year plus a Personal Pensionable Allowance of £41 per annum 'to bring your total emoluments up to your present salary'. The hours were forty-four a week, based on an attendance of five and a half days a week, which included working on Saturday mornings. As a graduate with a good degree it seemed a disaster to be categorised as a Grade II clerk. I challenged the decision, citing my qualifications and experience, but without success. As I did not have another job I decided I had to accept, to soldier on and hope that my lot would improve.

There followed a year from February 1948 when I was based at the Old Queen Street offices in Westminster still continuing in Districts Department. Whitfield Parker was still in charge, but Roberts had left to be replaced by R.B. Jefferies, a kindly Welshman who had been a district welfare officer until he lost a leg in a car accident and was moved to a desk job. I shared an office that was long and narrow and overlooked an alley behind the building; my companions were Sam Powell and Will Owen. The job I was given was to complete a giant survey of welfare facilities in all the coalfields, based on returns made by district officers. I found it difficult to get the returns in from them, let alone analyse them. It was just another boring desk job.

Powell and Owen lit my day. Sam Powell had been a youth officer for the City of Worcester and had come to the Commission hoping to widen his experience. He was soon disillusioned at finding himself not much more than a bureaucrat and was never happy in the job.

Fortunately he found himself a better one as youth officer in Aylesbury, leaving in November 1948.

Will Owen was a strong personality. Working with him I fell under his influence as much as I had with Harold Laski and R.D.V. Roberts. Owen came from a South Wales mining background and had been at Labour College at the same time as Aneurin Bevan, who was to become Minister of Health in the 1945 Labour government. Owen's ambitions were intensely political, and he was continually going over to the House of Commons to see Labour MP friends. Eventually he became MP for Blyth in Northumberland, a mining community. There he was well liked as a good speaker and a caring MP. I met him in the street once after he had been elected, and he said that being an MP was the best job he had ever had. He particularly liked overseas visits with delegations. Unfortunately he came a cropper when it was shown that he had dealt too favourably with the Czechs – Czechoslovakia was then a Communist country. I forget the details, but Owen had to resign and I don't think he lived too long afterwards. I wrote to him after the event and spoke to his wife, because I don't think you should desert your friends when they get into trouble. After all, he had been very good to me when I worked with him.

As well as doing the survey, I was assigned to work with Owen. He was given various organising jobs and used to take me with him as his assistant. One event I particularly remember was a concert of miners' choirs, staged at Harringay Stadium. I think the event was organised in conjunction with the *Daily Herald*, the Labour daily newspaper, for I remember going there with Owen to discuss the publicity arrangements.

I was assigned to look after the Biddulph Choir from Staffordshire and met them at Euston station to take them to a Farringdon Street concert hall for a rehearsal, which I think was led by Leslie Bridgewater. Afterwards I took them to Charing Cross and gave them a meal at the Lyons Corner House which stood at the western end of the Strand. Finally I escorted them to Hans Crescent, next to Harrods, to a large hostel created during the war for transient workers. Here they shared a large room full of beds.

I turned up there next day to take them to Harringay and, after a successful event, accompanied them on the Piccadilly Line from Manor House to Knightsbridge back to their hostel. Being late I took over a spare bed in their room and stayed the night. In the morning as they departed they presented me with about twenty pounds, the result of a whip-round. It was my first experience of how friendly and generous miners can be. What I especially remember was the sound of their combined voices singing as we waited on the tube station platforms for a train.

Not many opportunities arose to get away from my desk, but one occurred in May 1948 when Owen took me with him to help run a training course for district officers held at Barry, near Cardiff, on a Saturday and Sunday. Owen was anti-establishment and revolutionary in his thinking, and I suppose his influence was great and, in the parlance of the time, I, too, 'turned Bolshie'. On the Monday morning, instead of taking the train back to London I took off in the other direction. I made my way along the South Wales coast through Cardiff, Neath and Swansea, where I bought a pair of miners' boots. Leaving that bombed town I reached St David's and Haverfordwest. Travelling by bus I felt impelled to go on. When I reached the end of the peninsula I found a hotel room for the night. From there I made my way back to Carmarthen and booked into the Nelson Hotel. When I walked down the street most of the people were talking in a language unknown to me. In the evening I visited a circus and fairground. A local boy asked me where I was from. When I told him I was from London he ran from me like a scalded cat. I was astonished at the reputation of my city. The next day I went to see the nearby coast and Llanstephan, a place Dylan Thomas had visited. The day after, I went to see the anthracite coal country at Ammanford and Llandilo.

On Friday I decided to go home. When I reached Paddington I first went to see Elwyn Jones. 'I am going to resign on Monday,' I told him. 'I can't stand the office any more.' He agreed that it was what I should do. When I got home that evening I called on Stanley. He reminded me that our teacher Clifford Smith had advised us not to give up a job until we had secured another. I met Elwyn again on Sunday when he invited me to join him at Harringay Stadium for a performance of *Hiawatha*, which he was reviewing. In the Press Bar in the interval, talking to some Fleet Street journalists, I was astonished to learn that their pay was around £17 a week, compared with my own £8. I was envious, but by then I had realised that I had to keep my job, at least for the time being.

I seem to have made a botch of my explanations for my absence, as the letter I received on 29 June from Establishments Branch suggests:

I refer to the period from 31st May to 5th June 1948 during which you were absent from the office without authority. Your absence and the different excuses which you have produced to Establishments Branch and Manpower and Welfare Department have created a very unfavourable impression, and I warn you that such occurrences will not be tolerated again. We will now look upon the matter as closed and no further action will be taken on it unless there should be a recurrence at some future date.

This letter was followed a few weeks later by another giving me the appointment as a Grade II clerk. Perhaps the two things were connected. Certainly from that time I felt I had blotted my copybook with Establishments and I was not regarded as a reliable character. This view of me may have been enforced by my involvement with the Clerical and Workers' Union – I now served on the National Coal Board branch committee, union agitation never being looked upon favourably by establishment figures, even in a nationalised industry.

I suppose part of my defection in Wales was the wanderlust you tend to feel when you are twenty-four. In leave periods I went youth-hostelling in Gloucestershire and Worcestershire and then, with my college friend George Brand stayed in youth hostels in Dorset. When in London I went often to George's youth club in Pont Street, and there I met a girl who I went out with a few times but with no long-term results. I went out with Margaret Chalken, going with her to see *Coriolanus*, *The Cherry Orchard*, *Hamlet* and other plays. I saw Elwyn constantly, visited Jack Reading at his house in St John's Wood, met up with Tom Umpleby, now finishing his degree at LSE, called on Eric Ross at his lodgings in the Archway Road, attended the Proms, the cinema, cycled around Epping Forest from my Forest Gate home and enjoyed my social life.

As well as being involved in trade-union work I developed an interest in local politics in West Ham. This began when I joined the newly formed West Ham branch of the Fabian Society, set up by Michael Davidson, an optician who was to become a councillor and to serve as mayor. He lived in Earlham Grove, Forest Gate, where our first meetings were held. After the society began in May 1948, we held our first lecture meetings in June and July with Captain Swingler, MP, and the West Ham North MP Arthur Lewis as our speakers.

In September I was made secretary and charged with arranging speakers as well as dealing with minutes and correspondence. I was to keep this voluntary job until January 1951. Among the speakers for our meetings, often held in local schools, were my college friend's namesake Elwyn Jones, the MP for West Ham South, John Diamond, Hector Hughes, John Parker, Percy Daines and the Reverend Sorenson MP. I became the Fabian Society delegate to meetings of West Ham Labour Party Central Committee and was active in my local ward. Our ward chairman was Councillor Crone, a Thames lighterman.

West Ham was where the Labour Party had first emerged as a political party with parliamentary representation and when Keir Hardie was elected as the member for West Ham South at the beginning of the twentieth century. The local party meetings often seemed to be strangely enmeshed in feuds dating from before the Second World War, with allegiance to the 'traitor' Ramsey Macdonald still a subject for discussion. At one point I was put forward – at the insistence of councillors I had got to know through the Fabian Society – as a candidate for local councillor. I was, however, not selected.

I supported the Labour Party because I thought that their policies, practised locally, had led me to enjoy a good education, and I felt liberated when in 1945 Clement Atlee was swept into power. I was enthusiastic about the creation of a National Health Service and thought that nationalisation might reinvigorate some of the country's industries and services. In the two and a half years I was involved, I felt I was working towards the improvement of the life of the people among whom I had grown up in West Ham. I attended national Fabian Society functions and heard talks by Herbert Morrison, Harold Laski, Ian Mikardo, Donald Chapman and Attlee himself. My energy waned only when I wanted to give time to other matters.

Trying to improve my position, I pursued employment opportunities from 1948 through to the end of 1951. In this time I had fifteen job interviews but not one job offer. Two were for WEA tutor organiser jobs, one in Southampton, giving me the chance of a harbour boat ride to see the giant *Queen Elizabeth* liner, and the other in Leicester. I had an interview at the British Council, but the man I saw did not think I had the right skin pigment for service in the tropics. Another interview was at the Board of Trade; one was at BBC Radio; a third was for a research job at Labour Party HQ, where I was interviewed by Michael Young (he had a plaster on his face to cover a shaving cut); and one was with Alison and Peter Smithson for a job in their architectural practice. In January 1949 I was summoned for an interview at the British Laundries Institute; in April to Odhams, the newspaper publishers; and in June to the Institute of Hospital Administration, where the man who interviewed me put me on his shortlist, but I still did not get the job. One of the more enjoyable interviews was in July 1949 when I was called to the model estate of Bournville along with five other applicants. I was not successful, but I learned something about the village and had the chance to delay my return with a short holiday. I took a bus from Birmingham to Shrewsbury, stayed overnight at the George and then went on to Chester. Next morning I travelled to Wrexham, Llangollen and Barmouth, a good, old-fashioned seaside town. Then I went on to Dolgelly and, using my hitch-hiking skills, made my way across a remote mountainous area to Newtown, Montgomeryshire, where I stayed at the Bear. There was very little traffic on the road on that section, and I walked quite a lot. I suppose I must have been carrying luggage of some kind, probably the small haversack I used on such trips. I had a fine restful weekend at the Bear, reading a book by Neville Cardus on cricket which I had bought there. On Monday I travelled via Shrewsbury, Wenlock and Bridgnorth to Birmingham and back to Euston by train.

A fortnight later, in August 1949, a few days after my twenty-sixth birthday, I left the British Isles for the first time, when, on impulse, I bought a British European Airways ticket to Paris for a week's holiday. I took an evening flight, landing at Le Bourget about midnight. The airport reception clerk booked me a room in a small hotel on the Left Bank, and I shared a taxi there with a couple of fellow travellers. I have wonderful memories of that week on my own in Paris. I explored this great city, walking, using the Metro, going on buses and taking Thomas Cook and American Express tours. The coach to Versailles seemed full of young American students talking about Henry Miller, the risqué writer of the day. Travelling on a Bateau-Mouche on the Seine I drank so much wine that I was very unsteady when I got off. *Tristan and Isolde* at the Paris Opéra, apache dancing, night clubs, nude dancers at the Folies-Bergère mix in my mind with paintings and sculpture. There were hardly any tourists, it being only five years since the Germans had been driven out and four since the war had ended. All cities are wonderful to me, but Paris is particularly special.

In 1950 letters to publishers and job interviews at Marks and

Spencer and at Granada Cinemas yielded no results. In 1951 I had another chance to travel when I went to Bristol to be interviewed by the South-Western Electricity Board; I did not get the job but saw Brunel's railway station and his Clifton Suspension Bridge. I went into the City for an interview with the North British Rubber Company, which would have meant going abroad and which I would not have taken if it had been offered. In April I was interviewed at British Calendar Cables for a research post and by an advertising agency in Soho for a writing job. I applied unsuccessfully for two internal posts at the National Coal Board and was interviewed for a Civil Service information officer post.

Part of my efforts to get a better job stemmed from the fact that by November 1948 I had met Teresa Coughlan, with whom I had started a relationship. As it happened a new post at the NCB, which I gained in 1949, was to lead on to exciting new work.

6

FILMING AND MARRIAGE

I ENTERED HOBART House, the headquarters of the National Coal Board, on 25 February 1949 and joined about six other ex-Commission staff in a crammed ground-floor office. We were now members of the NCB Manpower and Welfare Department. I am not sure what we did, but I think I was still lumbered with the welfare survey. Fortunately Board jobs were advertised in weekly staff notices. You applied, and if you were lucky you were shortlisted for an interview. Being only a Grade II clerk my chances of getting a good job were practically nil, but I saw a vacancy advertised for a Grade I clerk's job in the Public Relations Department and, on 18 May 1949, after a successful interview, I got it. In Public Relations I was to feel at home as I never had in the dour world of welfare work.

Hobart House employed several hundred people, and when I transferred into that milieu of new faces it was with a slightly different appearance, as I had begun to wear a wig. I had been going to the central Middlesex hospital since October 1947, attending a clinic dealing with skin disease headed by Dr Ray Battley. I had been treated with new ointments without success. When the National Health Service was created in 1948 it allowed the free provision of wigs (attacked in the press at the time), and the doctors now recommended that I wore one. They gave me a purchase voucher, which I took to the firm of Spaans. This time I chose a less ostentatious brown colour. At that time the wigs were made from natural hair (acrylic was introduced in later years), the source said to be Italian nunneries. You wore one for a month before it was cleaned by baking, and then you wore a second one issued to you. At first I felt self-conscious, but soon the wigs became part of me, something I was to wear until old age with hardly a thought, apart from the monthly chore of changing them. Free issue did not last very long; soon you had to pay a fee towards the cost when, every three years, they needed to be replaced.

The charges rose higher and higher, but it was money well spent. And of course I spent nothing on shaving and haircuts.

Hobart House stood on the corner of Grosvenor Place and Hobart Place and was a brick-fronted building with stone dressing built on an E plan. It backed on to a mews, where there was an entrance to an underground garage. The building faced the garden wall of Buckingham Palace and had been put up as a five-storey block only after the death of King George V in 1936, who apparently objected to his garden being overlooked. Its name derived from the Hobart family, which had occupied a town house on the site. One of its aristocratic members had become governor of Tasmania and so gave his name to the Tasmanian capital. James Lees-Milne, in one of his wonderful diaries describing visits to decaying aristocratic homes on behalf of the National Trust, says that the Hobart family called themselves Hubbard, so strictly we should have been talking about Hubbard House, but nobody did.

The Army had taken over the building during the war, displacing the firms that leased offices within. In 1949 they still occupied part of the building, and the canteen on the top floor (later renamed the staff restaurant) was used by attractive, uniformed Auxiliary Territorial Army women who worked as army chauffeurs. But these disappeared as the National Coal Board developed its organisation. From the commodious front hall, access to all five floors and the basement was by two large lifts and a staircase. Those seeking to keep fit would pride themselves on only using the stairs to go up to their offices. I enjoyed working in the not-too-large rooms, which had sash windows that you could open, avoiding the need for air conditioning. Later on, open-plan offices were introduced for some departments, with interior walls knocked through, but fortunately I avoided these when they became the fashion.

It was a pleasant area to be based. In the lunch-hour, being a walker, I could cross Eaton Square to Sloane Square with W.H. Smith's bookshop and further on Sandoe's bookshop, off the King's Road. I could walk through Cubitt's Belgravia to Sloane Street and Harrods or go the other way along Victoria Street to the Army and Navy Stores, an area I was to see totally rebuilt. Near by was old-fashioned Gorringe's department store. If one felt energetic one could circle round the Buckingham Palace estate to reach St James's Park, a most beautiful place, or progress further into the West End. As a Londoner I found it wonderful to explore all these different areas, with their complexity of architecture and appearance.

Just as war and evacuation had shaped my life from 1939 to 1948, so history determined my life from 1948 to 1984. I was to walk hand in hand with time: I lived, by chance, at the time of the creation of the nationalised industries and was able to spend my working life in the security one offered to me and retired when such industries were being privatised or closed down. I was to be a mid-twentieth-century type of public servant, a worker in a nationalised industry and thus a manifestation of socialist ideas within a political democracy. These ideas, along with increased social security measures, held sway despite Conservative governments from the mid-1940s to the mid-1980s, when the world began to change – a forty-year social experiment. Personally I gained the security of employment my father had always urged on me, and as a Labour Party supporter, the satisfaction of working for an industry owned by the country.

The National Coal Board came into existence on 1 January 1948. What it inherited when the government purchased (not confiscated) the coal-mining companies was a huge motley of properties and an industry that had been undercapitalised for decades. With the exception of the newer coalfields in the Midlands, the best cheap coal had already been mostly taken. Later owners had put little money into their businesses. Poor labour relations and bad social conditions epitomised an industry which was largely nineteenth century in its technology. In my view the NCB's achievement in transforming this situation for the benefit of the country has never been sufficiently publicised. Every nationalised industry was a target for the newspapers, so how could they trumpet their successes?

A pit begins to die when the first ton of coal is taken from it, ran the old saying. Coal-mining is an extractive industry; the more coal you take, the higher the cost of getting it as you have to dig further for it underground. Despite the Board's successful search for new undiscovered coal measures and the exploitation of new coal, the industry was contracting in size when I worked for it. Mines were closed or were amalgamated into larger ones, and the labour force diminished. In time, administrative divisions were abolished and job opportunities for those looking for promotion declined as well. New mining technology meant fewer miners were needed; output per man went up.

It was the post-war situation of a shortage of coal, and the need to supply it in quantity cheaply to help revive British industry, that was to sow the seeds of the coal industry's downfall in the 1980s. The key factor was government control of prices. They were kept down in order to help industry to recover after the war. The normal interaction of supply and demand to determine price was not allowed to happen. This did not matter when the ethos of life during the Attlee government was public service. When in the Thatcher years this ethos was replaced by the profit motive, the coal industry was seen as a commercial failure. The goal posts had been moved.

With government-restricted prices it was difficult for the Board to make a profit. In addition, it lost its market in gas manufacture and in providing coal for railway steam trains and domestic fires as competing sources of power arrived in the shape of natural gas, oil and nuclear energy. Lord Robens as chairman fought hard to keep markets but gradually the core business became the supply of coal to electricity generating stations. This was the policy of both Conservative and Labour governments, which saw coal as a national asset (an island of coal) which must be aided in case of war. This concept of coal as a vital national asset lost out in the Thatcher years with the move to privatisation. More mines were closed, and labour relations deteriorated as whole communities were devastated by pit closures. An ill-thought-out and not universally desired strike engineered by Arthur Scargill at the wrong time of the year played into government hands. Fortunately I had retired on 1 March 1984 before this destructive battle.

In 1949 there was a sense of excitement at being in an organisation in which nearly everybody was new to each other. Sir Arthur Street, the first deputy chairman, had used his skills to provide the administrative structure for the new enterprise. He created Divisions and Areas across the country, as well as the main departments. A hard worker, he was to be found dead of heart failure in his Hobart House office late one evening. The uniqueness of the NCB was in combining Civil Service practices and control through the Ministry of Fuel and Power with the necessity of producing coal for the market. Its personnel were to become a blend of administrators, professional specialists and engineers – earthy, blunt men from the regions who looked at nature in the raw and by hard graft overcame it. It was the engineers who became the dominant force in the early years when the overwhelming demand was for more coal. They were to pioneer inventions and technological developments that were to revolutionise British coal-mining and to raise it to the top of the world's coal-mining league, with eventually British machinery being sold to the coalfields of the world.

Efforts to integrate staff were made from the beginning. The first chairman was Viscount Hyndley, a short genial ex-civil servant who put himself out to get to know his staff at all grades by inviting them in groups for evening sherry at his Chelsea home not far away. Room 16 on the ground floor was the main conference room, and here staff assembled from time to time for morale-boosting messages or progress reports, a practice which continued until I retired in the 1980s. Room 16 was to play a continuing role in the history of the NCB; here conferences at all levels were held, from bargaining to press briefings, and staff social events also took place.

My knowledge of people in the building expanded when I joined the Public Relations Branch. It was part of the Secretary's Department and was seen as a channel for making knowledge available about the industry and its policies to the media and the general public including schools. It always had an important role to play when new policies or technologies were to be publicised or crises such as pit accidents had to be explained. In due course it was upgraded from branch to department. It had contacts with all parts of the industry.

I remember with affection that short corridor of offices where I was based for the next five years. Coming out of the lift on the third floor, you turned left through swing doors and then left again into a corridor which was a cul-de-sac. It had wooden flooring (later carpeted when Derek Ezra became chairman), and the paintwork was pale green. Closed doors lining each side of the corridor bore the names of their occupants.

First door on the left was that of the chief press officer who, when I joined, was Noel Gee, MC. Educated at Harrow and in the United States, Noel had served in the artillery and later in life was to go deaf. Many of the staff recruited to the Board in the late 1940s had seen war service. Noel Gee was a tall, good-looking married man with a charming smile, but he could get a bit desperate when a dozen things at a time demanded his attention, understandably. He later became a divisional board member in the Midlands and then worked for an oil firm.

An interconnecting door from his office led to the next room, where sat his secretary, the formidable Miss Doris Allen, and Noel's deputy, Fred Pullen. Fred seemed to be approaching the end of his press career (although, in the event, he was not to retire until 1959). He had begun life as a journalist for a newspaper in his native South Wales. He told of the time when, as a young reporter, he had done well with a news story. The editor had called him in to congratulate him and then asked him what his current salary was. 'Five pounds a week, sir,' replied Fred, expecting a rise. 'Oh! I'm glad! I am glad!' exclaimed the editor, to Fred's mortification. He could never escape his Fleet Street past and was always off there to keep up his contacts, in the traditional bibulous fashion, returning in loquacious mood. At weekends he moonlighted for the *News of the World*, helping to get it out on Saturday nights. When I had an article printed in *Tribune*, a well-selling weekly, he claimed to have heard about it in Fleet Street and always seemed disappointed I had not followed it up.

Another interconnecting door led from Fred Pullen's office into the Press Room, where about four press officers worked. The press made their enquiries here, and the press officers, each specialising in a different section of the Board's work, contacted the appropriate department, for instance, Production or Industrial Relations, for a suitable reply. The press were not allowed to make direct contact with these departments if it could be avoided. Competing newspapers, magazines, cinema newsreels and radio were treated fairly. In time one began to recognise in the building the formidable figures of industrial correspondents or even Fleet Street editors arriving for press conferences or convivial discussion. A web of contacts existed. Also in the press room was the stills librarian, Miss Peggy Ward, who met all the demands for illustrations. Every large organisation has to learn how to handle the media. In my early days, of course, there was no television, but radio reporters were involved and newsreels, especially at any dreadful time when there was a pit disaster. At that period there were about five newsreels producing twice-weekly editions for screening in public cinemas; the BBC also had such a newsreel when television developed its output after the war – it would be some time before live daily news programmes were instituted.

I was to see many different people in the post of press officer. One who joined the branch when I did was Geoffrey Kirk, previously a reporter on a Derbyshire newspaper and a member of the wartime

Royal Navy, who had survived the torpedoing of his ship in the Mediterranean. Although appointed as an assistant press officer (like me he had to sign into an Arrivals Book each morning), he was so cool and efficient, even ruthless, that he rose to be chief press officer when Noel Gee moved on. In due course he became director of Public Relations and worked very closely with the chairman of the Board. Geoff was a first-class swimmer and would try to fit in a swim if the day's work allowed. He had a difficult time during the 1984 strike, as, like so many other Board people, his heart was with the mineworkers and he was disliked for it. After he retired he spent more time at the cottage he had in Scotland and was to drown in tragic circumstances. He was in a small boat with two nephews, I believe, when he was swept away. He rendered very fine service and was always pleasant to deal with, in my experience.

Geoff Kirk's promotion to chief press officer was a fatal blow to Henry Donaldson, who had been senior press officer under Noel Gee and who had expected to succeed him. Suffering sometimes from malaria, which he had contracted during his war service in the Far East, Henry was a good talker of some charm and he got on well with reporters, but he lacked Geoff Kirk's intellectual ability and ruthlessness. Watching Henry Donaldson absorb the fact that he had reached the pinnacle of his career in his forties gave me food for thought. 'There is a tide in the affairs of men, which, taken at the flood, leads on to fortune' (*Julius Caesar*). But if the tide is not taken and you are passed over, and what lies ahead seems but a reproduction of what had gone before, with no light of possible promotion at the end of the tunnel, it is a different story. Some people seem to handle this situation with equanimity, settling for what they have got. Others find the loss of promotional hopes a great blow to their self-confidence. Office work gives great opportunities for studying human personality.

Each press officer had his home telephone bill paid by the Board and was expected to be on duty at night, on a rota system. The coal industry never ceased, working around the clock, unlike many factories; there were always men underground, and accidents could happen at any time. If a disaster occurred, all hell was let loose, with major officials and Board members alerted and the world's press pounding for information about men trapped or killed underground, anxious to get the latest news for their next edition or to take newsreel photos. If the press officer's phone rang an hour or so after he went to bed he often would not sleep again that night. Sometimes it was a newspaper seeking backing information for some scoop it had obtained. The media has no respect for anyone in pursuit of a story.

The press office was a large long room with four or five desks. At one of them sat Peter Heap, who was about my age (twenty-six) and, when he joined Public Relations Branch, was a clerk like myself. He had the interesting job of producing a daily information sheet for circulation to top officials and others summarising the main news stories of the day. He would choose and condense appropriately and had to have it out by noon. The news sheet could often help Board members and others answer press enquiries that might develop from that day's newspapers. This was backed by a system of taking cuttings out of newspapers for circulation.

Peter Heap, who did this job conscientiously and well (inventing amusing cross-heads for each story), was to marry Joyce Prebble who also worked in the branch. In due course in order to get promotion he took a job in the Industrial Relations Department, helping to produce an information news sheet among other things, but in due course he returned to assume the post of chief press officer under Geoff Kirk, a job to which he brought a requisite amount of toughness.

On display in the Press Room were all the newspapers, provincial as well as national, which were consulted by various people during the day. Under the long table where they lay stood bound volumes of *The Times* that someone had donated, but I don't think they were consulted too often. The Press Office also had charge of a tape machine issued by the Press Association which all day long spewed out news stories. From time to time a press officer would tear off a strip from the lengthening band of paper to hang it up in the Press Office. The machine stood on a landing and was thus accessible to any member of the Board's staff. It was popular during test matches when people such as Mr Turnbull, the director of establishments, would regularly pop up to obtain the latest cricket score.

Beyond the Press Office, on the left-hand side, was a pair of swing doors giving access to a staircase, designed no doubt to meet safety regulations. This back staircase proved handy for people who, for one reason or another, wanted to slip out of the office unseen., as a discreet disappearance could be achieved. The real artists of this manoeuvre were those who went boldly out of the office carrying a file; no one doubted they were visiting another department over business. It was advisable to return within a judicious amount of time, so as not to arouse suspicion. Of course leaving the building on a wet day without a raincoat could raise suspicion!

Beyond the staircase was a room then occupied by Bill Sykes and Monty Calman, to whom I was assigned when I first came to work in the corridor, although I did not share their room with its two facing desks. They were responsible for the production of printed publications, either books for schools or for other departments such as Recruitment. They were both men I could get on with, although they were like chalk and cheese in their characters. Monty, Bill's number two, was a short, worldly-wise individual of a somewhat cynical nature who was not particularly enamoured of the Board. He was a tall, fresh-faced serious Yorkshireman who was one of nature's idealists trying to cope with the realities of daily life.

I was to work for them only for a few months before Bill got another job as publications officer to the Health Education Council. Monty also left, and in their place the Board appointed a young professional designer of publications named Eileen Westcott. A fairly tough, determined girl, capable of holding her own with her clients, I found her friendly, and we used to have lunch together (at Lyons Corner House). But I was not to work with her. After he left, Bill Sykes, who had been helpful to me and thought I should have a more high-powered job, rang me up and invited me to lunch, over which we discussed the problems of issuing publications, especially for his new employer. We carried on meeting for some time. He was a very nice man.

The next room to Bill's was the corner one on the left-hand side. It was occupied by the head of public relations, later redesignated the director. In the first year of the Board's life, before I joined, the head had been Noel Newsome, a very active newspaper man who had apparently done much to establish the branch and to secure its place in the Board. His deputy was Clifton Reynolds, who had made his name as an author of a book on agriculture as well as his autobiography, which had just come out and which I read at that time. Reynolds occupied the matching room on the right hand of the corridor, in the corner, the two divided by a small room used by a shorthand typist. These end rooms had views west towards St Peter's Church in

Eaton Square and were well lit and pleasant. Reynolds did not stay very long in 1949. He used to dictate non-Board work to his secretary and at least once wandered down the corridor saying 'Anyone got a pack of cards? I have nothing to do.'

I just missed Noel Newsome but arrived at the same time as Sir Guy Nott-Bower, a civil servant who took his place. Referring to some newspaper scandal of the time, he sent a telegram in advance saying: 'I am not Hugh Gaitskell's nephew.' Sir Guy was a gentleman, with all that word means, treating everybody with civility and conveying a deep human understanding that was much appreciated. He was the top of our tree and I was the bottom, but we could stand side by side in the gentleman's urinals, he in his braces and without a jacket, while he chatted away. I had the suspicion at this time that he and I were the only two people in the corridor with university degrees (the war had upset lives), but I refrained from mentioning this. I was to continue to work under his leadership for some years and was glad he was someone I could respect.

Returning down the corridor on the opposite side there was a room occupied by the Exhibitions Section, which designed, had constructed, transported, set up, manned and handled exhibitions at locations across the country. These were intended to promote the Board and help with recruitment. The slogan 'A Job For Life' was coined; these were the days of manpower shortages and as many school recruits as possible were sought for the Board's apprenticeship schemes in electrical, mechanical and mining skills. Bill Akroyd headed this section, assisted by Dave Williams and Bill Parkin. Akroyd had been to Eton and used to tease Noel Gee that it was a better school than Harrow, which Noel had attended. Bill Akroyd was an extreme extrovert who had come to the Board after war service during which he had met Noel Newsome. One day he asked a group of us, 'Do you like my new suit?' He had had made an identical copy of the suit he had always worn, and we could not tell the difference. Bill's hobby at his home in Maidenhead was pottery, using his own kiln. In due course he became public relations officer at the UK Atomic Energy Authority. On visits to us he would practise his explanations of how the technical processes worked. David Williams, his number two, was a canny Welshman of left-wing views. Bill Parkin was the junior but shouldered a great deal of responsibility in getting exhibitions set up in time, often working long hours into the night.

When Clifton Reynolds left, his office was occupied by Lambton Wilkinson who came from Durham and was named after the aristocratic family that had ruled in that part of the world; the local legend was about a monster called the Lambton Worm. Lambton had been a miner and told tales of working underground; but he was a smooth-spoken individual, athletic, well dressed and with a great talent for public speaking. His job consisted of responding to invitations to give talks from schools, women's institutes and the like. After many of these visits a fulsome letter of praise for Lambton would arrive, indicating he was the right man for the job. Lambton was knowledgeable about music and architecture, having sung in a choir in the great Norman cathedral of Durham. His sons, when they grew up, emigrated to western Canada and there set up a steel works. Lambton eventually joined them and became a member of the company board.

Lambton eventually shared this end office with the branch secretary. When I joined this had been Lew Unger, who had interviewed me for my job. But Unger was soon to die of cancer and was succeeded by Norman Batley, a suburban man whom I liked for his steadfast nature. During the war he had served in both the fire service and in India. I always remembered him grumbling that after one had spent money furnishing one's house it was only a short time before one had to splash out again on replacements. Batley in his turn was to be succeeded by George Anderson, who put a great deal of time into running the Board's Social Club, especially the annual flower show for which he himself brought in carloads of produce and flowers. Overcoming the handicap of a limp, he busied himself around the building and was much liked.

A room next to them accommodated a typing pool of about five girls who did the typing for the whole branch. Some of them I found attractive, but the one I liked was already married, so there was no future there. She had a small scar on her forehead, which she told me she had acquired when buried under rubble during the Blitz.

On this side was the room at first occupied by Unger and shared by him with Kurt Lewenhak, the films officer, for whom I was to work, based in this room. Next door was the clerks' office where I was placed when I arrived, sharing the room with Bill Crisp and Bob Hope. I remember putting a copy of the American magazine *Life* on Bob Hope's desk and saying: 'Where there is life there is hope.'

Bill Crisp was ex-army, non-commissioned, who taught me basic skills, such as how to handle a file with papers secured by a green Indian tag if you want to insert and remove a piece of paper in the middle. I enjoyed my weeks with these two, perhaps because I felt comfortable with fellow working-class people.

Next door was the newspaper room, staffed by Gordon Macdonald and a woman called Brenda, whose surname I forget. They got in at eight in the morning and systematically marked up references to the Board. These papers were seen by the chief press officer and the press officers, used by Peter Heap and then left in the Press Office. Next day they were not thrown away but stored on wooden racks in an adjacent room.

Gordon MacDonald, despite his Scottish name, spoke with a Yorkshire accent, having been brought up in Keighley. We were about the same age and I always enjoyed his common-sense views on people. Unfortunately he was plagued with nervous ill health which saw him off sick a great deal and which did not enhance his reputation at work. He was to die early, in his late fifties. Brenda was a titch of a girl, about eighteen years old, who lived in Sudbury with her family. The love of her life was Bert, a driver on the Piccadilly tube line, who would occasionally collect her from the office. I think they married but later split up. Bert once offered me a ride with him in the driver's cabin, an opportunity I took advantage of, giving me a different view of tube travel. It was probably against regulations, but I suspect that Brenda often journeyed home this way.

In charge of this newspaper section was Sid Pepper, a character of great individuality, who reminisced about his days with the Eighth Army in the desert. He would chat to his staff at length, who included Joyce Prebble. Pepper would ramble on about his army service; in addition his talk would have a moralistic tone, laying down precepts for his staff. His weakness was that he could not throw newspapers away, intending always to do important research, and so the piles grew and grew. Ultimately this was to be his downfall. Many years later Lord Robens took over as chairman and demanded a room-by-room tour of the whole of Hobart House, intending to meet as many staff as possible. Eventually he reached Sid Pepper, now housed in a ground-floor office of his own which he could hardly enter because it was filled with newspapers. Despite Sid's view that they represented valuable raw material for research, Lord Robens would not have it, and so the papers disappeared with, I think, Sid not long after.

Another part of Public Relations Branch was on the fifth floor of Hobart House where the magazine *Coal* was produced, edited by a Scottish newspaperman called Robertson and known as Robbie. He was to be succeeded by Alan Delafons. The magazine did not survive the appointment of Geoff Kirk as director of Public Relations, as he closed it down (Delafons left) and set up *Coal News*, which was to win awards as the best industrial newspaper in the UK. Before this happened, when *Coal* was still in production, I met Sid Chaplin who worked for it at this time. Sid began life as a Durham miner but turned to novel writing with great success – his first was called *The Leaping Lad*, published at about this time. He wrote articles for the *Manchester Guardian* and other outlets in his spare time. He was to become Public Relations Officer for Northumberland and Cumberland, and when, in the 1970s, I sometimes had to visit Newcastle for work he always invited me over to his house, with his wife Renee plying me with food. One of his sons, Michael, was to make his name as a television writer and director.

With my admiration for writers, I was thrilled to meet Sid, and it was probably with his encouragement that some news paragraphs I submitted were printed in issues of *Coal*. By this time I had been assigned to work for the Press Office, following the departure of Sykes and Calman. This was clerical work, handling mail and so on. I sat opposite Gordon MacDonald, watching him mark the newspapers, with Brenda cutting out items for circulation. This hapless life was made tolerable because at the same time I had been asked to look after the needs of the Board's films officer, my first involvement with films, a job which in due course was to provide exciting work and promotion.

This opening came about because Kurt Lewenhak, the films officer, wanted to work for the Board for one day, or half-day, a week, as he wished to go freelance in order to undertake creative work; he had secured a contract to write scripts for the steel industry. I was seen as a suitable person to look after day-to-day film affairs, combining it with the Press Office routine work.

In appointing a films officer and sponsoring films about the coal industry, the Board was in tune with the times. Making public relations films about work had begun seriously in the 1930s, mainly inspired by the Scot John Grierson, who headed an important film unit, first at the Empire Marketing Board and then at the General Post Office.

Grierson is credited with the term 'the creative use of actuality' as a definition of 'documentary'. A documentary movement grew in the UK as large industries such as the Gas Light and Coke Company and Shell Oil began to sponsor films, often with social overtones, as a public relations exercise. It was difficult to get these films shown in commercial cinemas, but 16mm gauge film projectors and prints allowed them to reach local audiences, sometimes with the aid of mobile vans. During the 1939–45 war film played an important role in disseminating information and boosting morale and was also used by the armed services as a training medium. As well as information shorts shown in cinemas, documentary extended into feature films with such titles as *The Way to the Stars*, depicting service life and sacrifice.

Kurt Lewenhak was a burly, extrovert person, often known as Lew. An LSE graduate of left-wing views, he had done radio work in Germany while in the Army where, I think, he met Noel Newsome and Bill Akroyd, all three of them ending up in the newly created Coal Board. The film-making programme he set up followed this wartime feature film trend, with titles aimed at the general public, depicting miners in a good light; cinemas were seen as the main outlet for them. The result was feature-length films such as *A Man's Affair*, about a young Kent miner's love affair; *Blue Scar*, a Welsh mining family story made by Jill Craigie (Michael Foot's wife); and *Tinker*, about mining apprentices, made by Herbert Marshall, a well-known left-wing figure in the arts at this time. A Swiss-made colour cartoon called *King Coal* emphasised the country's desperate need for coal to help it recover from the war. These all achieved some cinema success.

When, in 1949, I was assigned to work for Kurt Lewenhak, he had two documentary-style films in production. *Nines Was Standing* (the title refers to a coal seam where work was at a standstill) was designed to show how a colliery joint consultative committee worked, with consultation between mineworkers and pit management. This twenty-minute film was made by Humphrey Swingler through Green Park Productions. There were three Swingler brothers, and it amused me that I met all three in three different ways. As well as Humphrey, whom I was to see more often when I did film journalism, there was Stephen, the MP who had come to address West Ham Fabian Society, and Randall, whose English Literature lectures I was to enjoy at Morley College evening classes. The other film Lew had in production was

The Miner, a portrait of a miner's life. This was being made for the Board through World Wide Films by another respected film-maker called Jack Holmes. World Wide Films had been set up before the war by Jimmy Carr and was to prove the most durable of documentary film companies.

I am not sure if either of these two films secured any cinema screenings, but one that certainly did was *Mining Review*. This monthly ten-minute film was in the newsreel format and usually contained four separate stories. Its aim initially was to make miners in different parts of the country aware of belonging to a nationwide industry and to show men in one coalfield what was happening in another. The stories covered developments with new technology as well social activities. The series ran, without a missed issue, from the late 1940s until the 1980s and became an enormous database of film, showing life in Britain over four decades. The material is now deposited in the National Film Archive.

Mining Review followed the tradition of wartime government information shorts and got regular distribution to cinemas by National Screen Services. The bulk of the screenings were in the coalfields, but it was also taken by West End and Home Counties cinemas. During the war the Crown Film Unit had been created to make government shorts and features, and it was Crown that made the first six issues of *Mining Review*. Owing to production difficulties it was transferred to the DATA Film Unit, based at No. 21 Soho Square. This was a co-operative established by a group of film-makers, chiefly by Donald Alexander, who in due course was to succeed Kurt Lewenhak as the Board's films officer. The Documentary Technicians Alliance Ltd was 'concerned with the production of documentary films with social significance'.

Relevant films made by other sponsors also existed, and when I became 'Assistant to the Films Officer', my office nomenclature for my new responsibilities, I inherited a pile of 16mm cans containing these films. Chief of these was *Buried Treasure*, an explanation of the three-shift system of coal-mining, which had been made in 1939 for the Coal Utilisation Council. Films are either good or bad, an unpredictable outcome when the film director starts work, and *Buried Treasure* was widely seen as a good film and went on being used for a long time, especially when schools needed an explanation of mining techniques.

Best of the other titles I inherited was *The Cumberland Story*, made in 1947 by a man who has come to be seen as one of the most important of Britain's documentary film-makers: Humphrey Jennings, famous for *Fires Were Started*, *Diary for Timothy* and other films. Sadly Jennings died in a fall from a rock while filming in Greece in 1950. His film was one of four sponsored by the Ministry of Fuel and Power. Another film was *Coal*, made for the Department of Army Kinematography for training soldiers. *The New Mine* was made for the British Council about the new Rothes mine in Scotland as an aid in promoting Britain. *Under New Management*, about the nationalisation of the coal mines, was made in 1948 for the Ministry of Labour. *Charley's Black Magic* was a cartoon made in 1949 for the Economic Information Unit when coal was seen as vital to the nation's recovery.

All these films, as well as those made for the Board, were loaned out on request to schools and societies that had 16mm projectors, and I began to build up this film lending side, buying more copies direct from the film laboratories and learning how to check and rewind films before sending them out. I devised a catalogue of films available from the NCB, which I had printed for me by the Board's internal printing section, with a copy of the Board's crest on its neat brown cover. As bookings grew, another clerk called Gerald Acres was brought in to handle the dispatches as well as Branch clerical work.

Divisions were also supplied with these mining films for coalfield use and their film libraries given replacements as necessary. They also asked me to arrange loans of films on relevant subjects. At Hobart House I organised weekly staff film shows with borrowed short films. I also found myself interviewing casual callers, people wanting a film job or wishing to sell projection equipment or to film at a colliery.

I was soon involved with film production matters, helping companies such as World Wide with film library shots or answering questions from Jack Holmes, the director of *The Miner*. My most important role was working with DATA on the production of *Mining Review*. This was managed by a committee, meeting weekly to choose stories. On the Board's side were Henry Donaldson and Peggy Ward from the Press Office, Kurt Lewenhak and myself, the appointed secretary. The representatives from DATA varied: at first Donald Alexander and Leslie Shepherd, later Francis Gysin, Jack Chambers, John

Gaudioz and Jack Holmes. Leslie Shepherd had a fascinating ability to talk and write at length – sometimes to Donald's exasperation. He lived in a flat near King's Cross reputedly full of books. Leslie was to settle in Dublin and to become an expert on early ballads. Most of his rare books were donated to the Writers' Museum in Dublin.

All this made life much more enjoyable. My contact at DATA was Pamela Brown, and with her I cleared the way for filming to take place by contacting the appropriate coalfield people, sometimes making available the Board's special set of lighting that had to be used for underground filming on safety grounds. I soon asked to go on location with a DATA crew to get a better idea of what filming was like. This led to a one-day location trip to the County Agricultural Show near Cambridge. Director of the unit was Peter Pickering, and the cameraman was Wolfgang Suschitsky, already famous as a stills photographer. Born in 1912, Su, as he was known, was to do feature film work, being lighting cameraman on titles such *Get Carter* (1971). His son, Peter, was also to become a features cameraman of note.

In March 1951 this growing film work led me to write a memo to Noel Gee listing all the jobs I now did and pointing out how difficult it was to carry out clerical work for the Press Office. This situation was resolved when, on 31 May, Lewenhak resigned and I was made a full-time worker on films. Union negotiations leading to changes in job nomenclature led to my being made a clerical officer grade II with a salary of £532 a year (inclusive of London Location Allowance), better than my previous £442.

Donald Alexander joined as the Board's films officer on 11 May 1951 and stayed until mid-1963. He was to revolutionise the Board's film work and to give it a whole new level of importance. Like Lewenhak his appointment was as freelance consultant, engaged on the understanding that he would spend at least one day a week on his advisory job. His employer was Film Centre, which John Grierson and Sir Arthur Elton had set up in 1937 to be a consultative body promoting documentary films and their use. Grierson had left Film Centre by the time Alexander, joined it but Elton was still there; other documentary film-makers who worked for it for a time included Edgar Anstey, who was to become films officer to British Transport, and Paul Rotha.

Donald Alexander had been born in 1913 and was ten years older than me. He had gone to a public school, Shrewsbury, and then to St

John's College, Cambridge, where he had gained a first in Classics. When he graduated in the 1930s, documentary film was emerging as a new art form and as a medium concerned with social problems. Film societies were formed at universities and some amateur film-making undertaken. Donald, the son of a Scottish doctor of medicine who practised in Suffolk, had a strong social conscience. (I suspected that he had been in and out of the Communist Party, as was common among many young intellectuals, as it was seen as the only bulwark against the Fascism rising in Europe.) Donald went to South Wales and, using a borrowed 16mm camera, made a film about the dereliction and unemployment of the Rhondda valley. I believe some of his shots of people scrabbling for coal on waste heaps were used in Rotha's *Today We Live* (1939) and are still used in new documentaries.

Donald accepted a job offer from Rotha and worked for his company, Strand Films. Just after accepting Rotha's offer, he was offered a job by John Grierson, which he had to refuse. This led to a certain coolness between Alexander and Grierson. When in the 1950s I asked Donald, somewhat naively, what he thought of Grierson, he replied that 'he had once been a great man', thus consigning Grierson to the past. After a wartime period as a forester, Donald set up DATA. In my view, though, his finest achievement was to get the National Coal Board to adopt an extensive film-making programme and to persuade them to set up its own professional internal film-making unit. Over the next three decades it helped retrain the workforce and introduce new machines and technology.

I was to work for Donald Alexander as his number two for the next twelve years. He was a strong-willed man of very independent views, despising pretension, and I was soon to learn that I had to assume while working with him that Donald was always right. He took this attitude even when discussing films with Board members, one of whom once observed that 'we are not making this film according to the gospel of Donald Alexander'. Donald was forceful but not arrogant, and much of his attitude stemmed from his very quick and decisive brain. Some people tend to be secretive rather than talkative about themselves and Donald was like this. He could easily lose his temper, was sometimes seen as a bully and could never put up with fools or foolish behaviour, however grand the status of the person concerned.

This assessment of Donald's character leaves out his essential kindness and understanding. He was one of nature's teachers, and I saw many a young film director benefit from his coaching. He had a good eye, appreciated how a film should be made and applied logic to their structuring. His life was determined to a large extent by his social conscience, having no time for those who sought privilege. He relied upon the companionship of his second wife, Budge Cooper, herself a film-maker, who was a great character. On location filming, she sometimes shocked mining people with her swearing . She was physically very attractive.

I felt happy when working for Donald. Once more I had been fortunate in being placed with someone of high intelligence; this always brings out the best in me, as I try to match their quickness of brain with my own. Others in my life who had this attractive mental agilitu were Elwyn Jones, R.D.V. Roberts and later Francis Gysin and Denis Kensit. When Donald retired in 1963 I think I can say that I loved him, despite all the stress he had caused me over the years we worked together. This affection was rooted in admiration. He was to die in July 1983 just short of his eightieth birthday. I was especially indebted to him because under his tutelage I became efficient at my job.

When he arrived, Donald soon began to make policy changes. He supported the continuance of *Mining Review* and its cinema distribution, but he gave up making feature films for the cinemas. Instead he commissioned short educational films such as Derek Mayne's *Under the Surface*, about science and the miner, Sam Napier-Bell's series entitled *Coalmining as a Craft* and his history film, *Nine Centuries of Coal*. These were primarily for 16mm distribution to schools and other audiences, although *Under the Surface* secured cinema distribution, as did *Plan for Coal* made for the Board by DATA.

Donald also had five films made about five different collieries where reconstruction programmes were carried out, mainly about haulage improvements both above and below ground. These were commissioned from DATA Films and were produced and directed by Francis Gysin. Having met Gysin through *Mining Review* work it was good to have contact in this way. I had discovered through *Mining Review* meetings that Francis had a brain as fast as Donald's, and I used to enjoy the battle of wits between them when they were discussing the titles for each of the four stories in the reel. Francis was known for the nicknames he bestowed on people he worked with: Donald was 'The Duck', Leslie Shepherd 'The Sheepdog' and John Gaudioz was 'Pinhead'; Robert Kruger, the film editor, was known as 'Squarehead' because of his surname.

Outside film-makers were helped by Donald with facilities and advice. These included Philip Leacock who, through Group Three, a production company set up with government blessing to help British film-making and headed by John Grierson, made a film about a mining disaster, basing it on an event at Knockshinnock in Scotland. It was called *The Brave Don't Cry*, and I was able to visit the studio where it was made to watch filming take place.

Another film-maker Donald helped was Lindsay Anderson, who began his spectacular film-making career by making sponsored documentaries. One of these was for a mining machinery firm and was called *Trunk Conveyor*. It involved working underground, and Donald lent Lindsay the underground film lights and provided the services of John Reid as lighting cameraman. I had already met Lindsay Anderson at Basic Films, the unit set up by Leon Clore with whom we had dealings. I was to meet him by chance on and off until his death. I was always intrigued by the fact that we had both been born in August 1923. The son of an army officer serving in India, he had been educated at Cheltenham and Oxford. He had a reputation for being prickly, but I always found him polite and helpful. We once sat together in a studio watching a Polish short, a special screening he had set up for me when I was reviewing short films.

Donald soon found me other jobs to do. He asked me to set up a professional 16mm film-lending library as a development of the primitive system I was running. Issuing films was time-consuming, and he advised me to visit existing film-lending libraries to see how they did it. This I accomplished, starting first with the British Gas Film Library, run by Miss Wood, which happened to be situated not far from Hobart House. I went to see a number of others, including the Petroleum Film Board Library, and following their practices devised a series of booking forms. Donald negotiated with Leon Clore for his company, based at No. 18 Soho Square, to hold the film stock and to dispatch the films on receipt of our booking forms. A contract was made with a Basic subsidiary called Graphic Films. The system was up and working by August 1952, only a few months after Donald's arrival.

I continued to make the bookings myself for a few weeks, using the new forms, until the Board appointed a film librarian. The first to fill this post was a charming young Australian girl called Valerie Grieg, who had been trained as a ballet dancer. Soon she was a target for a press officer, John Anstey, who invited her out to the theatre. John was a man of great charm with many friends. I remember him returning to the office and describing how he had had lunch with Glynis Johns, a film star whom I admired. In January 1953 Valerie was succeeded by Mrs Phyllis Major, and then assisted by young Mrs Audrey Smith. Phyllis was one of those ladies who liked rearranging domestic furniture, and many a time Mr Major came home to find everything in a different place. But Phyllis was efficient and a joy to work with. The library system based on the forms was to continue until the library was closed down in the 1980s.

In 1952 Donald also made me responsible for checking the quality and acceptability of the first 16mm print of each monthly issue of *Mining Review*, created after the 35mm copies had been issued. This meant a pleasant monthly visit to Kays Film Laboratories based in Oxford Road, Finsbury Park, where I saw Reg Dace or more often his assistant Les Webb, who was in charge of 16mm grading. I usually went first thing in the morning, arriving later at the office. I continued visiting the laboratories every month until 1966.

A year after his arrival Donald persuaded Sir Guy Nott-Bower, to whom he reported, to submit a paper to the Board recommending two things: first, a three-year programme of film-making, producing instructional and technical films to help explain and implement the changes in coal production methods; and, second, that half of this film-making programme be undertaken by external film units and the remainder by a new internal Board film unit to be known as the NCB Technical Film Unit. The Board accepted the paper, and the new policy was put into place.

The method was for departments such as Production (later called Mining), Industrial Relations (responsible for industrial training), Medical Services and so on to make bids for specific films to be made, financed from a new Technical and Instructional Films Budget administered by Public Relations. A working group of departmental representatives met, discussed and agreed yearly which subjects should be covered. Production Department was allowed a greater number than other departments because that was where the greatest need lay. This system was to continue in operation for at least thirty years and always worked well. The films officer would chose subjects from the lists and assign a scriptwriter or director to the task, asking for the department to nominate the person with whom he would liaise during its production. Scripts were approved before filming and rough cuts shown to the department before the film was completed.

The success of this film-making programme depended essentially on the giant size of the coal industry. It offered potentially large audiences because of the vast labour force and was able to transmit the same information across a wide geographical area, as coalfields were to be found from Scotland to Kent from the Midlands to Wales. New technical solutions to mining problems, and approved methods of working to be taught at all levels, could thus be standardised across the country. It was the ideal medium to meet the Board's communication needs.

As the films were made and distributed, the sponsoring departments soon realised their value and pressed for more. The films proved their worth in a short time. In consequence the number of films made increased each year.

Donald, with whom I had worked for just a year, was bold enough to make me his right-hand man in the work we had to do. As the Technical Film Unit was put together, he made me its production manager. He could easily have engaged an experienced man already working in film production. But he did not, and I am grateful for the confidence he showed in me. He made me responsible for budgets and financial controls overall as well as continuing with responsibility for the film library, and my days became very busy. My career so far had not been very successful: I was still fighting a lack of self-confidence, despite periods of ebullience and exuberance when a different self began to emerge, and he must have been aware that I had a lot to learn, not only about film-making but the basics of being an efficient worker. Under his tutelage – and perhaps aided by my marriage to Teresa, I began to be more self-reliant. The more you do, the better you become was, I was to find, an important message in life.

Before I recount how work developed from 1952 I ought to sketch in my private life. Evacuation had ended for me early in 1948 when I returned home to Forest Gate to live with my father and mother, as I have recounted. My father retired from the Post Office in June

1949, being awarded an Imperial Service Medal for his long service, but soon found himself a part-time job with a local estate agent in Green Street, Upton Park, collecting weekly rents. He carried the cash in a large leather bag concealed under his coat and was instructed by his employer to give them the money if he was attacked; fortunately he never was. My mother had carried on working in a bank at Aldgate, in continuance of her wartime work, but was soon to give this up and to return to being a local agent for Spirella, supplier of made-to-measure corsets and foundation garments for ladies. I was to become accustomed to my mother ushering portly ladies into our front room and shutting the door while she measured them or fitted them with a garment that had arrived through the post in response to an order.

I left home before eight in the morning and quite often did not return until midnight, staying in town after work to go to evening classes or theatres or cinemas and meeting my friends. It was at this time that my school and college friends began to get married, which meant they devoted more time to their spouses and had less time to devote to friendship. Stanley married in 1949, living in Shepherds Bush at first in a flat. Soon he insisted on the three of us lunching together in the West End regularly, usually at a Lyons Corner House. I also continued to meet and lunch with now-married George Brand, who worked for the War Crimes Commission before landing a good job with the United Nations in its Human Rights Division; for this he had to sail to New York and set up home there. Daphne Brook also married in 1949, so ending our visits to the theatre together when she was in London. In 1951 it was the turn of Elwyn. Jones to marry and with it our good years of friendship after the war virtually came to an end. Stanley, whom I had known since schooldays and with whom I had shared rooms in Cambridge, remains my oldest friend, and I have continued to meet him over ever since. Graduating post war, after he had finished being a Bevin Boy, he got a job as an organiser with the Jewish National Fund and then as an economist for a tobacco firm (even though he never smoked). In 1952 he set up, on borrowed money, the first of his laundrettes (which had just begun to appear in the UK). These he developed into a chain over the years to turn himself into a prosperous businessman. He won a doctorate in later life with his thesis on the business side of laundrettes, which was published by Duckworth in book form. He was also to have two sons and become a JP.

Marriage was the norm, for in the 1950s living with a partner unmarried was not the done thing. Nor were dating agencies a common phenomenon. My own life changed on 14 November 1948, my father's sixtieth birthday, when I met Teresa Coughlan, my future wife. I used to go to dances – a popular way of meeting people of the opposite sex at that time – and in the *New Statesman*, the weekly left-wing journal which I read regularly, I saw an advertisement for a dance in Kensington Square at an International Youth Club. And that Sunday night I went along.

There is something about white that attracts me, and a girl in a white blouse was sitting on a chair at the side of the dancing area. I asked her to dance, and she accepted. We spent most of the evening dancing together, and I asked her for her name and number. I misheard her name as Pauline and got her phone number wrong as well. Standing in a phone booth in Charing Cross Road a few days later I could not understand why there was no reply when I rang. Had she taken a dislike to the yellow wig I had worn to the dance (this was before I got my better ones some months later)? I was to learn that she did not like wearing glasses and, as she was short-sighted, had not had a clear image of me anyway (one of my fond memories is seeing her trying to identify the correct seat number in a theatre as we made our way along the row – she peered very close).

That first dance was on a Sunday. There was another at the same venue the following Saturday. Fortunately we both decided to attend, and so we met again; this time I got her name and phone number down correctly. On chances such as this is the pattern of our lives determined.

Teresa lodged at No. 101 Gower Street, a Catholic girls' hostel, and taught at a girls' secondary school called Barnsbury in Islington. The following week we went to see *Paisà*, the new Italian film then showing at the Academy cinema in Oxford Street. From that time forth our friendship developed, and we met once or twice a week. Although I was to go on my own to Paris in the summer of 1949, the following year we went there together (by boat and train this time) and spent a week in the same hotel but in separate rooms. I was nervous of the propriety of this and avoided telling my parents that she had accompanied me to Paris, concealing photos I had taken of her on the Eiffel Tower and elsewhere.

My hesitation in telling my parents also stemmed from the fact that Teresa was an Irish Catholic, while my father had been in the habit when I was young of buying Protestant Truth Society booklets that decried the Papacy as the Antichrist (oh, the curse of these islands and elsewhere: the divisions between so-called Christians). I took her home for tea and wondered how her direct manner would go down. Teresa had been made an orphan in the influenza epidemic after the First World War (she was born in 1918) and had lost her parents when only a few years old. She had been brought up on a small Irish farm by relatives before moving to Liverpool to live with an aunt so that she could get a good education at a 'posh' girls' school. A very intelligent girl, she then went to a teachers' training college. I think this experience of loss had led her to develop a tough outer skin. It took some people time to discover that beneath her sometimes scathing personality there was a kind, helpful and honest girl. She was totally straightforward and never afraid to speak her mind. I always knew where I was when I was with her. I found this directness extremely refreshing.

From the the start ours was not just a platonic friendship but a romantic one. We would kiss and cuddle near her hostel door before saying goodnight – she had to be inside by eleven and visitors were not allowed. In the school holidays she returned to Liverpool. Her aunt lived above a family pub in Scotland Road, a rather tough area, where Teresa would now and then help serve in the bar. To attempt to impress her with my continuing interest at the end of 1950 I sent her a telegram (on the advice of her friend Anne) to say I was coming up for a weekend visit. We explored Manchester together and in one café were able to buy a bowl of soup for a penny.

Although we were good friends Teresa never seemed to want to marry, a suggestion that came up from time to time. I don't think she was sure I would be a good match or even that she wished to marry at all. So we sometimes talked about ending our friendship and not seeing each other again. In autumn 1951 we spent a weekend at a hotel in Streetley. It rained the whole time. We decided that this should be our final time together. But the next Friday we went together to the Unity Theatre and kept on seeing each other. In November 1951 Teresa left Gower Street to share a room at No. 39 Belsize Gardens, rented from a Mrs Tcharney, with Anne Murray, a pretty round-faced girl from Glasgow who was one of Teresa's hostel friends. (Others were Anne Delane, Florence Hayes and Ethel Smith, some of whom I sometimes met while Teresa was in Liverpool during the school holiday.) I developed the habit of going up there every Saturday and spending the day with Teresa, exploring Belsize Park and Hampstead.

At Christmas 1951, before she left for Liverpool, we again decided to part. But from there she wrote a letter telling me she loved me, and I responded; to which she wrote again saying that she only wrote the letter because she didn't want us to separate. We never did part, for I saw her again when she returned to London, and we resumed our outings together. We went to Stratford-upon-Avon together in 1952 (oh, the joy of seeing John Gielgud playing Angelo in *Measure for Measure*) and went on cycling holidays in Hampshire and East Anglia (still a good way of getting around before mass ownership of cars gathered momentum).

During these years Teresa still resisted my proposals of marriage (my parents, to their credit, never lodged objections to a Catholic daughter-in-law). We talked about going our separate ways but never did. Suddenly, towards the end of 1953, Teresa said: 'Oh, all right, let's get married if you want to.' We broke the news to my family, and I bought her an engagement ring.

In January 1954 I registered with Douglas West, a letting agency in Earls Court and had their daily accommodation lists sent to me at Hobart House so that I could get on to the phone in the lunch-hour and pursue possible flats. This paid off when we found a flat in Archway Road, Highgate, at the top of a three-storey 1870s' house. We were the first applicants, and the landlady was pleased to learn that we would get married if we got it. There was no argument about the rent because it was controlled in those days of post-war housing short-ages. Teresa moved in right away; furniture was obtained from my home and from my friend George Brand.

Our marriage took place on 20 February 1954 at the Catholic church in Maresfield Gardens, Swiss Cottage, with a small wedding breakfast in a restaurant near Belsize Park tube station. Our marriage turned out to be a happy one. Moreover it was beneficial to me in building my confidence, making me more decisive as I absorbed Teresa's attitude to life.

I enjoyed the 1950s. Despite continuing rationing, dowdy and dilapidated buildings, abandoned bomb sites and without much modern technology, life was relatively uncomplicated. Newspapers had very few pages; reports of crime and disaster did not dominate; celebrities and popular songs were of a different kind; roads were not clogged with traffic; and the built environment was not altered to meet traffic needs. The railways still served remote parts, and the jet airliner had not yet appeared to create a mass tourist industry and to redistribute the world's population in great numbers. No doubt being a happily married thirty-year-old contributed to my sense of well-being.

I particularly remember 1951, the year of the Festival of Britain. Teresa and I visited the South Bank exhibition site, remembering that it had previously been one of London's derelict areas of bombed housing where we had once cuddled in privacy. We went to see Battersea Park and the entertainments created there for the Festival, as well as Lansbury's model housing at Bethnal Green. We journeyed up to Harlow to see the first buildings of the New Town, designed to distribute London's population further out.

We became avid attenders of evening classes, then available widely for modest sums, although you usually had to endure long queues when enrolling. To help her with her school work, Teresa studied drama at the City Literary Institute off Drury Lane, where I attended creative writing classes given by various journalists and writers such as Rupert Croft Cooke. But I got greater satisfaction at Morley College, opposite Lambeth North tube station, where I joined an Art History course run by Dr Fraenkl and an English Literature course given by Randall Swingler.

Swingler made a great impact on me over the next two years as I heard him each week speaking about writers such as D.H. Lawrence, T.S. Eliot (whom he disliked) and Turgenev. Swingler would pace up and down 'like a caged tiger' while talking but demonstrated a wide knowledge analytically presented. A published poet, he was a well-known Communist writer who, it would seem, had endured the strict regime of a public school which he had come to despise. He married a charming wife who was a pianist. One Christmas he invited the class to join his friends at his home, a Georgian terraced house, in Islington's Compton Terrace; with his wife playing the piano to us, it was a memorable evening. Morley College is, of course, famous for its music making and teaching, and one evening the composer Michael Tippet sat at the back of our class waiting for Swingler to finish before they went off together. This was before my marriage, and I made friends here but not friendships that survived.

In those post-war years great theatrical offerings existed in the West End, especially at the New Theatre in St Martin's Lane (later the Albery) where Laurence Olivier, Ralph Richardson and Michael Redgrave were to be seen. I shall never forget Olivier as Hotspur, brought in hanging upside down on somebody's back after his death; the magic of Richardson as *Peer Gynt* (the strange playing the strange); Robert Helpman as *Hamlet*; and Olivier as *Richard III* and as *King Lear*, all at the New. I have discovered a notebook listing 'Plays Seen Before 1952', and these amount to about 250 in number. To pick out plays seen only at the New these included, as well as Olivier in both parts of *Henry IV*, Thornton Wilder's *Our Town*, Ben Jonson's *The Alchemist*, Alec Guinness as *Richard II*, Bernard Miles in *The Taming of the Shrew*, Bernard Shaw's *St Joan*, John Clements as *Coriolanus*, Aldous Huxley's play *The Gioconda Smile*, Molière's *Tartuffe*, Michael Redgrave in *Love's Labour Lost*, Turgenev's *A Month in the Country* and Alec Guinness again as *Hamlet*. This was just one venue. There were all the other plays in all the other theatres, including the Old Vic after it restarted, where I shall always remember Donald Wolfit as *Tamburlaine* (I had once gone out to Wimbledon to see his *King Lear*; I sat behind him on a bus once, going through Trafalgar Square, and he reminded me of a red-faced butcher in his physical appearance off stage). Marlowe is rarely to be seen, despite that wonderful poetry, and I was always grateful for the chance to see *Tamburlaine*.

A favourite theatre was the small Arts Theatre in Great Newport Street where the Alec Clunes frequently performed. Here I watched plays by Bernard Shaw, Ibsen, Pinero, Vanbrugh and lesser-known playwrights to widen my theatrical experience. Here I saw *Macbeth* played by Alec Clunes and Christopher Fry's *A Phoenix Too Frequent*. At the Piccadilly I saw Godfrey Tearle and Edith Evans in *Anthony and Cleopatra*, John Hawkins and Anthony Quayle in *Othello*. Another loved theatre, destined to be demolished, was the St James's, where I watched productions of Turgenev and Chekhov, Rattigan's *Adventure Story*, Fry's *Venus Observed*, Olivier in *Caesar and Cleopatra* playing opposite Vivien Leigh, as well as in *Anthony and Cleopatra*, and also saw Orson Welles play *Othello*. The early 1950s were a rich time for London's theatre.

In association with the 1951 Festival, there was a series of lectures on literary subjects given on Saturday afternoons at the Victoria and Albert Museum. My most vivid memory of these was seeing Roy Campbell, the poet, a rumbustious man (wrongly seen as Fascist) imparting great enthusiasm and brio in his talk. It was a tragedy that he died a few years later in a car accident. I still read the three volumes of his collected poetry.

My continuing love of drama found practical expression again with the National Coal Board drama society, one of the many social clubs set up soon after the Board was formed, for which modest funding was given. The play this time was J.M. Barrie's *Dear Brutus*, which we staged after several weeks spent at lunchtime and after-hours rehearsals. The venue was a rather dowdy Kensington Hall where we opened for about three or four performances in November 1951. By this time Donald Alexander had arrived at the office, and thanks to his own interest in drama he did not discourage me for disappearing for rehearsals. I played the part of Coade and was kitted out with shorts for Barrie's rather weird, magical play. I enjoyed going to Spaans, my wig-maker in Lisle Street, to buy stage make-up sticks. It reminded me of the theatrical make-up outfit I had been given as a present when a boy, when I used to plague my parents with my imitations of pirates or clergymen.

Another National Coal Board social club that was to prove more important was the A Circle, 'A' standing for art, architecture and antiques. It was supported by quite high-status officials in the Board, such as E.L. Turnbull, director of establishments, and by the Board's chief legal adviser. I was soon on the organising committee, which planned a regular programme of talks and visits. Here I began my long experience of organising coach outings, something I was to continue with my local history society after I retired. Through these outings I came to see just about all the country houses around London as well as visiting London venues. These days this sort of cultural excursion is quite common, but in the post-war years it was less so. The first coach outing I organised was to Luton Hoo, where we were met by Sir Harold Wehner, who showed us his wonderful art collection (much of it to be seen today at the Rangers House, Greenwich). We visited Sir Kenneth Clark's house at Hampstead and in 1950s visited Hertfordshire to see Henry Moore's house and studios. The sculptor turned out to be a down-to-earth Yorkshireman, and I was to chat away affably with him for some time in one of his rooms. We went through his grounds looking at his sculptures. Another visit was to Smith Square to see the private art collection of a member of the Sainsbury family. It was there that I saw my first paintings by Francis Bacon – a powerful experience, as the powerful images somehow attacked the spirit and made me fearful of looking at them.

Jack Reading was a significant member of the A Circle with plenty of ideas and personal connections who has always been a great promoter of the arts. In his job at the Coal Industry Social Welfare Organisation (which occupied premises in Hobart Place directly opposite Hobart House) he was to do much to promote artists such as Tom McGuiness, a Durham coal-miner who in his spare time produced oil paintings of great merit. Jack staged a show of his work and, like other NCB employees, I bought one which still hangs in my house. Later McGuiness was taken up by a London gallery, and the prices of his paintings soared. In later years Jack arranged for the Tom McGuiness Bequest to be displayed at Bishop Auckland. Jack remained a personal friend all my life. Another A Circle committee member was Phillip Gibbons, a member of the Board's legal department, who had always been a modest patron of the arts. One of his early purchases was a figure by Henry Moore; when Phillip retired he sold it and it brought him enough money to buy a period house overlooking Clapham Common. Through his contacts Philip introduced Eric Atkinson to the society and we adopted him. Again I bought one of this artist's paintings. After Eric had made his name, with one of his paintings bought by the Tate, he taught at Leeds and elsewhere but then emigrated to Canada, where he continued his career. I enjoyment my involvement with the A Circle during my time at the Coal Board. I wrote short articles now and again for its magazine, which ran for many years. These A Circle bulletins, a set of which I keep, provide a good view of an arts experience and show the value of such clubs within corporate bodies.

I continued to pursue my ambition to be a writer, signified by my attendance at creative writing classes, and looked for small opportunities to have pieces published such as in *Coal* magazine and in the bulletin of the A Circle. My first nationally published article followed my reading of a new biography of D.H. Lawrence during the 1950 Easter holiday. This was by Richard Aldington and was called *Portrait of a Genius But* . . . (It cost me 15s. – such a book would be published at a much higher price today.) I was overwhelmed by Lawrence's life story and when reading his books (published that year in a series of paperbacks by Penguin) by his prose style. I was determined to get to the Midlands to see his countryside.

Taking annual leave from the office, I took the steam train to Nottingham (the rhythm of the rails, different from today's sound, seemed to echo verse as I travelled up, or maybe I just wrote some to it). I booked into a hotel and took the bus out to Eastwood, Lawrence's birthplace. Today it is the target of organised tourist trips, and I believe there is a plaque to Lawrence and a museum. But in those days local people I spoke to professed not to have heard of him; I suppose in 1950 he was seen as a 'dirty' writer who had brought shame to them. Fortunately, through my Penguin copy of his *Selected Letters* I was able to identify his homes, which I photographed in black and white (light seeped into my Kodak box camera so they did not turn out too well).

When I returned I wrote up the story of my visit (including an encounter with a gamekeeper in my search for the farm Lawrence used to visit) and showed it to Elwyn Jones. He slightly edited it and suggested I sent it to *Tribune*, the left-wing weekly which, like the *New Statesman*, mixed political and literary articles. They printed it. This was good for my morale and was noticed by others. At Christmas the *Mining Review* committee bought me a book token in recognition of my work for them, and they wrote inside it: 'We suggest more D.H. Lawrence' – a wish, alas, not fulfilled.

Elwyn Jones was to put me in the way of more writing work. Through doing reviews for the magazine *What's On* he became acquainted with Roy Walker, editor of a fortnightly subscription journal called *Theatre* (which incorporated *Theatre Newsletter*). Roy and his assistant editor Ian Le Maistre were based in a one-room office at No. 77 Dean Street in Soho, and as well as doing theatre reviews for them Elwyn helped get out each issue by stuffing envelopes. Young June Austen was the full-time assistant who kept the place going. Elwyn invited me to help with these evening envelope-stuffing sessions, and soon I was going there after work once a fortnight to assist in getting copies into the post.

Afterwards Elwyn, June and I, and sometimes Roy and Ian, would go across the road to the Dog and Duck where gin and tonic was consumed to revive us. (In those days if you wanted to use the pub's basement toilet you asked at the bar for the key – perhaps the same system still exists?). June was an attractive girl whom I liked but she had become totally enamoured of Elwyn who seemed to have a powerful effect on nearly every woman he met. She was not interested in me, and, although we did go to the theatre together a few times, we were just friends. After I married Teresa she came over for meals, and we kept in touch until she disappeared into Broadcasting House and another job.

I was given plays to review for *Theatre*, but these were mainly of theatrical productions at the smaller club and other theatres in existence at the time, such as the Questors at Ealing, the Kew Theatre and the New Lindsay in Notting Hill Gate. From time to time I was given a West End show to cover. These I found rather overwhelming, wondering what national newspaper critics would say about the play. But it was good practice in writing succinctly. I set myself to answer in my review the questions: 'What was the play about?', 'What was it trying to achieve?' and 'Did it achieve it?'. I had to address these issues in terms of writing, acting and production values. Having free tickets to theatres was a great help in taking Teresa out, for I was not flush with money.

I was given other journalistic jobs by the editor, such as writing an article on the production of a Bernard Shaw play at the Lime Grove television studio. In those days plays were not pre-recorded but transmitted live, and it was fascinating to see how this was done. It was the first time I had been to a television studio.

Roy Walker was a highly intelligent man who wrote books on Shakespeare, such as *The Time Is Free*, about Macbeth. He seemed to find life very stressful. He was analysed by a psychiatrist and afterwards advocated that everyone should do the same. Eventually he retired.

Ian le Maistre, the deputy editor, was a sociable man, and in 1953 he took me out to lunch with Richard Findlater, the famous writer on the theatre of the day, and with Bob Edwards, editor of *Tribune* who later was to have important posts in Fleet Street.

Money was the problem with the magazine, and appeals for financial aid were made from time to time to our subscribers. Once I saw a cheque for £50 signed by J.B. Priestley in the office. Eventually the magazine had to cease publication. Before it folded Walker asked me to compile an index of the contents, which I did. It was used in bound volume of issues sold to subscribers. For some reason I had to consult a book or two in the British Library, then in the British Museum. Walker lent me his reader's ticket, and I remember a Saturday morning spent in that place sitting under its great dome and the feeling of awe I experienced. In later life I was to acquire my own ticket.

7

FILMS FOR THE COAL INDUSTRY

DONALD GAINED APPROVAL in mid-1952 for his film-making proposals and set up the internal film unit. He named it the NCB
Technical Film Unit to disassociate it from Hollywood for those with
no knowledge of film as a working tool. This was not an unfounded
fear, as some people made jibes, and when film technicians began to
be seen in the canteen and elsewhere the more staid members of the
Board's staff were astonished by men with beards and women in
trousers. 'Why don't you get yourself a decent Board job, Gay?' was
said to me.

In the autumn Donald took on as our first film director a New
Zealander named Alun Falconer. He was born on 18 August 1923, the
same day as myself, and was slightly plump. 'Let me have men about
me that are fat,' said Donald, quoting *Julius Caesar*, Perhaps he had
suffered from thin men in his past. Alun had far-left views and had
gone to Communist China, about which he was writing a vast novel,
which sadly never got published. He was creative and energetic, and,
as the unit grew, he became an associate producer looking after our
directors. He began to invent plots for feature films, inviting us to
choose the film star most fitted to a role. Eventually he was to sell a
feature film script to the film trade union, which was putting money
into encouraging new writers. Called *The Man Upstairs*, it went into
production directed by Don Chaffey and starring the young Richard
Attenborough. Other members of the cast were Bernard Lee, Donald
Houston and Kenneth Griffith. After its release in 1958 Alun resigned
and worked for a new commercial television company before, as a
freelance, writing plays for television. Unfortunately a heart attack
killed him in 1973 at the age of fifty.

At the same time as Alun was engaged, Donald also took on Lionel
Griffiths as our first cameraman. He was a young photographer whom
Donald had met while making steel films in South Wales. Lionel
came from Taffs Well in the valley of the Taff just north of Cardiff and

had a good photographic eye. He was also temperamental and moody something I was to encounter with many technicians. He was mostly shy and pleasant but at times could get into a black mood and make hostile comments. He was married for a time but was essentially a loner. I was fond of him and remember when he came to my home in March 1955 to take a still photograph of my four-month-old son. Lionel worked for our unit for many years but also freelanced. In later years he lived in St Giles High Street and died there after returning from a night out drinking by choking on his vomit.

The units we sent out on location usually consisted of a director (who could also be the writer of the script); his assistant, who made the practical arrangements for each working day, including food and transport; the lighting cameraman; and the cameraman's assistant, responsible for the dispatch of the daily rushes to London for processing overnight. Usually they took an electrician with them to set up the film lights. Our first full-time unit electrician was a burly Londoner, Charlie Burgess, who joined us in January 1953.

Purchase of film lights was undertaken by Lionel Griffiths, and for a short time they were stored at the Board's premises at Worton Hall, Isleworth. This had been a film studio, but it had been acquired by the Board as laboratories for scientific research work. There were about six lights, which had film industry nicknames such as 'Pup'. These were fine for surface filming but not underground, where tight control was exercised by HM Mines Inspectorate (based at the Ministry of Fuel and Power) as to what was allowed. One headache of my working life when underground filming was scheduled was to ensure the availability, in a condition that the inspector would accept, of what were called the 'safety lights'. This was a set of twelve heavy but fragile lights originally developed in the oil industry for underwater use. They had to be transported to the colliery, inspected on the surface and transported underground where filming was to take place. Often the inspector failed several of the lights, and filming was delayed as a result. This caused complications when short-term technicians had been taken on, say, for a two-week contract.

Our first filming location was Brierley Colliery, and here Charlie Burgess had some electrical junction boxes made up, deemed acceptable for underground use and known thereafter as the Brierley boxes. These were kept with the safety lights and were usually stored and maintained at a Midlands workshop. For bigger jobs, with surface filming, film lights, a portable generator and other electricians were hired, usually from a firm called Mole-Richardson; much of my life was to be devoted to hiring suitable extra electricians, some of them being more acceptable than others to the crew with which they were destined to work.

For safety reasons filming underground had to be by clockwork camera, and for this we used a 35mm Newman Sinclair, No. 415. Later on we hired another one on a regular basis from Ralph Elton, one of our directors, or rented extra ones from Ian Struthers or other technicians who supplied such equipment as a sideline. In the 1950s a new firm started up called Samuelsons, which soon came to be predominant in the hiring out of all kinds of film equipment. In the 1950s there were still some collieries known as 'safety pits' because they were gas-free, and this helped us with our work, on our shot-firing films for example. But mostly collieries were not gas-free, and electrical equipment, such as a camera, which could spark, might have set off an explosion. In these early years all our filming was on 35mm gauge, as projected in cinemas and used by feature film-makers; later on the Swiss-made Bolex 16mm camera was improved and more sensitive movie film produced, allowing filming on the smaller 16mm gauge. The problem was always to have enough light in the right place. Some of our directors experimented successfully in using, for certain scenes, light from the cap lamps which everyone going underground wore on their helmets, powered by batteries hung at their waists.

Other full-time recruits taken on early in 1953 were John Shaw Jones and KittyMarshall who were both to stay with the unit for long periods, Kitty until its closure in the 1980s. John Shaw Jones was a jack of all trades, older than the others, who had joined the film trade union when it began in the 1930s and who boasted an early number on his card. He was a large man with a grey beard and worked both as a cameraman and as a director. Kitty Marshall was our number-one film editor and was a person of strong personality. In due course she became a producer and always had an important role to play in the unit's affairs. Ron Fry was a young man working at Film Centre who was given his chance to get into film-making by Donald, who made him assistant director. It was the beginning of a long career in the industry for Ron, who later moved on to other film work, both in studios and on location around the world. To facilitate record-keeping I gave each production a number. The number was prefixed by INT for internal productions and by EXT for externally made productions (by other units under contract to us). INT 1 was to be *Area Workshops*, made in Scotland by John Shaw Jones. But production was delayed owing to disagreement among the engineers over the script. We were soon to discover that the demands of a film script often led to policy being clarified or defined by the sponsoring department so that statements made in the film would be acceptable throughout all the coalfields; scripts were sometimes the catalyst to determine internal policies. So the first film to be made was to be INT 2. I must have been unsure about my numbering system at the beginning, as this covered two films made as a pair for Industrial Training Branch and called *Setting a Prop* and *Hand Haulage*. They were introductory training films for apprentices, and filmstrips associated with them were also made. Filmstrips were a training aid, probably now forgotten but once widely used, that consisted of strips of 35mm film, perhaps 30, 50 or 100 frames, which were shown, frame by frame, with the aid of a filmstrip projector. They were rather like 35mm slides and were widely used in training establishments.

Filming on INT 2 began in January 1953 at Brierley Colliery by a unit consisting of Alun Falconer, Lionel Griffiths, Jack Fairbank (a temporarily engaged assistant director of fiery temper) and Larry Pizer, who was to shoot the stills for the filmstrips and who in later years was to become a lighting cameraman on feature films. On 20 January 1953, for me a historic day, I went to Humphries film laboratories in Whitfield Street, near Tottenham Court Road, to collect the unit's first can of rushes, sent down for processing the previous evening. They were to be viewed as soon as possible by Donald Alexander in his capacity as the film's producer, so that the unit could be told if there were any technical problems (camera scratch, for example) and whether the shots accorded with the script. In the early days the unit did not have its own viewing theatre, and one of my jobs was to hire a venue in Soho, usually either in Dean Street or Wardour Street. The Crown in Wardour Street, where the projectionist was Mr Frost, was the theatre we used for that first screening of rushes. Did we guess as we sat there that these rushes would be the first in what was to be thirty years of filming?

On Saturday, 31 January 1953, when location filming had been completed, the fortnight's rushes were screened to Alexander, Falconer,

Griffiths and myself at the Crown Theatre. For the first time I understood the complexity of assembling a finished film out of hundreds of diverse shots. Later I was to learn the importance of the role of the film editor in making a film.

Three more weeks' filming took place before editing began in March by Kitty Marshall. This was carried out at cutting rooms hired on a full-time basis at Cardin's in Endell Street, Seven Dials. Here Kitty assembled the film, in consultation with Alun. A rough cut showing then took place of the proposed film to the sponsoring department. The intended commentary was read out, giving the opportunity to alter the wording before it was recorded. Changes to the visuals could be made, but suggestions for new shots were usually resisted, as further shooting would mean extra cost and delay. After the film was completed, there would be a show copy screening to the sponsoring department, and copies would be made on 16mm size for distribution within the industry.

Over the years a variety of people, usually actors, were chosen to speak the commentary when it was recorded. On this occasion Ewan MacColl, the folk singer, was chosen, and it was his voice on our first films. He was a friend of Donald's and was to do much work for us over the next few years. I had to agree the fee with him and arrange for his invoice to be paid. I always found Ewan a very pleasant man and have happy memories of him. It was about this time that Ewan was to make, with Charles Parker at BBC Manchester, those famous radio ballads about working life at sea and on the railways. We used Ewan in some issues of *Mining Review* to sing working ballads; about six were recorded and later put together as one edition. Howard Goorney, John Shrapnel and John Slater were among the actors used for commentaries.

To help me understand my job in my first year I sought practical experience of filming and so at the August Bank Holiday weekend of 1953 I went with the unit to Rawdon colliery, near Ashby de la Zouch. The headstock at the top of a shaft was to be moved across to another shaft. The work was being undertaken during the holidays to avoid loss of coal production. Donald Alexander was in charge of filming, and camerawork was to be done by John Reid and John Shaw Jones, with Tony Maher (a temporary appointment) as camera assistant and myself as assistant director. Merriment broke out among some us when we saw an advertisement on the side of a railway bridge describing the local coal as 'Hot, clean and economical' with its perceived sexual undertones.

John Reid was another great character to work for us. Described by Donald as one of the three best documentary cameramen of the time, he had a distinctive, cultivated voice (orphaned, he had been sent to boarding-school) and was known by Francis Gysin's nickname for him as Reid of England. Reid had worked for Francis many times, first meeting him in Manchester on a Rotha film, *A City Speaks* (1947), after the then Captain Reid had first come out of the Army. Reid had charm and was very persuasive. He was fond of drinking (in fact, he was an alcoholic), and one night we went out late in the evening to a country pub and he persuaded the landlady to let us carry on drinking well past closing time. I always remember that Sunday sitting out in the rear pub garden guzzling beer well after midnight.

Even more vivid a memory is of going to a miners' pub near the colliery and drinking the strong local brew on an empty stomach and being completely overcome by it. I found a nearby field and lay down in the August sun and slept. Reid discovered me and took photographs of me on the unit's Rolleiflex, fast asleep, dressed in pit overalls and a safety helmet. I later managed to confiscate the negative and prints, and these have remained at home ever since. Reid and Shaw Jones did not quite hit it off, and Reid would tease Shaw Jones by quietly singing 'Bearded like the pard', a phrase from those famous lines in *As You Like It*, beginning: 'All the world's a stage'. Shaw Jones did not like being teased about his beard but never seemed to find the right phrase with which to hit back.

The unit stayed at the Queen's Hotel in Ashby de la Zouch, which in 1953 was run by a remarkable bachelor. In the bar on the first day Reid began chatting to this owner in his inimitable way and extracted the information that every year he drove through France for a holiday. 'In your Rolls-Royce,' said John as a joke. 'Yes, as a matter of fact I do drive a Rolls – it's in the garage at the back.' Reid was astounded to be caught on the wrong foot. In 1953 television broadcasting was still in its infancy, but the hotel owner had a set in an upstairs lounge, which he allowed us to watch. This was an early model in which the picture was projected upwards on to a screen via a mirror. In memory it seemed superior to the smaller more conventional box models which were usually to be seen in people's homes.

In fact I can claim to have been one of the first in post-war Britain to watch television regularly. I had seen a television before the war in the window of a local electrical shop. But in 1952 my brother Ernest made us a set. He did this by buying the parts and constructing a wooden cabinet to put them in (he was skilled in both electricity and carpentry). This he gave to my parents (I don't think he had a set in his own home), and from that time I watched programmes, transmitted live, such as *Animal, Vegetable or Mineral* and live dramas, in one of which appeared my former school colleague Bryan Forbes. Broadcasts in 1952 were only by the BBC, and transmission times were short.

The filming of the move over of the headstock at Rawdon colliery in late evening went successfully and resulted in a short coverage film useful to other colliery managers and engineers faced with similar problems. I enjoyed my time away as assistant director very much. A grimmer experience of location work was in 1954 when I volunteered to be the assistant on a unit filming underground so that I could discover what such work was like. This was when Alun Falconer directed a film he had scripted called *Building a Strip Pack*. These packs were built up by miners to support the roof after the coal had been taken, and filming was to be at the coalface.

The location chosen was a pit called Craghead, close to a small town called Stanley in Durham. This was a thin seam pit; that is to say, the coal was laid down in seams not more than three feet six inches high (just over a metre), so that it was impossible to stand upright at the coalface: you crouched, knelt or lay. To reach the coalface you had to walk upright for about a mile along an underground roadway and then bend down to walk doubled up for a good distance more. In the early days of the Board in 1953, standardisation of equipment, including safety helmets, had not yet been established, and miners worked according to local custom the way their fathers had done. So they went into the pit here wearing cloth caps. We were issued with black pit helmets (white only became the standard colour later), and I seemed to knock my head every few yards on the beams that supported the roof while I walked slowly along the roadway. By contrast the local miners whipped along the roadway in their cloth caps at great speed and never hit their heads.

The Board had inherited a traditional form of longwall coal-mining that used a cycle of three shifts to obtain the coal. One shift would undercut the seam of coal by machine, and it would then be brought down either by shot-firing (explosives) or by mechanical picks; another shift would put up timber supports and move forward the face conveyor; and the third shift (usually the morning one) would load the coal by shovel on to the conveyor. The product was carried by the conveyor to the gate or road at the end of the coalface, where it was transferred either on to another conveyor or into small mine cars, usually called tubs. Where the coal had been taken there was a void known as the goaf, and this would be lined at the sides with stone; packs would also be built along the gates leading to the face, the stone coming from ripping the roof. These packs helped the pit ventilation system bring air to the coalface, otherwise it would have been lost in the goaf. The goaf was an unsupported space and often the roof of stone above it would fall with a tremendous thud. I always found this impressive, rather reminiscent of the Blitz when I heard or saw it.

An alternative system was retreat mining, and another was bord and pillar where 'rooms' were excavated into the coal; the latter was not common in Britain but was in the United States. Coal was also obtained by opencast mining, where coal was excavated from huge deep pits by heavy machines; this was much more profitable but did more damage to the environment and was not favoured by the mining unions who represented the great workforce of miners working underground.

It was to be the replacement of the traditional longwall three-shift system that was to be the Board's main achievement in its first decades, parallel with similar development work going on in Germany. The new methods of working meant that coal could be obtained with a smaller workforce. Newly designed mining machines were mounted on to face conveyors set next to the coal seam, and they moved continually up and down it, ripping the coal off so that it fell on to the conveyor and could be taken out of the pit. Thus every shift became a coal-winning shift, although setting roof supports over the excavated area of coal had to be done. This was facilitated by the development by Board engineers of steel roof supports of a squat, heavy design which could be lowered from the roof and moved forward automatically by the use of hydraulic power. These changes began in the 1950s, and films were made by our units to explain these machines to colliery managers across the country so that they could be persuaded to install them, their advantages being put to them by area mechanical engineers who were charged with mechanising the mines. The films were, of course, also used to train the machine operatives and their supervisors (known as overmen and deputies) as well as the workshop maintenance crews.

The earliest machines tried out were known as ploughs and scraper boxes, and Donald went across to Germany to film some of these in operation there, producing films on them in 1954. We also made an hour-long three-part film on the A-B Meco Moore Cutter Loader, a British machine earlier in date and massive in size, which we issued in our first production year of 1953. But ploughs and scraper boxes, although made and used in Britain for many years where mining conditions suited them, were to be overtaken by the Anderton Shearer Loader. This consisted of a revolving drum with picks mounted on an ordinary cutter to shear the coal, with a plough loading the coal on to a conveyor. It was invented by a Lancashire engineer called Anderton as a simple machine using existing devices. It was to prove one of our most enduring and successful machines. The unit made a 16-minute film about it in 1955.

The Board's engineers, working at our research establishments, devised many different face machines and improved and developed powerful roof supports. They were all manufactured according to the Board's specifications by mining machinery companies such as Huwood, Joy Manufacturing and Richard Sutcliffe and sold to the Board. These manufacturing firms were able to expand because they could also sell these British-designed products to foreign countries. Sales of British mining machinery were achieved around the world, continuing the ethos of the Industrial Revolution. This was a reversal of the situation obtaining when the Board was created, for then it had to import machines from abroad, such as the Dosco Continuous Miner from Canada.

But in 1954, on location in a thin seam pit in County Durham, we were involved in making a film for the Board's training centres about the traditional craft of pack-building. In Stanley we stayed at the King's Arms hotel, my companions being Alun Falconer, Lionel Griffiths, Charlie Burgess and Geoff Hermges. Geoff, who was Kitty Marshall's husband, had been a stills photographer in the Board's scientific research establishment, but he wanted to become a cinematographer and he was allowed to come along as a camera assistant, like myself, for the experience. On this job I made the hotel bookings, handled the cash float, organised daily arrangements to suit Alun and took upon myself, for the experience, the task of sending the rushes down to London. This meant a bus into Newcastle and getting the metal box on to an overnight train. I remember the awful aching of the limbs after a working day underground when I made these journeys; but at least they allowed me a look around Newcastle – any big city fascinated me. We returned to Stanley for a second week after we had completed underground filming, this time to film at a training centre called Morrison, where we were able to get shots in easier conditions. On the last afternoon, after work had finished, I went to a Stanley cinema and saw Doris Day in *Calamity Jane*. Whenever this film comes on television I am reminded of that happy, restful afternoon in a Durham cinema.

I had also gone, earlier in 1954, to a more relaxed location. A comparatively new pit in Nottinghamshire called Calverton had been chosen for a visit underground by Princess Margaret. The unit was asked to cover this for possible use in future films. Lionel Griffiths, Charlie Burgess and myself stayed at the nearby Hutt Hotel and were able to film the visit. I remember how diminutive Princess Margaret looked as, clad in white overalls and surrounded by a posse of men, she entered the pit cage to make the descent. This was in April 1954 and was the first time I had been away from Teresa after our marriage in February.

Films were also now being made for us by external units and given my EXT code. One that lasted a long time was about shot-firing, directed by Max Anderson through Basic Films. Max was a well-respected film-maker who had made some notable documentaries for Realist Films, such as *The Harvest Shall Come*. He was a short, likeable man with left-wing views, but he became exasperated over the shot-firing films, which dragged on; unfortunately the miner chosen as shot-firer discovered that he was the key figure and that filming could not take place without him, and he would sometimes delay his arrival on location, rather like a temperamental film star. The project was eventually finished, the processes of firing shots explained in a methodical way for training purposes. The rough cut of this film was screened to Sir Humphry Browne, director of mining, and to Sir Andrew Bryan, HM Inspector of Mines. Browne was a key figure in producing the Board's Plan for Coal on how the industry was to be developed. Donald's rapport with him over a film about the plan was helped by the fact that they had both been at Shrewsbury school.

Donald was quick to get films off the ground and when the *Pack Building* film was shot in July 1954 it was numbered INT 13. As more films were made we took on more technicians and acquired more equipment, so we found that more space was needed. When it began, the Film Unit was based in one room on the third-floor Public Relations Branch corridor in Hobart House. It was becoming obvious that this was not enough, and in consequence we were moved, in March 1954, to No. 2 Grosvenor Place, a property about ten minutes' walk away where the Board already had offices. No. 2 was at the northern end of Grosvenor Place on the corner of Grosvenor Gardens, opposite St George's Hospital, now the Lanesborough Hotel. It was one of a row of grand mansions built in the 1860s in the French Renaissance style for aristocrats who wanted to live close to royalty; the frontages faced the wall of Buckingham Palace gardens. If I remember rightly it was the Earl of Buccleuch who had resided at No. 2 Grosvenor Place.

This mansion, which was to be demolished in the 1960s, had a porch and foyer which led into a high-ceilinged hall, in the centre of which was a grand staircase with ornamental lights at its foot. The upper floors were occupied by departments such as Staff or Scientific, by the Board's Operations Research Unit, staffed with mathematicians and scientists, and by a Translations Section. In due course the grandest room was to be taken by one of the Board's most well-known employees, Dr Jacob Bronowski, who previously had been at the Board's research establishment at Stoke Orchard near Cheltenham. Bronowski was to come to prominence with his television series *The Ascent of Man*, seen as being on a par with Sir Kenneth Clark's series *Civilisation*.

To reach my new office I walked by the left-hand side of the staircase to a tiny lift once used by servants. This ancient contraption took you up a couple of floors to a corridor that led to a group of offices, previously the live-in rooms of the upper servants. The one I finally settled in (shifting people's offices around is a game constantly played in large corporations, as departments wax and wane) was Room 21. This had a big window that overlooked the mews at the rear. I sat at one of the two desks in this bow window, the other one being for Donald whenever he was in town. Other desks were occupied by Donald's secretary, with her typewriter, and later by Alun and Kitty as producers. A room off it was used by scriptwriters and directors.

The unit was also given the basement area, formerly used as kitchens and for storage. Here, from January 1959, we had cutting rooms for the editors, so we no longer rented Endell Street, and we turned another large room into a film theatre with a projection box. This saved money renting theatres in Soho and also saved a lot of time, having projection facilities in-house. It was used constantly for rushes, editing work, rough cuts and show copies. Beyond the theatre towards the back of the mansion was another large area, and this was made into a studio. Here models were constructed and filmed; small rooms off it were used by camera and other technicians, and film lights and camera equipment were stored here.

For the theatre we engaged a full-time professional projectionist. Two or three different people held this job. Projection boxes usually have no windows and tend to be claustrophobic if inhabited all day and can ultimately affect one's health, I believe. All our projectionists were to prove personalities with very definite attitudes about everything; one had to gain their co-operation for things to go smoothly when periods of pressure occurred.

As the unit expanded, my job got busier and busier. In the first place I was responsible to Donald for the general administration of the people in Film Section, several of them full-time Board employees; for running the film library and film distribution; and co-ordinating with most Board departments on work in progress or on distribution problems. Second, as production manager I had to hire technicians and see they got paid, buy film stock, book hotels (until the assistant directors took over this task), see that transport, film lights and electricians – and sound recordists when required – were engaged, arrange cash floats and check expenses claims. I had to assist in the purchase of cutting-room equipment and in general deal with personal problems cropping up among unit people. I had to arrange rough-cut approval shows to departments and delivery shows and, as we progressed, prestige shows to press and others in outside cinemas. I had to help the external unit with facilities for film-making and work with Donald on the contractual and invoice arrangements. I had to prepare an individual budget for each film before it was made and get it accepted by a rather pedantic member of Finance Department, whose queries just before a unit was going on location might cause delays. In addition I had to administer the overall budget.

To a somewhat surprised Donald, who had expected to have to fight Civil-Service-type bureaucracy, the Film Unit was given almost *carte blanche* in its affairs by the Board. It could hire, fire and spend – indeed work like a small private business within the larger organisation, free of restrictions. This was partly due to the confidence in Donald of those above us. His great business sense, which perhaps owed something to his Scottish ancestry, meant that he was very prudent in all his dealings with outside firms and people and knew the value of money. We were of course subject to Finance Department and Audit scrutiny but not unbearably so. Staff Department delegated to us the contracting of staff on long- or short-term notice, either by letter of appointment or on an invoice basis.

Donald would select a subject to film from the agreed list (submitted by a department and endorsed by the Working Group on Films) and would choose a suitable scriptwriter and a director for it. They would then decide on the cameraman they wanted, either from within the unit or from outside. Taking on the technicians was my responsibility, and I had to suggest an assistant cameraman and an assistant director, putting up names for the director's and producer's acceptance. Sometimes finding assistants created endless work. Often it became a negotiation with the Association of Cinema Technicians (ACT), later known as the Association of Cinema and Television Technicians (ACTT). The union operated a closed-shop policy, something it had won after battles with unscrupulous producers in the mean years in the 1930s when exploitation occurred; eventually tight agreements setting down employment conditions and minimum rates had been hammered out between union and producers' association. For somebody who wanted to be a film-maker, the catch was that they could not get a job without a union ticket; and they could not get a union ticket without a job. You had to get a job, then you could apply and try to get a union ticket – only given after vetting and scrutiny.

The union acted as an employment agency, and if you did not have an assistant available you rang and asked them for a list of names. Bunny Gardner and Bessie Bond were the great yea-or-nay people at the union who gave you names. Some of the people on the list were unemployed because film units knew that for one reason or another they were not the best of technicians and could cause delays and loss. Nevertheless I had to phone such people to find out their availability; fortunately, when offered work underground at minimum documentary rates (lower than for feature filming) they frequently declined the job. Of course you could get good out-of-work assistants as well, and we took on many worthy people. Parallel with this search for suitable employees, we interviewed promising people who were looking to become film-makers but who did not have a union ticket. Sometimes they had made an amateur film and displayed real talent. If we were lucky we were given reluctant permission by the union to take them on. As the unit grew in size, we could take advantage of the union ruling that units could take on trainees in limited numbers in proportion to the number of union members that they employed. Several good people joined us in this way.

As film production expanded, much time had to be given to crewing. I think that by this time the phone on my desk had been changed to direct dialling, but it could still have been the old system of picking up the phone and waiting for a Board switchboard operator to ask you what number you wanted. As technicians were often at work during the day, they had to be contacted in the evening. This was made easier for me in May 1955 when I was finally allocated a telephone at home by the Post Office, which ran the service at that time. The aftermath of the war meant that there was a huge waiting list for phones; efforts with the Board's communications officer to get me some priority for industrial reasons did not succeed. The phone, when it finally came, was a shared line with somebody else up the road; if they were using the phone I would get an engaged signal and would have to wait until they were finished. It was to be October 1966 before I was allocated a phone at home that was not shared. The problem seems to have been a shortage of main distribution cables; neighbouring streets had overhead phone wires held up by tall poles which were connected to individual houses by other wires, but my road was always serviced by underground cables. The metal pavement level covers to junction boxes still bear the Post Office Telephones name.

Getting to know if a potential recruit was any good was facilitated by phone calls to other production managers. Particularly helpful was Philip Aizlewood at Basic Films, who seemed to know them all. It was with sadness I was to hear that he had died by drowning while on holiday. It was often useful to check a name with a previous employer before taking them on. I wrote the letters of appointment and Donald signed them, until it was agreed that I might as well sign them myself.

In 1955 the approval for a three-year film-making programme was to be considered by the Board. By then the departments were aware of the value of our films (made in black and white) in training all levels of employees in both new and traditional mining techniques. The Board therefore gave approval for the continuance of film-making. By then Donald and others had realised that making films about coal-mining subjects, especially underground, could be done best by an internal unit; after all, the people who made the films through external units tended to be the same freelance people the unit itself employed. Gradually the external units were dropped. The main ones had been Basic and DATA. DATA was eventually wound up in 1961 and its assets and staff taken over by the Board's Film Unit.

No further work was done by Basic, but this important film company was not particularly perturbed. It had been founded by Leon Clore after he had served in the RAF photographic reconnaissance unit during the war and was to be an important centre for British film-makers. Clore had worked for the Crown Film Unit, and he attracted good people to interesting projects. His associate company Countryman Films made the *Conquest of Everest* in 1953 (Edmund Hillary's great triumph in Coronation year). He provided Tony Simmons with the wherewithal to make his prize-winning *Sunday by the Sea* and was to go on to make feature films such as *The French Lieutenant's Woman*. Karel Reisz, Lindsay Anderson, Tony Richardson and later John Krish, Jack Gold and Stephen Frears were helped by being given work by Basic at the start of their film careers.

Clore was a rather abrasive man, and I cannot say I took to him, but he was a great supporter of talent and a kind man at heart. My dealings with him were partly over the film library and partly over the films he was contracted to make for us. Sam Napier Bell was the director there I had most dealings with; I always remember Sam's astonishment when his son became a very successful name in the world of popular music, earning more in a week than his father earned in a year.

Concentrating all work within our unit led to it becoming larger. Already, by the end of 1955, we were employing at least a dozen technicians on a full-time basis, and it was only a couple of years or so after we had got started. I applied for membership of the ACTT as a production manager and was granted my union ticket. I was then able to tell Staff Department (formerly known as Establishments) that the union minimum rate for the post was higher than the salary the Board was paying me. Donald supported me, and the union wrote a supporting letter to the Board. In reply the Board pointed out that, as a full-time Board employee, I enjoyed other benefits such as sick leave that were not available to film technicians. In a compromise my engagement by the Board changed in January 1956 to being on a temporary basis on ACTT terms of employment. Fortunately I was allowed to continue my membership of the Board's superannuation scheme, so ensuring a pension when I retired. This may have been the deciding factor for me in making the change, although I thought the change from permanent to temporary employment was worth the risk to secure more money, about £270 per year extra. My weekly salary went up to £19 3s. 3d. and was to go up by about a pound a year regularly under union agreements. This arrangement was to last three years.

So from early 1956 until the end of 1959 I was wholly engaged in the work of production manager as a temporary ACTT employee. I therefore gave up my other work, including supervising the film library and our accounts section (which together employed four or five full-time Board employees). This enabled the Board to move in Anne Russell to take charge of these; she also looked after the budget . This suited her very well as she had just lost her post in Public Relations on the monthly magazine *Coal*, as it was being replaced by *Coal News*. Anne moved in with us and stayed three years as administrative head.

Anne took over my desk opposite Donald, who by then had also acquired a small office in the basement where he could work alone or interview people in peace and quiet. I moved to another desk in the same room. The other desks in the room were occupied by Kitty Marshall as producer (although she often worked with the film editors in the cutting rooms) and by Donald's secretary, supplied by the Board – at first a girl called Micky King, then the neat and efficient Rita Gardner.

Anne was a congenial person to work with. Her career had included working as a journalist on the *Evening Standard* before coming to *Coal* magazine. She was married to a wealthy husband who worked in the City, and they lived in an elegant house in nearby Brompton Square. I remember one of the days she invited me home to lunch, which we took in her garden and where I was so plied with red wine that I was unable to do any work in the afternoon.

Anne was a *bona fide* media person, as we all tended to be – we were not stuffy office types. Her hobby was going over the road to Harrods which held lunchtime auctions where she sometimes bid for strange boxes of oddments, hoping to find something good inside. Now and then she took me with her. She was good at her new job, and Donald was sometimes petulant because of the speed with which she took action and returned documents to him, the ball once again being with Donald.

In due course Anne had a baby, and I carried on her work for three months while she was off on maternity leave. She returned but soon resigned, in October 1959. Anne's post had been named 'administrative head' of Film Branch because Donald, although films officer and in charge, was not a Board employee and therefore not strictly accountable. It was thought that a separate Board employee was needed to take administrative responsibility.

When Anne resigned, her post was advertised internally through the Board's weekly news sheet issued to all employees. I applied and after an interview, competing against other candidates, I was selected to be administrative head of films on a general administrative Grade IV scale which yielded me £1,350 a year. At long last, after my first appointment as an administrative assistant to the Miners' Welfare Commission in 1944, I had returned to being designated and paid as an administrator.

In the event, carrying on the two jobs of administrative head and production manager, which had been simple enough when we started in 1953, was not now possible because of the expansion of work. Within a few weeks Donald and I were interviewing ACTT technicians for the post of production manager. We were successful in recruiting David Kenning, a grammar-school-educated man from west London. David had joined Technicolor film laboratories to gain his union ticket (laboratory employees all held them, although the union could be difficult if they thought that working in a laboratory was just a trick to get into film-making). David was a clever young man who proved very efficient at his job. He was to resign in April 1964, after five years, to take up a good position in BBC Television's sports department (he was a keen hockey player and a sports lover). Unfortunately soon after moving to the BBC he was killed in Spain in a car accident while on holiday.

By 1960 Donald's drive and intelligence had created a very successful enterprise. One of my tasks was to produce a printed film catalogue for film borrowers and users both, within and without the Board. The one I compiled at the end of 1959 showed the extent of the achievement. In the previous seven years, ninety films had been made, sixty-four of them by the NCB Technical Film Unit, the rest by outside units. In addition, the catalogue listed 160 issues of *Mining Review*. An end section to the catalogue listed twenty-three non-NCB-sponsored mining films from various sources, copies of which we bought and stocked for loan. Most loans were on 16mm gauge, the 16mm projector being widely used. Copies on 35mm could be made available if required. Later experiments were made with making available films on 8mm, the size used by some amateurs.

Life with Donald could be fraught. He was in the habit of coming up to London from Newbury where he lived (later he moved to Wiltshire), arriving from Paddington at about half past ten. We would hear his footsteps down the corridor, and we would all bend over our desks and avoid his eye. This was because Donald could be in a bad temper in the mornings. You felt his strong personality as soon as he entered the room. The first conversation might be characterised by Donald being brusque, especially if he had been asked to do something that he had not done and was being pressed on the subject. His classic defence was: 'Why didn't you remind me?', so transferring the blame on to someone else.

Because in those early years he was often only in for part of the time, he placed on his desk an A4-size, thick-covered notebook in which were written messages about people who had rung him or decisions awaited from him. When action was taken, the entries were ticked off. In the beginning we all scribbled in this book, but when Rita Gardner became Donald's secretary she was designated to write down Donald's messages. All enquiries had to be routed through her. When I left I took with me two such books , and they give a good idea of the work we were doing and the people who contacted us.

They show that by 1960 the Board had installed an internal telephone system called PAX. So most desks had two black phones, one allowing outside calls and the PAX phone enabling internal calls within Hobart House. This was a great advantage. A code book of numbers was issued with the phone; as changes of staff were frequent, this constantly had to be updated. For contacts with NCB employees in the coalfields a centrally supplied teleprinter service existed. You wrote a message rather like a telegram on a standard form and put it into your out-tray for collection and transmission. To save labour costs, individual out-trays tended to be replaced by central collection points. As well as trays for papers, many people had on their desks a glass flask and beaker filled with water issued by the Board. Not everybody used them, but I remember I had one and used it for years. The Board also issued white hand towels and bars of soap to be kept in your desk. The towels were changed each week for laundering. The rumour in the early days, when Board members were discussing economies, was that one had suggested reducing the frequency of issue of bars of soap.

Donald often said he was not a civil servant and did not intend to act like one. So his attendance at his desk and his dealing with messages was often arbitrary. He always decided what he should do and where he would be and not what others wanted him to do or be. Donald would often spend days in the basement studio, where he enjoyed devising complicated models from scraps of materials, working out how they could be filmed and used in explaining a method of mining or something we had to explain visually. He would avoid coming up to his desk, being immersed in what he was doing. I would only go down there if something urgent had come up and try to interrupt him for a decision; this was sometimes not easy. I usually found it was best to do this – and to tackle Donald on thorny subjects – in the afternoons after he had been for his lunchtime beer at a nearby mews pub. At these times Donald was usually in a much more receptive and mellow mood.

Another of his passions was a huge flowchart board which he had made and mounted on the office wall. On this we were supposed to move pins and stretch tapes to indicate the stages and target for the completion of each film. I am not keen on these devices, finding it much easier to use pencil and paper to plot, when you can sit and ruminate at your desk rather than stand up at a board moving cumbersome pins and tapes. Fortunately Donald accepted in due course that the board was not a success.

When I first worked as production manager in late 1952 I began an A4 notebook in which I ruled lines so that I could record the names of the technicians working for us. Each week I was able to enter how many days on which production they had worked so that I could calculate the labour costs of any film, a useful guide in budgeting future ones. David Kenning took over this book in 1960 but stopped using it at the end of that year in favour of recording systems of his own. I now have at home that old ragged blue notebook and can read the names of all the technicians who worked for us until the end of 1960. In those first eight years, eighty-six different names are recorded, each of them taken on either by letter or invoice and paid off when finished or kept on long-term engagement. The latter, of course, included Kitty Marshall.

Each of these eighty-six people was a character in their own right. For my recording system I used to go round asking each week what they had spent their time on the week before. This meant that I was in constant touch with everybody on our books, and I soon regarded each of them as a friend. I greatly enjoyed their company, especially the variety of their temperaments. They were all, in their own way, creative people, and I felt I was in an environment that suited me, being able to bring order to it when I could.

This office efficiency, such as it was, did not come to me all at once, and without Donald's tutelage and supervision I might well have made a hash of it. This was especially so in the early years, when, distracted by marriage, I sometimes found it difficult to concentrate on work. I have always been a slow starter, but if I can build up habits and routines, then I have a base from which I can develop and gain competency and confidence. Fortunately I also have within me the need to work, and steady endeavour brings results. Donald was tolerant of me, teaching me especially the importance of being decisive. The influence of Teresa was also significant, as I gradually absorbed her forthright outlook on life. So I think I went on to become a success in my job.

I cannot mention all the technicians who formed the unit in the 1950s and 1960s, but a few can be singled out. Among the first to be recruited was negative cutter Mrs Sexton, who was based in Studio Film Laboratories, the firm that did much of the unit's processing work in its early years. Mrs Sexton cut the precious 35mm film negatives to match the edited film after it had been finalised. From this, 35mm copies could be struck and master film obtained, from which a 16mm negative and print could be made. After Mrs Sexton retired in 1961 the post was taken on by Mrs Pye, who worked for the unit for many years, based at SFL, 71 Dean Street. When the unit was formed, not only picture but sound was recorded on to film. Soon afterwards magnetic sound tape was introduced and editors had to learn a new technique.

The cutting room was a very important stage in film-making and we were fortunate in having first-class editors. These included Sarah Erulkar, wife of a Shell Film Unit film director named Peter de Normanville. Sarah celebrated her partly Indian origins by wearing a sari most days. She was joined by Betty Gooch in November 1957 as an assistant editor, and the team was strengthened by recruitment of qualified editor Kitty Wood in September 1958. She was a small, pretty woman, always immaculately dressed. She was married to a music composer who lived in Scotland and retired there in due course. In January 1960, as work expanded, Laurel Gemmell came as another editor. She was from a family of film technicians; after long service with us she retired to Italy.

Among the directors working for us was Peter Whale, whom I originally engaged for a short-term job after the fastest interview imaginable. He was a veteran of newsreels who was to become editor of *Mining Review*. Francis nicknamed him 'Moby Dick'. Bob Kingsbury was a young, well-liked New Zealander who sold stills to magazines and more or less began his directing career with us. Sadly he was to injure his back in an underground roof fall while filming; later he returned to documentary film-making in New Zealand. David Pitt and Phillip Owtram were two intelligent young men Donald recruited as directors. David Pitt married Betty Gooch and stayed with us for most of his working life, despite abilities and ambitions in other directions. He made some very good films for us and occasionally freelanced elsewhere. Sadly Betty was to die comparatively early.

Philip Owtram, like other members of the unit, came over to us for dinner, bringing his wife Brenda, a talented woman who worked at the BBC. He was to leave to make films in Nigeria for Shell. Alun Falconer would also come to us for a dinner with his wife Mary, or we would go to them, as they lived near by in Crouch End and later Highgate. Another guest was Rod Barry, a friend of Alun's. Barry was the son of Dora Russell who had been married to Bertrand Russell. A left-wing idealist, his mother had written a book called, I think, *The Tamarisk Tree*. Rod had volunteered to work underground at a Yorkshire colliery while still in his twenties. Unfortunately a roof fall trapped him. As a result he was lost the use of his legs and had to use a wheelchair. Rod applied to his employer, the National Coal Board, for a job in the Film Unit and was taken on by Donald as a trainee editor. The cutting room at Endell Street was adapted so that he could enter the room and work in it while remaining in his chair. He was a very likeable and intelligent young man, with many friends. After some time he moved on elsewhere.

Ralph Elton was another director who was to make some good films for us. He was younger brother to Sir Arthur Elton, and Ralph came to us after working in Malaysia with John Shaw Jones. Pre-war he had been recruited to the General Post Office Film Unit by John Grierson. He was a large, shaggy sort of man who suffered from lung problems developed in the East. Sir Arthur Elton was not only a leading documentary-film figure but also a baronet, a hereditary title. Ralph and his brother lived at an ancient house called Clevedon Court in Somerset, reputed to be the oldest domestic building in the country. In the 1960s when competition between fuels for domestic heating was becoming intense, Arthur, who worked for Shell Film Unit, had oil central heating installed in his half of the mansion whereas Ralph, who worked for us, had solid-fuel central heating installed in his half.

Ralph was a sociable person and would invite unit people down to Clevedon Court for the weekend. When he joined he said to me, as production manager controlling expenditure, 'I have only two weaknesses: I always travel first class and I take taxis; if I drive I lose concentration after half an hour.' Ralph must have been raised by servants, for he was always leaving scarves and sweaters around, which he just expected to be collected and returned. Married, he envied the fact that a cockney like me could father a couple of children whereas his efforts to raise a family were unsuccessful. He was quite outspoken about this – Ralph would say anything he liked. He was a kind, good man with a brilliant photographic eye. He was better as a cameraman than as a director, it was thought. But good editing and producing could result in excellent films from him. Owing to a weakness in his chest he was to die far earlier than he should have done.

Another extrovert character we took on was John Fitzgerald, who had spent much of his early life in Australia but who had returned to London and worked as a milkman. He obtained a job as a clerk in Public Relations, from where he successfully negotiated for work with the Film Unit and somehow managed to get a union ticket. He was to prove a very resourceful director who made many films for us underground before returning to Australia. There he was to continue to make documentaries, including some on Australian coal-mining. It was about two in the morning in November 1958 that John Fitzgerald rang me to tell me that there had been a road accident involving a unit vehicle and he had fractured his pelvis. Continuing phone calls kept me out of bed the rest of the night. Fortunately he recovered well.

I had had to deal with a road accident before, back in 1954, when Ron Fry had been taken into hospital in Worksop, Nottinghamshire. His widowed mother was not on the phone, and I had to travel out to her home in Harringay to tell her about the accident. Ron asked me to be careful, as his mother had a weak heart and it was with some trepidation that I knocked on her door. Luckily it was just a minor injury. Next day I went up to Worksop to collect the float and settle Ron's accounts.

Another trainee taken on by Donald with the union's permission was Rodney Giesler, a bright young man with a German father and an English mother who had gone to an English naval training school at Pangbourne and who had ambitions from an early age to be a film-maker. Donald was impressed by a 16mm film Rodney had made and gave him the opportunity to learn everything, from cutting room to film library to assistant director. Rodney, a great acquisition for the unit who remains a friend today, has told the story of his career with great panache in a lengthy interview with John Legard, recorded in 1994 for the history unit of the film trade union. (His interview tapes join a growing collection of tapes made with leading British film-makers.) Rodney was to direct five films with us before being offered a job by Shell in Kuwait. In subsequent years he set up his own film unit, Auriga Films, towards the latter part of his time making films for a large Norwegian enterprise.

Talking of his time with our unit, Rodney says:

It was marvellous training. A marvellous discipline. Donald could be quite ruthless if you started waffling or if you put a shot in the wrong place. He'd write against your remark 'Round objects'. At that time on a production coalface, the Power Loading Agreement was in operation, and the coalface crews were all on piece rates. And God help anyone who got in the way of the conveyors. It's quite extraordinary to see a crew working on a coalface with a huge vicious-looking power loader on an armoured conveyor. In other words, the conveyor being the rail track: the thing it runs on. And the roof support team working. They worked as a rhythmic team, and if you got in their way, you're not popular. Filming underground was a very specialised job. The main problem was safety . . .

Rodney gives a vivid description of a day on location on an underground film, getting up at 4.30 a.m. and getting back to the hotel at eight at night and having to argue with Donald and the union about how many of these hours could be regarded as overtime. But Rodney adds, 'I remember that unit for the total friendliness of it. No one was biting anyone else's back. There were no jealousies. It was a marvellous training ground and a very happy time.'

Other directors who worked for the unit were Robin Carruthers, Ferdinand Fairfax, Prue Lancaster, Nestor Novera, Robert Vas, Stanley Goulder, Terry Trench, Norman Prouting, Ean Wood, Euan Pearson, Hayden Pearce, Joan Duff, Dick Mason, Peter Pickering, Budge Cooper, Mike Morgan, Jack Ellit, Sean Hudson, Ezra Dearing, Francis Beiber (as editor), Brian Salt, Geoffrey Bell, Ralph Bond, Pierre Henfrey, George Roman and Maurice Kauffman. Cameramen included Ron Bicker, Peter Henessy, John Rhodes, Cyril Arapoff, Eric Chamberlain and Eddie Tilling.

Assistant directors were numerous and included Ken Little, an indomitable cockney who was able to supply location units with food in any circumstances. His side activity (of which officially I was not aware) included delivering milk before coming to work. Later he was to move to Anglia Television, and I learned a year or so ago that he died in the late 1990s. The names of some of the assistants always stay with me, such as Chris Sutton, Roger Pennington, Jack Krantz and Brian Probyn. In 1957, after Charlie Burgess took retirement, we engaged John Gillard as the unit electrician; previously he had been a house electrician at Hobart House. He was to stay for a very long time and in due course could lay claim to having gone down more coal mines in the British Isles than any other employee of the Board, as he used to go on location all the time with our units when they worked underground.

Much of the organising work in setting up locations was now undertaken by the assistant directors employed for each film. They worked closely with the director, and they were liaised with David Kenning, thus relieving me to take on other tasks, such as improving film use now that a substantial number of titles were being deployed around the coalfields. Donald arranged for someone in each of the Board's nine administrative divisions to be nominated locally as divisional film liaison officer, an additional responsibility to his existing job. (Although plenty of women worked in our unit and were employed in Hobart House and in administrative jobs, the industry was predominantly male, and women were not allowed by law to work underground, so precluding them from most engineering and other jobs in coal-mining. So I use the term *his* job because it was men that I always dealt with when working with divisional people.)

The creation of divisional film liaison officers was designed to improve the flow of information. Local users could be made aware of what films were in the pipeline and at the same time they could let us know about local problems in getting films seen and kept in good condition. They could also suggest new subjects that they would like to be seen covered by film (although this was decided officially through departments reporting to the Working Group on Films). Donald arranged for quarterly conferences of these officers, which gave them the opportunity to meet in London and to exchange experiences .

To increase our knowledge of what went on in the coalfields, Donald asked me to visit each division in turn for a couple of days each. He quite rightly argued that making films was not an end in itself. They were useless if they were not seen by the audiences for which they were intended and in conditions that were adequate. We still relied, of course, on the department sponsoring the film to make sure its own coalfield people used it as they intended. Donald instituted a statistics collecting system to see how frequently each film was viewed and used as an educational tool; maintaining this became another of my tasks.

I was at first apprehensive about taking on this field study (lack of self-confidence was something I still had to contend with, although the extrovert side of my nature was emerging). But in August 1961 I began my tours, visiting South Wales to stay in Cardiff and being driven by R.J. Williams, the divisional film liaison officer, to training centres and to speak to film users. My old taste for travel was whetted again. By going down early by train (I had yet to learn to drive) and by returning slightly late I found that on my divisional visits I could do some sightseeing. At Cardiff I took the opportunity to visit Llandaff Cathedral with its magnificent Christ statue by Epstein, my favourite sculptor, and also to take a tour of Cardiff Castle with its wonderful period interior.

I realised that the Edinburgh Festival was on and swiftly arranged to fly up, securing a hotel just off Princes Street. I think the Festival in the 1960s was not as large as it is now, with the so-called Fringe still in an embryonic phase. I enjoyed reading *The Scotsman* newspaper over breakfast, at which of course I ate porridge, and had useful meetings with many Board people. This was my first visit to Scotland since I had hitch-hiked there with Stanley Bloom in 1946. Edinburgh is very beautiful. At the end of each day I used time to the full, fitting in two theatre visits each evening. I saw the official production of Shakespeare's *King John*, was fascinated by the singing of Dominic Behan, Brendan Behan's brother, and greatly enjoyed the exhibition of Epstein sculpture staged for the festival.

In September 1961 I stayed in Wolverhampton, where the actor John Slater (who had featured in *Passport to Pimlico*) was appearing on stage in *Simple Spyman* at the local theatre. I knew him quite well, as he had spoken the commentaries for nearly every issue of *Mining Review*. I went round to see him in his dressing-room and watched the play. The main meetings about films were held in Himley Hall, a former stately home used as the headquarters of the Board's West Midlands Division. I was looked after by Mr Innel Clement, the local public relations officer, who also acted as divisional film liaison officer. Somehow before leaving I managed to escape to the Five Towns of Arnold Bennett (actually six) and saw the house where Bennett had lived. Bennett, with his magnificent novels, many of which I had read, was one of my literary heroes, despite Virginia

Teresa at Camber Sands,
Rye, in 1953, just before
our engagement

Outside the National
Gallery in the 1950s

Top: Upton
Avenue with
post-war pre-fab
houses built on
the Vi bomb
site. No. 77, is at
the far end
of the surviving
Victorian terrace.

Right: Teresa with
Richard, our first
child, and Olu,
our lodger

Top: On location
at Rawdon
Colliery, August
1953. Standing are
John Reid, me,
Tony Maher
and John Shaw
Jones. Donald
Alexander
(1913–93), the
second NCB
Films Officer,
crouches in front.

Right: John Reid
found me drunk
in a field at
Rawdon.
Unfortunately he
had the film unit's
Rolleiflex camera
on him.

Above: At Calverton Colliery, Nottinghamshire, with the film unit's electrician, Charlie Burgess

Below: My press pass to the 1958 festival in Belgium

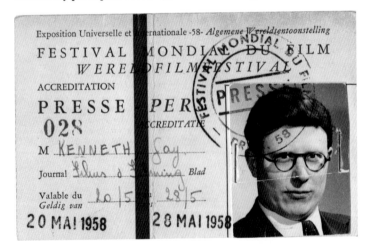

Left: At my desk in the Film Unit

Below: Francis Gysin (1921–95), the third NCB Films Officer, in 1992 after his retirement
Courtesy of Joanna Gysin

Unit cameramen Lionel Griffiths tested his lighting skills in 1955 by taking my picture.

My father and mother outside No. 77 Upton Avenue in 1965

Above: Sam Goodman in Germany in 1965

Below: West German Short Film Festival at Oberhausen, February 1965

Above: Film festival banquet in Rouen. Opposite me (second from left) are Gloria Tessler and fellow journalist Ken Myer.

Below: Stanley Bloom and his wife Salome with Teresa on a visit to Cambridge in 1963

Above: On the Rhine on the Ruhrkhole boat; I can be spotted on the left, in the second row, among German apprentices and their leaders.

Below: German mining apprentices at Cardiff University, 1972. Area NCB Manager, Bill Cleaver (centre) was a famous rugby player.

Above: Colleagues John Quin and Bob Roberts on a visit to Gullick Dobson mining machinery company in Wigan, Lancashire, 1973

Below: Mining machinery exhibition at NCB Swadlincote, 1974

Above: A research visit to South Wales, 1977, while writing the training manual *Basic Mechanical Engineering*

Below: Fire-fighting at Grassmoor Training Centre, Chesterfield, 1982. I had written a training manual on the subject for the NCB.

Top: Retirement day
for Irving Halle and
me, 1 March 1984

Left: My mother
with Teresa and our
children, Oonagh and
Richard, 1974

Above: Hornsey
Historical Society on
a weekend visit to
Portsmouth in 1991;
outside 1 Mile End
Terrace, Charles
Dickens's birthplace

Right: Leading a
local history walk
in Muswell Hill,
September 1979

Above: My mother celebrating her ninetieth birthday with her two sons, 1983

Below: My family with my five granddaughters, 1994

Above: One of the books on local history I have written since retirement.
This was published by Tempus in 2002.

At home in Muswell Hill in 2009

Woolf's views. I was also glad to have seen the coal-burning pottery kilns.

In October 1961 I went up to Newcastle to visit the Northumberland and Cumberland Division where my acquaintance Sid Chaplin was the public relations officer. He invited me to his home in the evening, where his wife Renee laid on refreshments and where we had a long chat, a practice that was happily to be repeated on future visits to that wonderful city. That evening Sid broke off our conversation to see an edition of a new commercial television programme called *Coronation Street*, which a friend of his had scripted. On this visit I had some useful meetings, met some great characters and was taken on a car ride through that imposing northern landscape. We passed through Blyth, where one of the Board's chairmen, Sir James Bowman (a much admired figure), had been brought up, then we pressed on to see Seaton Delaval, a huge mansion designed by Vanbrugh, one of my heroes as both architect and playwright. The building seemed in a neglected state and looking forlorn, albeit grand.

In November 1961 I went to Manchester, not visited since I had been there with Teresa ten years before. One evening I went out from the hotel to the suburb of Sale to see Fellini's *La Dolce Vita*, which I had missed previously. Another evening I took the bus to Rochdale. In my boyhood, Gracie Fields, the Lancashire singer of renown, had been much admired by my parents, and I had always wondered what the town she was born in looked like. I remember standing in the market square, flare lights burning on the many outdoor stalls in the dark air of winter and those, strong, distinctive Rochdale voices sounding all about me, reminding me once more of the diversity of the country in which I lived. Also on this visit I was able to visit the Rylands Library and see the film version of Shelagh Delaney's play *A Taste of Honey*, which I had seen on stage at the Theatre Royal, Stratford. Photography was by Walter Lassally, whom I knew through film work, he, too, having been given early opportunities by Leon Clore at Basic Films.

On Friday afternoon, the last day of my three-day trip, I was taken by Ray Purcell, the divisional film liaison officer, out to Old Boston Training Centre. This was reached via the East Lancashire road, notorious for its fogs. We encountered one on this November day on our return journey, with unfortunate results. As we crawled along we came to a halt because of a crash in front of us. After waiting for some time Ray decided to pull out and overtake the lorry standing in front of us. As he did so a truck in the outside lane emerged slowly out of the fog and hit his car. The slow speeds meant that it was only a minor accident, but it was enough to disable the car.

It was by now gone four o'clock and my aim was to catch the 5.55 train from Manchester to Euston, which I think was the last one to London. I left Ray with his car and walked through the fog, just fields on either side. Luckily I came to a roundabout which cars were negotiating extremely slowly in the fog. I was able to run beside one and beg for a lift, the driver having the windows down so as to see better. He gave me a lift but explained that he was only going to Ellesmere and that his vehicle might break down at any moment as there was something wrong with the engine. Fortunately it did not, and he dropped me at a bus stop. A double-decker came but was only going as far as Salford, on the west side of Manchester. I took it nevertheless and from Salford managed to catch a taxi to take me to the station. I ran on to the platform with my bag and again was able to jump aboard the train as it was pulling out.

In November that year I returned to Newcastle, this time to visit the Durham Division. I was looked after by Bill Gatenby, our divisional film liaison officer, who, because of a bad back, had to wear a special corset all the time. I enjoyed his company and made some useful contacts. I also had the chance to enjoy the magnificence of Durham Cathedral and to see it in its wonderful setting.

In January 1962 I went to Mansfield where my wife's sister Agnes lived, working at Mansfield General Hospital. She gave me an evening meal, and we spent some enjoyable time together talking about family and other matters. I stayed at an old hotel in the centre of Mansfield and remember the tall rail viaduct spanning the town and its vibrant open-air market.

I covered the South Yorkshire area, in the North-East Division, and visited Doncaster, Barnsley and Sheffield in the course of my journeys. I was to return again to Mansfield in November 1962 to visit the East Midlands Division, based in a mansion situated north of Nottingham called Sherwood Lodge.

I continued making these visits from 1961 to 1965, for each one making a detailed report, and in follow-ups I tried to solve problems. One result was that Contemporary Films, to which we had switched from Graphic Films for the handling of our film library dispatches, was contracted to visit every divisional film library each summer to look after its 16mm film prints, some of which were in poor condition, and to provide replacements. This maintenance procedure was a good investment. The statistical monitoring system was improved, and film usage was seen to have increased. I devised and distributed a regular *Film Bulletin* to keep a wide range of people informed about our new films and film equipment.

Forms of projection equipment were being marketed that were more portable; a survey of projectors across the country was undertaken that helped determine where more were needed. Donald, meanwhile, was insistent that the money put into film production must not be wasted by the underuse of the films being made.

In the 1960s marketing imperatives intensified for the coal industry in the face of competing fuels, and a greater drive to sell coal and our other bi-products began in earnest. Use of film by the Marketing Department became an important part of my remit. In 1960 Lord Robens had been made NCB Chairman by the Conservative government and he tackled marketing with zest, his personality being particularly suited to the salesman's task, as well as being good at providing morale-boosting leadership within the industry.

Marketing Department now asked us to make films for them. The word 'Technical' was dropped from the unit's name, and we began to make films in colour, which was possible now that Technicolor processing was proving more successful. One of the first of the marketing films aimed at general audiences we made was *Arthur Clears the Air* (1961), directed by Gerry Bryant, with a dream sequence filmed in a studio. Films on the installation of solid-fuel central heating systems and the Aga cooker for the domestic market were backed by films aimed at industry, promoting the use of solid fuel to heat factories or to power industrial processes. Small portable film projectors were tried out by marketing people and bought in bulk. These enabled salesmen to travel around and show films to potential customers.

Another important customer for the Film Unit was the Board's Medical Service, headed by Dr Rogan. Working with his assistant, Dr McLintock, we began a series of films about first aid, designed for use by those working underground. These covered wounds and bleeding, asphyxia and artificial respiration, fractures, burns and eye conditions. Several of these were directed by Budge Cooper, Donald's wife. By the mid-1960s we were making staff instruction films on how to supervise – for sales office staff and others – and, significantly, in 1969 we produced a film called *Computers for Management*. The Board was a pioneering industry in the use of computers, being the first to base its payroll on computers, and the film showed how the board utilised its computers to service all levels of management. This was well before the explosion of computer use in the 1980s and 1990s; and of course, as far as film-making and distribution were concerned, well before the development of video for production and screening.

The unit expanded further in 1961 when *Mining Review*, the long-running monthly newsreel, was taken over from DATA Productions and that firm was wound up. This reduced costs and tightened up arrangements. DATA technicians were taken over and incorporated into the unit, although some left voluntarily. The producer for the now in-house reel was Peter Whale, the ex-newsreel man, commonly called 'Moby'. He was assisted by young Lucy O'Sullivan, and editing was taken on by Robert Vas. Born in 1931, Vas was a Hungarian who was later to make his name with a dozen films showing his talent, including one about the documentary film-maker Humphrey Jennings for the BBC in 1970. He was given his first chance to be a professional film-maker by Donald, starting in the cutting rooms. He could be a very emotional man. I actually saw him jump up and down in a rage and burst into tears; he was eventually to commit suicide.

Distribution of *Mining Review* to cinemas had significantly increased. Originally its distribution had been handled by National Screen Service; this firm had been dropped by Donald and a new company set up in 1956 called DATA Film Distributors, employing DATA Production's accountant, Bill Chartrey, and a new recruit, selected by Donald through interview, called Sam Goodman. Born in Meard Street, Soho, and a cockney to his fingertips with the gift of the gab and Jewish chutzpah, Sam talked up bookings by constant personal visits to theatre owners and managers. Within a couple of years Sam had increased circulation from 400 bookings a month to 1,000. Many cinemas closed in the 1960s and 1970s, as television stole their audiences, but in 1979 *Mining Review* was still reaching 650 screens out of a total of 1,300 UK screens. Sam also secured cinema distribution through DATA Film Distributors for half a dozen of the Board's other films in versions adapted for public audiences.

Among films shown in cinemas was *The Big Meeting*, about the annual Durham Miners' Gala, a great event in the mining industry attended by Labour government ministers and ending with a wonderful procession into Durham Cathedral. Donald led a weekend team in the making of this. Also shown in the cinemas was *Songs of the Coalfields*, commissioned from DATA by Donald in 1957, featuring Ewan McColl. Also made in 1957 and shown in cinemas was *New Power in Their Hands*. This was scripted by Donald Alexander and edited by Kitty Wood and used existing film material to show the revolution in coalface working methods that had taken place in the previous decade, so that over 90 per cent of British coal was now extracted by power loading machines. While the unit made the bulk of our output, Donald still commissioned occasional productions from other units. Most notably he contracted Derrick Knight in 1963 to make a film about the medical rehabilitation of miners who had been injured at work and were being restored to working health at one of the Board's rehabilitation centres (originally established by the Miners' Welfare Commission). Knight took his title from the Bible and called it *A Time to Heal*.

Television was becoming a powerful medium in the 1960s, and demands for mining shots for news and other programmes increased. I was asked by Donald to set up a stock-shot library. Film editor Mollie Bodger was put in charge, and a scale of standard fees for the use of our material was devised. This brought in a small, steady income. The use of our library shots had to be monitored because they could be used again without paying us a fee if the purchaser was sloppy or less than honest). One of our clients was the BBC, and it led to Mollie and I visiting Alexandra Palace where the BBC made its twice-weekly newsreel. Here we discussed a system to prevent double use and non-payment of royalties. Afterwards we were taken into the BBC canteen where we saw some famous faces, including Robert Dougall. This was a handy visit for me, as I lived only about ten minutes' walk away, and Mollie was able to come home afterwards to meet Teresa.

The library of stock shots was useful because we now had a sizeable amount of film material in our ownership. This was a reflection of our continual steady output and was accompanied by an increase in the size of the unit. In the early 1960s it had at least thirty employees and was to develop into the largest industrial film-making unit in Europe, constantly turning out two dozen films a year, including a dozen *Mining Reviews*.

By 1963 Donald had done over ten years as films officer and was now fifty. Most of those years he had worked full time, making films on location, sometimes abroad, as well as producing them and, through his administrative skills, making sure that the unit's worth and value was well established and its product used to practical effect. That summer Donald received a letter from Francis Gysin in Venezuela asking him what job opportunities existed in the UK, as he wished to return. Donald saw at once that here was his natural successor.

Born in 1921, Francis Gysin had been head boy at Highgate School before going to Cambridge to take a degree in languages – he and I must have been there at the same time. His father was of Swiss nationality, and so Francis had held a Swiss passport and had not been affected by call-up papers. Fluent in several languages, he was involved with Cambridge University Film Society and developed film-making ambitions as a student. He began as a protégé of Paul Rotha and was associate director on *A City Speaks* about Manchester and on *Land of Promise* (1946).

When DATA was set up in 1948, Francis joined it, making a film about Scottish universities (his mother was Scottish), and working alongside Donald Alexander on *Mining Review* stories as director. This was when I first met him, when he came to Hobart House for the production committee meetings. He was living in Finchley, and I remember going to a party at his house. Then Francis was offered a job as Shell's films officer, in charge of its Venezuelan film operation, soon establishing a successful film unit making films about oil. He quickly developed the ability to speak Spanish. Married to Kathy and with two young children named Christian and Joanna, he became concerned with the violence on the streets of Caracas and decided it was not the best place to bring up his children. Hence he wrote to Donald, seeking help to engineer his return to the UK.

Donald tendered his resignation in October 1963, overlapping work with Francis for a month and leaving at the end of November. Donald had caused me a lot of stress, and sometimes on Saturday mornings at home I was glad that that I did not have to deal with him

(Saturday-morning working being abolished at Hobart House in September 1956). Despite this I felt quite emotional at his departure. He had changed my life since he had appointed me to the production manager post, had been personally kind to me, and I came to appreciate his creative but practical, down-to-earth attitude.

I soon found that life with Francis was less stressful. Possessed of a fast-working brain, he was quick at decision-making and paperwork. Like Donald he could not tolerate fools or pretentious people, but under a tough, cynical exterior he was a kind and thoughtful person, solicitous when staff were ill and visiting them when hospitalised. He gave people job opportunities if he thought they were worth it.

He was notorious for giving people and things nicknames. His soubriquet for Hobart House was the 'Bordello'. For me it was at first 'Tiger' (I think he meant right-hand man), but he already had a cameraman called Tiger – Ken Reeves with whom he had worked at DATA – so he changed mine to 'Phantom'. I think that this was due to my practice of putting work papers on his desk while he was out of the office – 'The phantom has struck again'. During the rest of the time I knew him, until his death in 1995, he called me Phantom, never Ken. One soubriquet I never quite understood was his referring to taxis as 'Cardiffs'. According to John Reid, this began when young woman we employed in the film library, who had been a model, he called the 'Tall Girl'. We had an editor called Kitty Wood and a film director named Euan Wood; to distinguish them Kitty was called 'Clean Wood' and Euan was called 'Dirty Wood'; Euan was of course of very presentable appearance but Kitty had a special ability to look totally immaculate.

Francis was also notorious for his ability to run things from a bar stool, a reputation he gained while at DATA. I still smile when I pass the Carlisle Arms in Soho, for it was there in the early 1950s that I first saw Francis at the bar, taking on somebody for a location job. Francis continued this practice throughout our period of working together. His usual tipple was Teacher's whisky (always ordered as a double), although he preferred Scottish malts when available. He regularly bought bottles of wine in Soho for home consumption. Alcohol appeared to have absolutely no effect on him. He was never drunk, as far as I could tell, and he hardly ate anything at lunchtimes except a sandwich at the bar. Paradoxically, in one way he was the opposite of

Donald; Donald was mellow after lunchtime pints, whereas Francis was more equable in the morning with his brain working at its fastest and in the afternoon could be more argumentative. I learned to bring knotty problems to Francis in the morning, whereas with Donald I had raised them in the afternoon.

Francis remained my friend all his life. He retired a couple of years after me from the Board and instituted a practice of meeting friends in the Coach and Horses in Soho every Tuesday lunchtime. Fate dealt him a hard blow when his wife was killed by a motor cycle near their home less than a year after his retirement. An ex-continuity girl, Kathy was totally devoted to him. It was in the Coach and Horses that I was to have my last drink with him. He had just had an operation, but he had insisted that his daughter take him to the pub. Two days later he died, aged seventy-four.

Not long after Francis took over from Donald, in November 1963, the Board gave up possession of No. 2 Grosvenor Place. In a more prosperous Britain, recovering from the war, the property developers began to have their field days. Large areas of London were bought up piecemeal, and vast new buildings replaced characterful old properties. Conservation was not the order of the day then. No. 2 stood next to Murdoch House, Grosvenor Crescent, home of the Gas Board (and named after the inventor of gas lighting), and this corner was acquired by a developer who knocked down the fine 1860s mansions and built an office block. Across the road in a mews, behind the still surviving St George's Hospital, was a riding school whose horses trotted in Rotten Row. The old began to exist beside the new.

The Film Unit and the film library were transferred to offices near Marylebone Station that the Board already occupied for use by its Coal Products branch. These were Nos. 26–28 Dorset Square and consisted of a modern extension built on the back of a period house built in 1892, once the home of the Grossmith brothers, authors of *The Diary of a Nobody* of 1892. We were allocated the basement area, with the film library installed in offices on the ground floor. The use of the basement by the unit had to be planned, for at that time it was an open space without dividing walls. Francis, David Kenning and myself worked out where we needed offices, theatre, cutting rooms and studio space. These alterations were carried out, although the ever-critical Francis was appalled at the standard of building. We moved in on 4 May 1964. David Kenning did not come with us but resigned to take up his BBC post. Instead we took on John Reynolds as production manager. There had been a firm of chain makers called Reynolds or Renolds, and Francis immediately decided on 'Chain' as a nickname for John.

I had two and a half very good years in Dorset Square, a happy working time. It also gave me a new area of London to explore in the lunch-hour, and I now discovered idiosyncratic Bell Street, with its bookshops and art galleries, the Baker Street area, with antiques shops selling Staffordshire flatbacks which later I was to regret not buying, and if you walked far enough you could reach Marylebone High Street or the Wallace Collection, thought by many to be the best house in London. North of Dorset Square were, of course, the open spaces of Regent's Park.

Lunch-hours were occupied by Francis in pubs with work colleagues, and as soon as we arrived in the new building he did a survey of local hostelries to select his regular. Francis never liked being on his own, and this trawl was conducted with a group of fellow drinkers: John Reid, cameraman Eddie Tilling, who worked a lot for us, and John Reynolds; I reluctantly tagged along as I wanted to know where Francis was likely to be. It has always been my practice to use my lunch-hours for specific excursions, hurrying to film shows, art exhibitions or bargain bookshops or meeting up with old friends – if necessary working overtime if the hour overran.

With Francis as my films officer I had to choose between continuing my varied activities away from Dorset Square or missing out on possibly important lunchtime discussions about work. Somehow I got by. Francis realised that I would accompany him a couple of days a week but not every day.

He was unimpressed by the public houses near the new offices, and for a while he drove the unit's vehicle – by then we had been allocated transport by the Board – to a pub we had frequented while in Grosvenor Place. This was the Kinnerton Arms in Kinnerton Mews, just off Wilton Place but which was referred to by Francis as 'Cracknell's', after the name of the pub manager. The vehicle was a Dormobile, painted in the Board's trademark blue, which could be conveniently parked near St Paul's Church on a bomb site (where the Berkeley Hotel was later built). I vividly remember the somewhat hair-raising journeys down Baker Street, Park Lane and around Hyde

Park Corner into Knightsbridge, especially on the way back after Francis had been drinking whisky solidly. Once I was alone in the driving cab with him when another vehicle ran into us at a junction. We survived unscathed. This was on the way to the pub before Francis had had his lunchtime booze.

At other times we had to work at Kay's recording studio on the borders of Maida Vale and Kilburn, and then we would head for the Clifton Arms. Among the crowd would be Cyril Arapoff, one of our cameramen (famed for his stills photography, books of which have been published), Langton Gould-Marks, a large man with a bushy beard, talented at talking, who earned his living as a freelance consultant and scriptwriter, and Bob Ash, one of our assistant directors, married to a New Zealander woman film director named Margaret Thompson. I got into the habit of drinking tomato juice at these sessions to make sure that I could work with a clear head in the afternoon. I still maintain that if there is a good ambience in a pub and one is with a convivial group of friends one can have a perfectly enjoyable time without the need of alcoholic stimulants.

Eventually Francis settled on drinking in a pub on the north side of Dorset Square. This was a stone's throw from the office and thus made working life easier. You could slip out of the office and discuss a problem with him at the bar. Francis was decisive and efficient and ran the Film Unit with brio; he was greatly respected throughout the Board by staff in all departments and by Geoff Kirk, his boss. Working in a pub was just his style.

The basement offices in Dorset Square were, of course, below street level. I would look up from my desk to see the feet of pedestrians hurrying by along Melcombe Place, near Marylebone Station. In early morning and late afternoon a flood of humanity would flow by, trousers and stockinged legs visible from our window, the restless constant movement to and fro of travellers. My desk was by a window and opposite me sat Rita Gardner with her typewriter, then secretary to Francis. At a desk on my left sat John Reynolds, when he was not elsewhere in the building or out on a visit. Donald and Francis let me use their secretary, and I dealt with the morning mail by dictating letters to Rita. John left in 1966 to join World Wide Film Productions, and a replacement Production Manager was required. I recommended that Rita should be offered the post. She was a meticulous, accurate, hard-working young woman who knew the work of the Film Unit inside out and was perfect for the job. Although rather astonished at her promotion out of a secretarial grade, she proved a very efficient manager and was to stay in the post until the demise of the unit. Rita's old job was given to Joyce Gilder. When either Rita or Joyce was away the Board would supply a temporary secretary. These varied in competence, but most were efficient enough.

When you came down the stairs from the reception hall into the basement, our corridor of offices was on the left, on the left-hand side, opposite the side wall of the cinema theatre. My office came first and next was our accounts section. This was headed by Phil Mullins, recruited from Finance Department when we were still at No. 2 Grosvenor Place. His assistant was Ron Hunt, a reliable member of the team, who helped with invoices and with the film library. At one stage Ron got another job within the Board on a higher grade, but he got so bored with it that he successfully negotiated a return to his old job with us. In a former career Ron had worked in clothes retailing, and at weekends he would earn extra money by doing similar shop work. Sadly, lifting heavy bolts of cloth damaged his back and led to problems in later life. He lived at Portslade, near Brighton, and travelled up and down each day. He never got a seat, so he carried a small wooden stool that he sat on in the train corridor.

Next to accounts was the *Mining Review* office. Peter Whale and Lucy Sullivan (who had run it while we were in Grosvenor Place) had resigned, and Francis replaced them with John Reid as producer and Maureen Lee as his assistant. I had known Maureen at Hobart House, where she worked in Public Relations Department. I found her easy to get on with and occasionally would have lunch with her. John had an alcohol problem and would sometimes arrive at the office in the morning saying he had been made to sleep in the spare bedroom the previous night. His wife could not tolerate his drinking, nor could his young teenage daughter. His alcohol dependency put a great strain on his marriage. He went through a period of giving up drink, but he tended to be morose. Francis was perplexed at his abstaining from alcohol, as the two had worked and drunk together for over twenty years. In due course John returned to drinking, this was the end of his married life, which ended in divorce. Sometimes he used to ponder aloud whether his life would have been different if he had not worked with Francis, which was was hardly fair on the latter. At any rate most of the time John exuding considerable charm and was great fun.

In the 1970s production of *Mining Review* was to pass to Robert Kruger, who had edited it when it was made by DATA. He was to prove very competent as a producer. He always had an interesting book on his desk – he read widely, and I always enjoyed conversations with him. His beautiful wife worked for the Gulbenkian Foundation and would sometimes call for him at the office. Robert continued to freelance as an editor, taking time off from the Board to work elsewhere, often in Holland where he had built up contacts. He worked for Paul Rotha. who made films about Hitler and the Nazis, and Robert edited these brilliantly. Maureen Lee continued to be the assistant on the reel. In Robert's time colour film was introduced. Sometimes issues were made on a single subject instead of four. Sponsors, including the Metropolitan Police and Marks and Spencer, were found who would pay to have a single-reel issue about their work made for cinema distribution. This policy reduced the cost of the reel to the Board.

Next to the *Mining Review* office, at the end of the downstairs corridor, was Francis's office with his single desk, although often he was elsewhere talking to technicians, visiting the cutting rooms, at Hobart House or in the adjacent theatre, viewing material or hosting visitors.

Film library staff and their racks of reserve films settled into their ground-floor offices. Phyllis Major had been succeeded in 1954 by Edna Brown, who had previously worked in the Board's secretariat. Edna lived in South Kensington and was one of the old school, with a plummy, cut-glass accent. She was to become a friend of my wife and myself, visiting us at home. Later, when she retired and moved into a residential home near Queen's Gate, we stored trunks for her, including her family silver. She once told me about a certain Lady 'So-and-so' who was clearing her Kensington house, and, thanks to Edna, I bought a fine antique table and a good, if worn, carpet. I went on visiting her for many years. Edna became a sort of honorary 'auntie' to some of the technicians, helping many of them with their personal problems.

After Edna retired she was succeeded by Kath Gent, who had been Edna's assistant. Tragically, Kath was, after her retirement, killed in a cycling accident. She was followed by Vicky Pitcher, a forthright middle-aged woman who had served in the WAAF during the war. She, too, became a good friend. After her retirement she and her husband left the Home Counties and retired to their native Lancashire. She died not many years later of cancer.

Working in Marylebone meant we were adjacent to the British Transport Film Unit, headed by Edgar Anstey, with whom we had some dealings over joint film shows. This meant I became friendly with Edgar's number two, Charles Potter. Charles would take me out to lunch and we would exchange film-maker names and gossip; this was to our mutual advantage. I had a great respect for him and was sorry to learn subsequently, after his retirement, of his death.

Under Francis, production continued to expand. In addition to the technical instruction films we made for departments, we also produced films for general audiences. These included *Master Singers* (1965) by Robert Vas, *Portrait of A Miner* (1966) by Dick Mason, an Australian director of great competence, *Coals! Coals!* (1967) by David Pitt, about the old days of domestic coal use and distribution by horse and cart, and *The Cathedral in the Village* (1968) by Robin Carruthers, about wonderful Southwell Minster in the mining county of Nottinghamshire.

Lord Robens, chairman until 1971, put great emphasis on safety, which became an even more important Board concern, even though the era of the great mining disaster with hundreds killed had passed owing to the introduction of safer techniques. The most tragic event was the coal-tip landslide which overwhelmed a primary school at Aberfan in South Wales in 1966. I remember sitting at my desk in Dorset Square and hearing the news. I could not prevent tears running from my eyes.

Robens was criticised that day, but he was the chairman who promoted safety, and it was his experience in the coal industry, controlled by a safety inspectorate and regulations, that led to the Health and Safety at Work Act. The Health and Safety Executive set up under this Act has done much to improve safety standards in working practice, and its origins lay with the coal industry.

Film was used to promote safe working, and a series of dramatic films illustrating hazards was made by David Pitt and others, with often grisly reconstructions of people being killed. Robert Kruger became producer with special responsibility for a series of safety loop films, some of them designed to be used on Scopitone machines. The

Board also began to adopt closed-circuit television (CCTV), which was just becoming available, and created mobile closed-circuit television vans for safety campaigns. For the first of these touring campaigns we recruited a husband-and-wife team, the man as the technician, his wife as presenter. They would set up at collieries and use CCTV to show safety messages in the canteen or elsewhere at the pit.

Lord Robens had a natural understanding of film and was always ready to be filmed. He could give an interview on film to the exact number of minutes required by the producer, an achievement greatly admired by Francis. Recording would take place in our theatre, with Robens hurrying in and out without fuss, with always a friendly word for anyone he met. He also encouraged the use of film in management training; this was not yet a widespread practice.

8

FATHERHOOD AND
FILMS AND FILMING

LIFE IS MULTI-LAYERED. The earnest involvement with film-making at the National Coal Board was one strand, family life a second and creative activities a third. Perhaps I put those in the wrong order. For me, settling down in married partnership with Teresa, an intelligent woman and my best friend, gave me confidence and a base. In our first months we explored Highgate, went regularly to the theatre and took a belated honeymoon at Easter in the Scilly Isles, flying there in a propeller-driven De Havilland biplane. There were only a few seats, and I was behind the pilot; he kindly dropped the plane down when he saw that I wanted to photograph the islands.

Teresa soon became pregnant, and we acquired a 1929 three-bedroomed house not far from Alexandra Palace, moving in on 23 August 1954, just after the overland railway to the palace closed down. Each working day I would take a twenty-minute walk from my house to Wood Green tube station. We had been helped to build up the necessary mortgage deposit for the house (which cost less than three thousand pounds) by a loan from Agnes, Teresa's sister. Richard was born on 30 November 1954, finally delivered by Caesarean section after Teresa had had a difficult labour. Oonagh, our second child, was born on 26 May, 1957, also by Caesarean.

In our new home, with a baby, we had to work out how to pay the bills once Teresa no longer had an income from teaching. For the next ten years we took in lodgers, supplied by the University of London. These included Olu from Nigeria, who qualified as a medical doctor while she was with us. She then tried to find a position in a British hospital, which proved difficult at first. 'I'll have to paint my face white to get a job, I think,' she said. This was the mid-1950s. Eventually she found a good position in a hospital in West Ham. Then she married a fellow Nigerian and went back to Nigeria to practise. Meeting her many friends I was to discover how jolly Nigerians can be. Our friendship continued for many years (Richard was a pageboy at her wedding), and she visited us when she came back to the UK. Olu was followed by Asra, from Pakistan, studying at the Institute of Education before going home to head a school. She was with us from September 1956 until May 1958 and, like Olu, became a family friend. In due course we had other lodgers, from the Gold Coast and elsewhere, including a delightful Welsh girl called Betty Owen, who also studied at the Institute of Education. Her boyfriend, Keith Morris, a music student, met me one evening at the tube station to drive me home and asked if I knew that President Kennedy had died. It was the first I had heard of his assassination. Our last lodger was Hilary Walker, a medical student, who was with us for two years until June 1964, when we reluctantly had to reclaim the room so that our two children could each have their own space.

Despite the income from lodgers we were still not very well off, so in 1955 Teresa decided to return to teaching, with a local woman engaged full time to look after Richard. But then Teresa was pregnant with Oonagh and had to give up teaching again at the end of the 1956 summer term. When she went back to work, at first as a supply teacher, it was at primary rather than secondary schools, so that her hours coincided with our children's school attendance. But this was not until 1965. In 1966 she settled permanently as a primary school teacher at Tetherdown, a Muswell Hill school based in Grand Avenue. She was to stay there for fourteen years.

We kept up a social life, with visits from friends and relatives, and carried on going to the theatre, although less often and using baby-sitters. Nevertheless we managed to see Beckett's *Waiting for Godot,* Anouilh's *Waltz of the Toreadors,* Brendan Behan's *The Quair Fellow,* Miller's *A View From the Bridge* and Osborne's *Look Back in Anger* and *The Entertainer,* among other plays. Gardening became a new occupation, as did household maintenance. Two small children kept us busy.

Photography has long another hobby of mine, with the pleasure of mounting my pictures in albums, captioned and dated. Turning over the pages, I can live again those happy family days of outings, holidays, visitors, school events and parties and realise what an important part of my life was raising a family with my wife. Arguments and rebellions took place, of course, but that was part of sharing a home. With these photographs I can see how our two babies progressed into university graduates. I also see the maturing beauty of my wife –

as well as the changing fashions in clothes. Having children, whatever the problems, can bring great joy.

With a busy job and full home life, what was I doing about my ambition to be an author? I wrote essays, stories and poems when I could but never had anything published – I never tried very hard to get into print, perhaps through fear of rejection or lack of time. A thick blue notebook I began to keep at this time served as a place to comment on books I had read and to jot down feelings and trivial events – a sort of sporadic diary with sometimes months or years between entries. The writing impulse is strange; it is always present in me, but it needs direction and must be channelled into some useful outlet such as a letter, article or a work of fiction. At that time I was able to harness my impulse to write to produce some hack journalism. My motivation was income as much as anything.

Such work came my way through the kindness of Peter Heap, my colleague from Public Relations who, like me, was to serve out his career at the Coal Board. He knew a man about our age called Ken Clark who worked in trade journalism (perhaps they were at school together). Peter worked regularly for Ken Clark in his spare time and had been offered more jobs than he could comfortably handle, especially some rather boring chores like compiling catalogues, and he suggested that I took these on. I gladly did so, having a rather romantic attitude towards journalism and writing and being glad of the money.

Ken was editor for a group of magazines serving the clothing industry, published by United Trade Press, which was based in a post-war office block in Gough Square, just off Fleet Street, near Dr Johnson's house. His remit included the production of an annual edition of *Hard's Year Book,* providing addresses for clothing industry firms and people. Each year it had to be updated. Soon Teresa and I were working together in the evenings and at weekends on the painstaking and tedious task of correcting one set of copy against another. Suppliers of clothing were listed under categories, and Teresa and I chuckled over 'Chef's Check Trousers' – the work was so boring that we would attempt to find amusement in anything. Luckily we could listen to the Proms at the same time.

I began working for Ken in August 1955 and continued for seven years. Fortunately the work became more interesting, as he asked me to write up reports on one-day conferences, which I was able to do by taking a day's annual leave from the office. I produced articles and undertook other dull writing jobs, including summarising new patents taken out, such as for a new bra design. However, it brought in money – although not much – and gave me the chance to meet other journalists. On one memorable occasion Ken rewarded me by taking me to lunch at the Wig and Pen Club in Fleet Street, where I got drunk; this was in the office lunch-hour, and I returned to my desk barely fit for work. Ken was a stickler for accuracy and would tell me off if I slipped up over a fact. It was a good training.

More importantly I embarked on another type of journalism in 1954 which was to continue until about 1986 and which was to shape the way I was to spend free time. This was writing about short films and documentaries for the monthly magazine *Films and Filming*. It began with Donald Alexander, who would engage writers he knew to prepare scripts for projected films, using people such as Arthur Calder Marshall. Among these was Peter Brinson, who at this time shared a flat in Gloucester Terrace with Tony Simmons, who had been evacuated with me to Brentwood in 1939. Peter was a tall, good-looking, well-educated man who had emerged from the war with the rank of lieutenant-colonel. His main interest was ballet, and eventually he was to head a ballet school; this was after being director of the London office of the Gulbenkian Foundation.

While writing a script for Donald, he was offered the post of editor of *Films and Filming*, soon to be launched to join a group of similar magazines, which included *Books and Bookmen, Dance and Dancers, Theatre and Theatre Going*. These were published by Hansom Books, the brainchild of Philip Dorse. Hearing of this venture, I took the initiative and wrote to Peter asking if he would employ me to cover short films for the new magazine. This he agreed to do. He was not editor for long, but his legacy for me was decades involved in film journalism.

The first number appeared in October 1954 and contained my first piece. This was a very short column headed 'Documentaries', in which I reviewed Tony Simmons's *Sunday by the Sea*, which had won the Grand Prix for the best short film at the Venice Film Festival in 1953; Lindsay Anderson's and Guy Brenton's *Thursday's Children*, about deaf children, which gained circuit release and helped establish Lindsay Anderson's name; as well as titles from the Petroleum Film Bureau, such as *Powered Flight*, and the first of the Coal Board's films, *Coalmining as a Craft*. From March 1956, when Peter Baker was editor, my small column was upgraded to a full-page article, although it did not appear in every issue. IWhat I wrote about was left entirely up to me. Seeing films when and where I could became part of my routine, together with weekends spent writing up articles.

In practice this meant that many lunch-hours and early evenings were spent attending press shows. In fact I expended a lot of time and effort for very little remuneration, and as Hansom Books was always late in paying I often had to wait for what little I got. I suppose I got hooked on the glamour and camaraderie of this journalistic life that contrasted with, yet complemented, my day job at the Coal Board. It introduced me to other industries and made me new acquaintances and some good friends, many generous with help and advice as well as just being fun to be with.

Alun Falconer argued that I should not devote my energies to journalism for such small financial returns but should produce material for television, where there was an expanding market in the 1950s and 1960s. Although I did try writing a play, under the influence of John Osborne, this effort when submitted came back with a rejection slip. Somewhere along the line I did not make it as a serious author. I suppose I enjoyed life too much, with an interesting job, a good family life and a regular job in journalism that gave me a creative outlet, a social life and a byline in a national magazine. Such activities took most of my time.

Tolerance by Donald and Francis and by later bosses at the Board was the key to my continuing my film journalism for so many years. If I was in Finance Department there would have been no link between my full-time work and my journalistic activities. But Donald and the others saw the value of my contacts in the film-making world, and I was able to bring my colleagues useful information about the films of others, technicians and developments in film production. Donald related this to his early experience when the pioneer documentary film-makers used to show each other their work; indeed, he tried to keep this going once we had our own theatre. So there was a useful flow both ways, for I used every opportunity to promote the Coal Board and to make its activities in mining, as well as in film, known to the people I met at press shows. My second job also ensured that I never felt trapped and isolated within the coal-mining industry; I think this made me a better and more useful employee at the Board.

Reporting on films sometimes gives ibe the opportunity to travel abroad to cover a film festival. Mostly these perks tend to be taken up by the editor, and I always remember how Peter Baker came back each year from the Cannes Film Festival tanned a dark brown and happy. Peter wrote a novel based on these experiences and, after handing over the editorship of *Films and Filming* to Robin Bean, mysteriously disappeared from view. I had an opportunity to go abroad myself in 1958 when I was asked by Peter to cover the film festival being run in conjunction with the Brussels World Festival, part of which was devoted to shorts and documentaries. Naturally I accepted. I would have liked to have taken Teresa with me, but Richard was four and Oonagh one, so this was not practical. I did, however, write to her describing what Brussels was like when I arrived after a short flight:

I spent from 11 a.m. to 4.30 p.m. at the Exhibition – what a colossal size. It is fifty times as big as the South Bank, and oh, your feet. This morning I took the overhead cable rail to the Foreign Pavilions, saw the Mines Pavilion and the British Pavilion. The latter is very good, although it could be a bit bigger. Attached are two pubs and very nice it was to have a half of the best bitter I've tasted in one of them. It is all very colourful and South Bank-ish. The site is sloping and wooded and there are hundreds of fountains, lakes, flowers and odd trees, either incorporated into the pavilions or gracing the avenues.

The avenues are jammed with people from all over Europe. The clothes are bizarre but not as chic as I usually see at Hyde Park Corner. There are all classes and the poorer Belgians (and French?) wear that usual drab black clothing. I never knew that there were so many priests and nuns; and if you were still teaching you wouldn't want to come here, for every few seconds you pass crocodiles of schoolchildren. Every school in Europe is here – boys, girls, young, older, uniforms, no uniforms, *thousands* of children all rushing the pavilions, buying ices, gabbling, phew! Well, South Bank all over again.

I have a book of meal tickets worth 100 francs each, two for each day (dated) and a list of restaurants at the Exhibition or in Brussels where they are accepted. No meal at a restaurant is under 95 francs basic, and if you spend more than 100 francs you pay the difference . . . I had lunch at the Dutch pavilion, then on to the USSR and USA pavilions, which are next to each other. The first sells souvenirs. Do you want any – lace, carvings, etc.? I bought a bar of Russian chocolate and saw my first Russians. They don't wear horns. The USA pavilion is very good. An enormous round building with part of the roof still open and in the centre an enormous pool. Here they were having a mannequin parade of some outrageous bathing costumes. They have colour television going and a hi-fi gramophone room where I sat for an hour in an armchair to rest my feet. After an ice milk and tea I got my exhausted self back to the motel about 5 p.m. having seen five pavilions only.

The film shows are run every evening, one at 6.30 p.m. and one at 9.30 p.m. with an hour between. These two shows are repeated next day, one at 11 a.m. and one at 3 p.m., so if you miss the evening shows you can catch up again next day. Costs are so outrageous. I have just translated every item of my expenditure into shillings and it has really brought it home to me. I just ain't going to spend unless I have to – but you have to. Total expenditure to date is £5. Two eggs for breakfast were two shillings and sixpence. Bus to the Exhibition was 9d. Overhead rail was 20 francs which equals three shillings. Half a beer was one shilling and sixpence. Ice milk and tea was four shillings, and so on. I won't bore you. If I get away with £20 I will be lucky, excluding any purchases.

It seems so odd to be on my own you know. I have washed my nylon socks. I must rush now or else I'll be late for Ken Clark . . .

It was by chance that Ken, for whom I did United Trade Press work, was also in Brussels at the same time, attending a congress. We were able to meet up and explore the city together. As a visiting film journalist I was staying at a hotel about seven miles away from the exhibition. The first time I left my room to attend the festival I noticed a row of small cars with drivers, which I realised were taxis, They each carried a tall pole with a pendant that said 'libre'. Ah, I thought happily, free transport to the exhibition; recalling my schoolboy French. When I reached the site I was surprised when my driver demanded a considerable fare. But the journey is free, I protested. 'Libre' meant free for hire, he explained; not free of charge!

Twenty-eight countries competed in the Short Film Festival (feature films were also shown, with a competition for the Best Film Ever Made, but I can't remember which won). Francois Truffaut's first ever film, a short entitled *Les Mistons*, won the prize for mise-en-scène. Truffaut was to go on to make some seventeen feature films, widely acclaimed, before his death in 1984, aged fifty-two. I suppose I saw him accept the prize?

I had always admired the early French feature films that I had viewed, and here I found myself enjoying not only *Les Mistons* but Paul Paviot's film *Django Rheinhardt* and Francois Villier's *Le Foulard de Smyrna*, about an imported silk scarf depicted as the carrier of the Black Death.

The British entries included films financed by the British Film Institute's Experimental Film Fund and one by the famous documentary film-maker Harry Watt, called *People Like Marie*, made for the World Health Organisation. Remarkably, the Grand Prix went to a British film. This was Shell's *Forming of Metals*, beautifully photographed and directed by Peter de Normanville (husband to Coal Board Film Unit editor Sarah Erulkar). This was good news, and so I took the initiative of phoning *The Times* in London, which carried a news paragraph about it the next day. This led me to writing an article for *The Times* on the Brussels Film Festival of Short Films, which they printed soon afterwards.

Returning home, I managed to get specialist magazines to take short reports on particular films shown at the festival – such as an item used by *Flight* magazine on the training plane the Jet Provost, which featured in one short. My report for *Films and Filming* was run as two articles in succeeding months. All this pleased Noel Gee, director of public relations, who had fully supported me in allowing me time off to attend the festival.

Actually the first film festival I attended was the year before, in 1957. I went as a Coal Board representative, for it was the first attempt by British industry to set up a festival of sponsored films. It was to be repeated in 1959 and eventually to lead to an annual festival, mostly held in Brighton, at which I was to be an assiduous attendee, doubling as Coal Board representative and film journalist (which gave me free attendance and saved the Board money). The 1957 and 1959 festivals were held in Harrogate, and Board films were in competition in several of the categories. My report for *Films and Filming* said:

> When captured, Field Marshall von Keitel gave one reason for the Allied victory as their quick and complete mastery of film education.

During the last war the British armed services were making an average of 150 to 200 films a year, and these played a vital part in training vast bodies of men suddenly called to arms. It was largely as a result of the Forces experience that documentary films, born in the Thirties, swept into use in industry after the war. The logical result, twelve years later, is a Festival of Films in the Service of Industry held recently in Harrogate for four days. It is the first of its kind in this country, although similar functions have been held in Belgium and elsewhere. In all 320 films were entered for the festival and the pre-selection committees chose 131 to be screened.

The films were backed by 72 different sponsors, mainly industrial firms ranging from giants such as Shell, ICI and Unilever downwards. The government was represented by seven films made through the Central Office of Information and through the British Productivity Council, a sorry reflection on the first sponsor of them all. Of the categories into which the films were divided, two, Public Relations and Sales Promotion, attracted over half the original entries. Thereafter a diminishing number were entered for Industrial Productivity, Training, Health and Safety, Human Relations, Careers, Sales and Dealer Training and Films for Use in Schools.

It was to be some time before I was invited to another festival abroad. This was in 1965. Geoff Kirk, by then director of public relations, invited Sam Goodman and me to attend the Oberhausen Film Festival in Germany, a prestigious annual event where we had entered some editions of *Mining Review*. Sam Goodman was anxious to try to make some distribution contacts for the reel, Germany having a coal-mining industry of roughly the same size as Britain. I presume that Geoff also thought of the trip as a reward for hard work by Sam, and, I suppose, myself. Francis Gysin did not want to go.

It was a memorable trip. Leaving London in its snow on Saturday, 20 February 1965, Sam and I flew to Dusseldorf on a Lufthansa flight and from there took a train to Mulheim in the Ruhr, where we had booked into a small hotel. Run by Hans and Margit, a young couple, we found it a friendly place to stay. We had separate rooms, but I doubled up and shared a bed with Sam one night so that Margit could take in an extra guest. On our last night they invited us to a nightclub party, connected with a local festival. Sam did not go, but I took up the invitation and danced the evening and early morning away with local German girls. One of them told me she could never forgive the British for their bombing of Germany, but the evening was enjoyable. I got home at 5.30 a.m. and had to get up two hours later to catch a taxi with Sam to the local railway station *en route* to the airport. When I got to the station, I realised that I had left at the hotel a nice suede trilby hat I had bought, having found continental weather in February exceedingly cold. I discovered I couldspeak enough German to get the taxi driver to take me there and back before our train arrived. I like the sound of the German language, but speaking it was easier for Sam, as he had been brought up to speakYiddish, which originates in a southern German dialect.

As a Jew, Sam had no particular affection for the Germans, and he pointed out to me that a drunk on a bus was spouting something of the old anti–Semitism that Hitler had promoted. I did not feel antipathy to the Germans I met, although I had been brought up during the war to hate Hitler and his country, and even today I cannot see a photo of his face without a feeling of revulsion. Strangely, I felt more at home in Germany than in France, and the language came easier to my tongue. Perhaps some remote Anglo-Saxon gene ticks within me; certainly it was in northern Germany that I once had the uncanny experience of passing a man in the street who was the image of my father, with the same skin colour, ginger hair and shape of face.

Sam and I went by tram to Oberhausen, registered on the Sunday and attended the festival opening. But he did not think sitting and watching films all day was lack exciting, and instead we embarked on sightseeing. Next day we took the train to Cologne where we saw bomb damage and the mighty cathedral by the Rhine. We returned slightly drunk to watch someYugoslav films. Next day we explored Essen, where I bought my hat, and on Wednesday we went to Bonn, visiting Beethoven's birthplace and looking at the Federal Parliament building. Here I dropped my Balda bellows camera, so next day we took it it to a Mulheim photographic shop for repair. Speaking perfect English, the man behind the counter examined it and laughed. 'This is a museum piece!' he declared. He sold me a Dacora, my first 35mm camera. When we were ready to leave he made a point of coming out from behind the counter to open the door for us. I thought that German sales staff were better trained and more polite than most English shopkeepers and assistants.

Somehow Sam had made contact with a distribution company

and so early next day we went to Duisburg for a prearranged meeting. That evening Sir Frank Roberts, the British ambassador, gave a short speech at the festival, but we won no prizes. Other British journalists were there, and I came across Paul Rotha, whom I had met before, looking red and florid with his companion, the actress Catherine Smith. So at least one doyen of British documentary was there. I returned home happily on Sunday afternoon and next morning went as usual to Kay's in Finsbury Park to check out the next print of *Mining Review*.

In October 1965 I travelled abroad to another film festival, this time in Rouen. I was a Board representative attending an international gathering of sponsors of industrial films. These festivals were run in the UK by the British Industrial Films Association, later to become the British and Scientific Films Association, with similar organisations operating in other countries. Rouen made a great effort to demonstrate cookery skills, and my main recollection is of going each day to a different superb French restaurant. I also saw films – after all, I was going to write it all up in *Films and Filming* – and was able to visit the Flaubert museum in the house in which he had lived, although the curator only spoke French and I found myself floundering when trying to converse.

Despite all the excitement and friendship working in the Film Unit brought, and despite being allowed to pursue a parallel career as a freelance film journalist, a worm of discontent began to grow within me. In 1965 I was forty-two. At this age a person is aware of the passing of youth and starts to sum up his life. I had reached the top of my salary grade and, despite increases won by the union, I felt I was stuck. Attempts to get my job upgraded to a higher salary band, supported by Francis and Geoff Kirk, resulted in my job being examined by Staff Department grading specialists, but they did not recommend an upgrade, so I started to look round for other job opportunities.

Before all this the year 1966 had brought many pleasures. An enjoyable by-product of film reviewing was an interesting social life. In April I had several enjoyable excursions. I went on a press party trip to Crewe to celebrate the electrification of the line to Liverpool and Manchester (steam trains being then being phased out); I travelled to Derby with Alec Hughes of the British Association for the Advancement of Science for a screening of films at the Coal Board's central engineering establishment at Bretby; and the Coal Board staged a press show at the Hammer Theatre in Wardour Street of our latest film, *Portrait of a Miner*. I saw films made for the Gas Council and British Transport and those collected by Derek Hill for his Short Films Service. I attended film selection panels for the British Industrial Film Association. Life seemed full.

The same year I finally learned to drive. Teresa and I had no plans to buy a car, although we were better off now that she had a regular teaching job in Muswell Hill. We had gas central heating installed in our home – a significant and welcome development that transformed our lives in cold weather, being very different from open-fire warmth, which penetrated only so far into a room. Taken for granted these days, it opened up the whole house for use in winter.

Harold Wilson was re-elected prime minister, and on Saturday, 30 July 1966 England won the World Cup; we watched the football match on television while visiting my parents in Forest Gate. In August we rented a house in Leichendam, near The Hague in Holland and spent two weeks exploring that country, amazed that everybody seemed to speak English. By chance, Robert Kruger was editing a film in Amsterdam and was able to visit us and share a meal. The house was neatly arranged and very tidy. Large and rambling, it stood by a canal, crossed by a bridge straight out of Van Gogh.

9

PAID TO WRITE TRAINING MANUALS

IT IS THE insidious newspaper advertisement that attacks the mind, even during a busy and happy life. A job is described with a tempting salary, and you agonise over whether to apply. An older friend of the family, whom we used to see socially, older than me, said, 'I've got past the stage of reading job advertisements in *The Daily Telegraph*.' In 1966 I had not yet reached that stage.

This was a time when the Civil Service was being urged to buck itself up and introduce a managerial intake with industrial and business experience. In May the Civil Service Commission put an advertisement in *The Times* with details of administrative opportunities for men and women aged thirty-six to fifty-two. These were appointments as principals in the administrative class of the home Civil Service; candidates needed to have had a responsible job in industry or commerce of at least middle management status. I decided to have a go. Nothing much happened during the summer, but then I was asked to take a written examination on 1 September 1966. When the results came I discovered that I had come fourth out of 862 candidates.

The second opportunity came in August when a job was listed in the Staff Vacancy Bulletin, in the Training Aids section of Industrial Training Branch. The successful applicant would assist in the production of an internal training magazine and other aids such as films, manuals and programmes for programmed learning. 'Drafting ability is required; experience of writing, training or education, or knowledge of mining or engineering would be an advantage. Apply by 2 September 1966.' Most importantly, it was grade III, one higher than my post in Films.

I found the advertisement when I returned from holiday in Holland and pondered whether to apply, my present working life being so pleasant. In the end I sent in an application just after closure date, which was accepted. The job was held by my old acquaintance, Peter

Heap, who told me he had given it up for another in the Coal Board because he could not stand the authoritarian manner of a new head who had been put in over the man for whom I would be working. He urged me to take the Training Aids job, nevertheless, saying I had a reputation for getting things done.

The Board moved faster than the Civil Service. An interview panel for three candidates, of which I was one, was arranged for 28 September. On 5 October George Anderson, the Public Relations Department secretary handed me a letter in our Dorset Square offices saying I had been offered the job. Now I was in a dilemma. Should I take it or stay where I was? And what about my Civil Service application? I told Francis of my success, and he urged me not to accept but to remain where I was. I felt guilty about letting him down, but it was my decision to make, not his, and the job would put me on a higher grade, so I decided to accept.

The Civil Service called me for a two-day interview at their Savile Row offices on 1 and 2 November. I took two days' annual leave and went along. There was an exciting mixture of tests, both written and oral, including a one-to-one session with a young man with a quick brain in which we parried arguments over a set problem. I was successful and was invited to a Final Selection Board on 1 December. I messed up this interview. Next day they sent me a letter saying I had failed. I came up with all sorts of excuses for my lack of success. I had been asked which department I wished to work in and I had said Education, whereas perhaps I should have said Ministry of Works, with a chance of getting into heritage buildings work. There were about twenty people on the panel and some seemed so far away that I could not make an impression on them. This was exacerbated by my deteriorating hearing, which had started to be a concern, and I could not always hear what was said. I had not been at my best.

My rejection actually solved a problem, for by this time I had joined Industrial Training Branch at the Coal Board, my last day in Films being Friday, 18 November. I cleared my desk, saw a *Mining Review* show copy and at half-past six went with Francis to Embersons' Wine Bar for a farewell drink. My seventeen years in working with films were over.

I already knew Denis Kensit, the head of Training Aids, with whom I was to work. By chance we had once travelled to Newcastle together on the same train, and he came to *Mining Review* rough-cut shows when he could. He told me he had persuaded Jack Cadogan, who was the head of the branch and chairman of the interview panel, to appoint me rather than one of the others. I think Denis wanted someone he knew he could get on with. For my part I admired his good brain, and I was pleased to work with one so intelligent and amenable.

He was Irish, the son of a musician who played in an orchestra in Paris, where Denis had been brought up in part, in consequence of which he spoke excellent French. He was a student of language and could tell a story with all the eloquence of the Irish, although he had no accent. He told me his father had given up his job in order to play chess. Denis was renowned for his stories. He always treated me cordially and at the end of my first year with him he paid me the compliment of saying he was very happy with my work.

Denis always amazed me at the way he could deal with intricate problems at great speed, but his general philosophy was that most things could wait for tomorrow. I was told on my arrival that my first job was to clear his desk. I looked at it. It was piled high with files, each one relating to some training matter. There must have been twenty or thirty of them, some coated with dust. I could just about see Denis over the top of them, as he was a slightly built man. It took me about a year to reduce the pile to about half a dozen.

He had taken his degree at Cambridge and returned annually to take part in a university run. He was a keen cyclist and he took his wife, son and daughter on cycling holidays. During the war he had served in an anti-aircraft unit and told a vivid story of being shelled across the Channel when stationed at Dover Castle. He joined the Coal Board when it was set up, working with Reginald Revans, of whom he had a high opinion.

Dr Revans, who lived to ninety-five and who had an obituary in *The Times*, spent several weeks living as a miner and learned the importance of team working. He developed Action Learning, a theory that a manager should learn on the job. Denis had worked with Revans on Basic English – needed when in the post-war period the Board took on foreign workers, such as Italians, and in the 1950s refugee Hungarians. These men had to be given crash courses in English in order to work safely in the mines.

At one o'clock Denis would eat sandwiches at his desk and read before going for a drink in a nearby public house, such as the Pig and Whistle on the corner of Wilton Street. I would eat in the staff restaurant and then often join him in the pub, enjoying his storytelling. This was a popular venue with an upstairs restaurant; one day I saw the film actor Jack Hawkins going up the stairs to dine. Another favourite haunt for Denis was Gordon's Wine Bar in Villiers Street. A group of us would take the District Line train to Charing Cross (now called Embankment) and walk the few steps to Gordon's. Although it was the 1960s it was still boarded up from wartime days, when it was common to board up blasted-out windows in case there was another bomb. We sat in the street-level front room where Denis would order a Marsala and some sandwiches, which were always tiny. After these outings I often returned to the Coal Board desperately hungry. But breaks like these made good working relationships.

Working to Denis were writers, book designers and administrative people involved in the production of a home-study course in Coal Preparation: the cleaning of coal before it is marketed, involving specialised processes. When I joined, the few of us were based in offices above a bank at No. 1 Chester Street, a stone's throw from Hobart House. The premises were rather gloomy, with narrow corridors and dark wooden panelling. My enduring memory of being there was receiving a phone call on Thursday, 30 March 1967 telling me that my father had died, aged seventy-eight. I felt shock and chill, as I had been with him just three days before on Easter Monday; Chester Street was never the same afterwards. Fortunately we were moved into Hobart House on 28 July 1967. My phone number was no longer Ambassador 3266 but became Belgravia 2020, as it had been thirteen years before.

Leaving Film branch and joining the Training Aids section of Industrial Training branch was a culture shock for me. I had been a big fish in a little pond. Now I was a little fish in a big pond. After being used to approving financial expenditure off my own bat, I had to adjust to submitting petty-cash slips for approval to people elevated several ranks above me. Moreover each day I had to get used to going into the office with important people, board members, heads of departments and the like, and to recognise that I was now comparatively small fry. I have come across several people who prefer working in small organisations because they cannot stand being insignificant in a large organisation. Personal pride is an important factor in many people's working lives. Fortunately I had moved from one creative part of the National Coal Board to another. We had an end-product, previously a film, now a training aid, a physical entity we could see as a result our daily labours, a satisfaction not enjoyed by people in other departments. I was to be called upon to get things done, from writing training manuals to running training courses. This I found, suited me well.

My new branch was responsible for the training of the industrial grade employees at collieries and elsewhere. This included mechanical, electrical and mining specialities and covered also training of under-managers, deputies and overmen. There were about eighty training centres, each with their own staff who had to be trained as well. Safety was a key aspect of training. Schemes of preventive maintenance, by which all machinery was inspected at regular intervals and dismantled even if it seemed to be working perfectly, were introduced and had to be explained. The high rate of back injuries, which could lead to significant loss of production as well as personal pain, meant the introduction of training courses in 'kinetic handling': teaching how to lift and shift weights in small spaces without damaging the spine. Special attention was given to dangers from gases, and every person going underground was given a mask called a 'self-rescuer', for which training was needed. The erection of dust barriers across all roadways had to be explained as a safety mechanism which reduced the impact of methane gas explosion. All levels, from mine management and the engineers down to supervisors, operatives, maintenance men and trainee apprentices, had to be trained both to improve safety and to increase output.

Training Aids covered a variety of media and techniques and changed and expanded as the decades passed. The first aids had been a series of red hardback manuals covering basic subjects such as roof support, underground transport and mining systems. To these were to be added filmstrips, 35mm slides, overhead projector transparencies, paper hand-outs, charts, diagrams and, of course, films. The ultimate was the creation of a 'training package', which comprised a varying batch of aids that could be used flexibly by instructors according to the target audience – from managers to apprentices straight from school.

Ensconced in a Hobart House office, sitting opposite Denis, my first years were spent in administration, helping Denis in the achievement of targets, handling our budget and running the Coal Preparation home-study course. When changing jobs I had been anxious about whether I could keep up my work for *Films and Filming*, but Denis had a tolerant attitude towards my going off to outside film shows and sometimes he would come along. After all, keeping in touch with training developments in other industries was part of our official remit.

In 1966 my first need was to get to know my colleagues. The writers were Bob Flanders, Ron Clements and Bob Roberts. The designers of the texts they produced were headed by John Quin, in post until I retired and still my friend. His assistants were Trudy Ward and Polly Dawes. Later members were to be long-serving Caroline Bradfield, John Branston and Philip Archer. The designers had the tricky job of assembling text and illustrations in a state ready for printing, and much measuring and use of Letraset transfer lettering was involved.

Denis reported to a grade I person in Training branch. Fortunately the brusque man who had upset Peter Heap had soon left to take a job in another industry and had been replaced by F.L. Edwards. Louis, as he liked to be known, was a charming man. A Cambridge graduate, he was married with two sons. He would take his children to a 'mini film festival' at weekends, visiting West End cinemas one after another. He was also passionate about opera and persuaded a group of us to buy tickets for an evening performance at the London Coliseum. This was to start a lifelong enthusiasm in me for opera, which I was to pursue especially after retirement.

Louis was only in this post until 1972, after which he transferred to Marketing Department and was soon making regular visits to Brussels in the course of his work, establishing European connections.

In 1970 Denis Kensit retired, and I became responsible for the work of Training Aids section, reporting to Louis Edwards. This included overseeing budgets, home-study courses and supervising the writing of training aids, their design and issue. Unfortunately I did not get an upgrading to Denis's grade II level, as Staff Department said that this had been a personal grading for Denis. After Louis moved on I reported first to Roy Grier, the head of mining training, and then, from 1973, to John Freeman, head of supervisory training, with whom I was to work closely. John came from Ashington in Northumberland and knew the footballing Charlton brothers, who were from the same mining town. John had had a tough early life in the mines but, ambitious and determined, had secured this headquarters job. In the years I worked with him I was the senior training aids officer, with a section numbering around nine or ten in number. John Freeman had his own separate staff of three to run supervisory training.

When I joined the section and worked with Denis, the new technique being tried was 'programmed learning', which had originated, it was said, in the work of an American behaviourist, Dr B.F. Skinner, who had shown that pigeons and rats could learn step by step if they were rewarded at each stage. If humans learned in short steps, and were rewarded by being told each time they got it right, they would be encouraged to continue their learning process. Machines had been developed for this – with great fuss being made in certain newspapers about 'teaching machines'. But the Board decided to avoid expensive machinery and to prepare printed manuals. A list of subjects within the mining, mechanical and electrical fields was drawn up and gradually, subject by subject, was tackled by a writer. His task was to prepare texts enabling apprentices to acquire and retain knowledge, step by step. The draft text was tested by the author at a training centre. The centre staff would monitor results with their recruits, and the text would be amended at problem points.

The Coal Board was only one of many organisations, companies and institutions, including universities, experimenting in the 1960s with learning methods. The Association for Programmed Learning was formed and was changed eventually into the Association for Programmed Learning and Educational Technology. It was a new ball game in academia: annual conferences were held, three of which I attended. At the Coal Board a course was set up to train people in programmed learning, led by outside specialist Derek Rowntree. I learned the techniques on this course, and, although I did not become a Board programme writer myself, I went out into the field with Bob Flanders to test such a programme out on apprentices. We stayed overnight in the Yorkshire town of Pontefract, famous not only for its castle but for its liquorice sweets.

After Denis retired I became responsible for the home-study course in Coal Preparation. This early form of distance learning had been set up soon after nationalisation as a way of training men at the plants and was designed to improve the quality of the coal coming out of the mines, ridding it of impurities before it was sold to the customer. The main need was to build more and better plants, which the Board did, but it was not easy to release operatives from work for training;

the home-study course enabled men to train up to foreman and super-visor level. It was devised originally by a privately run college set up in Highgate, north London. All the coalfields had specialised coal-preparation engineers, usually with chemistry degrees, and they were the controlling force for the study material, constantly updating it as new techniques were developed and setting the examination papers. Four times a year the engineers came to Hobart House for a day's conferences mainly devoted to the examination paper and its mark-ing. Denis had chaired these conferences, and I took over after he went. I also had to see that the study material was issued. When I joined, the team responsible under Denis was headed by Alloa Rowan. She was a cultivated woman whom I knew because we both were on the A Circle committee. She lived in South Kensington with her uncle, General Piggott. I had to deal diplomatically with her and was sometimes exasperated by the complexity with which she tied up the whole operation. She was supported by two women clerks. But some-how we got along, and I began to make my way through the trees to see the shape of the forest. Sadly, within a year or so, Alloa was attacked by cancer. She and her uncle bought a house in Whetstone, and soon she was running the course from home; I lived not far away and went up there for a morning to go over the work with her until she was forced to give it up. She was to die in August 1968, with her elderly uncle dying a few months later.

Alloa was followed in post by Dorothy Scott, helped by a young man born in Guyana named Vivien Lawrence and later by Mary Martin and Graham Leech, none of whom stayed very long. Things improved in 1970 when I was assigned a clerical officer as my assistant. This was Peggy Bowker, a middle-aged, hard-working woman who took over very competently the whole job of reproducing and issuing the lessons. This was before photocopying, and the great quantity of material had to be run off from carbons in the Hobart House duplicating section. Peggy became a valuable assistant, acting as my secretary, which was useful when I dodged out to see a film. She retired in 1981 but, sadly, developed illnesses which lead to her death a few years later.

The programme writers Bob Flanders and Ron Clements decided that they were not earning enough money and left the Board to set up as freelance consultants. In 1969, to replace them, we took on Eric Ross, who had worked in several Board departments. I first knew him in 1945 when he joined the Miners' Welfare Commission and our desks were in the same room. We both lived in Muswell Hill and were friends. Eric was a natural teacher; the son of a Methodist missionary, he was born in Africa and was to take a BSc in Economics like myself. His views were far more left-wing than mine, and he was active in many causes. He was to die, aged ninety, in 2008.

I had hoped to become a writer myself, but yet more administrative work arrived when Duncan Rutter became head (later called 'director') of Industrial Training in place of Jack Cadogan, who got a job as head of one of the industrial training boards which the government was creating at this time in order to increase the amount of training across the country.

Rutter had become an army major during his National Service and had joined the Board's Administrative Assistant scheme, designed to encourage graduates to take the middle and higher management posts. He had worked closely with the Board's deputy chairman, W.V. Sheppard, and had now secured this post. He had a quick brain and plenty of ideas. His downside was his preference for travelling rather than sitting at his desk, which many in the branch considered he took to extremes. I respected his brainpower; he seemed to have no fear and was a leader.

Following his appointment, Rutter felt he should get to know his staff better and discover their capabilities. He decided to give people special jobs on which they would report directly to him. For some reason he seemed to think I was the person to look after foreign visitors. He began by giving me the job of escorting two Romanians who wanted to study education and training in the coal industry. I went with them from one end of the country to another, including a memorable train journey across the Pennines from York to Manchester, seeing the great mills, chimneys and factories of industrial Britain in all their splendour, standing proud on a high landscape. I was to keep in touch with Aristide Budeneau, one of these men, exchanging cards and letters for many years. Les Roby, a colleague who worked with them in London, sent them food parcels when the country was in dire straits.

Rutter also gave me the job of organising the German exchanges and this I did, in 1970, 1971 and 1972. Under a scheme devised by him, a group of British apprentices was selected to spend a fortnight in Germany under the auspices of Ruhrkohle, the Board's counterpart in West Germany. Their itinerary included visits underground, to mining machinery manufacturers, research centres and the like. A tour of a brewery and a boat ride on the Rhine were among the entertainments. The British party was looked after by training officers and interpreters. I had to organise the selection, by areas, of apprentices – one mining, one mechanical and one electrical – and arrange the briefing in Manchester, carried out by Dr Manfred Fronz from Ruhrkohle. Rutter was careful of costs, and I had to put up the British apprentices in the Manchester YMCA, next door to the grand hotel where Rutter stayed.

He allowed me to join the British party for a few days on their visit to Germany. As well as making the travelling arrangements, I acted as one of the escorts, along with British coalfield training officers, journeying from Liverpool Street to Harwich in June 1970 and spending six days with them before returning on my own, catching a train from Essen to the Hook of Holland for an overnight ferry back to Harwich and another train. As during my previous visit with Sam Goodman, I felt at home in Germany.

I was at Harwich again early in the morning on 1 September to welcome the German party before handing them over to an area officer, Julian Edwards. We took them by coach to Cambridge from London, where I had arranged for a local German-speaking guide to show them round. In the market one of the leaders found a Nazi badge, which he said had been designed as a reward for mothers after giving birth. We lunched at the Dorothy Café; here I escaped for a while to explore the building. By chance I opened a door into the ballroom. I spotted some gold chairs lining the walls and recognised the place as being where, during my first days in Cambridge in 1941, I had attended the college Freshers' Ball. I could not understand why it all seemed so small, as if everything had shrunk.

I looked after the German visitors again in September 1971, escorting them to Scotland and staying in the Royal Mile in Mylnes Court, a medieval building used by the university as student accommodation. In 1972 I had a week with the British party in the Ruhr where we were well entertained and again looked after the Germans on their visit to the UK. This time I took them on a coach tour, organised in association with local area training officers. From London we took in, as well as coal mines, Cardiff, Warwick, Stratford-upon-Avon, Coventry, Kendall and Edinburgh, impressing one German leader at least with the diversity and beauty of the British landscape, enough to bring tears to his eyes when we finally parted. We stayed in Edinburgh, again at Mylnes Court, and the coach swept across the Forth Bridge to visit Longannet Power Station, with its adjacent coal site, and receiving a talk in German given by a manager.

After dinner on our return to Mylnes Court, the party walked up the road to Edinburgh Castle for the tattoo, which started at nine. The Germans had been told that it was the custom to pass round drinks while waiting for the performance to begin, and during the next hour I was offered sherry, whisky, beer and other refreshments. The party returned to Mylnes Court in merry mood and to consume the substantial crates of beer which they had already deposited in the building. Things got fairly raucous. One of the apprentices was thrown in a bath of cold water and re-entered the lounge dripping wet. The female warden saw him, the soggy carpet and the beer stains and ordered us all off to a lounge in the basement. I felt duty-bound to accompany them, and a gradually reducing group sat around in the bowels of the building with one apprentice then another rushing off to throw up. At past two in the morning I decided to call it a day and went to bed.

Next day was scheduled as a free morning for everybody before catching the 2 p.m. train to King's Cross. Breakfast was self-service in the refectory, and I was sitting with Hubert Muschner, the interpreter who had acted almost as my valet throughout the journey, carrying my bag and checking I had everything I wanted; he was a dear man. 'Did you hear what happened last night?' he asked. He told me that after I left the party in the basement the most charismatic of the leaders had eventually decided to go upstairs to bed. Staggering and befuddled by drink, he had pushed open a fire exit. As this was a medieval building in the heart of the Old Town his action immediately triggered an alarm at the fire station. Within minutes the fire brigade had arrived. Everyone was made to line up in the courtyard, including a group of research students resident there during the university vacation. 'I asked one student to go outside,' continued Hubert, 'but he demanded to know on whose authority I was ordering him up.' There was some bad feeling apparently. According to Hubert, the leader who had inadvertently caused the fracas appeared shortly after in a dressing-gown enquiring what was going on – a picture of innocence.

I digested this information over my porridge and bacon and eggs and feared the worst, recalling the sorry state of the carpet. I went to make peace with the warden. 'Don't worry,' she said. 'It won't affect your coming next year.' We smiled at each other, and we both knew that it would. Our party never stayed at Mylnes Court again.

My three years in charge of the German tours were great fun. After that Rutter handed the job over to Alan Whatmore, a new recruit to the branch. I remember in particular Dr Fronz, whom I saw most often. He spoke perfect English ('I learned it at school, no problem'), and I remember him maintaining on a train journey that the UK had nothing to lose by joining Europe. I tried to to explain to him that, as a former world power, it was not the case of the UK fearing to join something larger but of joining something smaller than the world-wide empire that we had previously controlled. I still have some mementoes given to me, including a clock made of hard coal and a letter-opener shaped like a miner's pick given to me by Ruhrkohle, and also a deputy's safety lamp posted after the tour by Hubert Muschner. Hubert had been a German prisoner of war in Britain who had married a Scottish girl after release and opted for a job as a colliery electrician. We had found our interpreters within our industry, as they needed experience of mining and its terms to translate for the visitors.

I looked after one more group of German visitors – in July 1978 – at Rutter's request. This meant a train to Nottingham and a bus out to the National Water Sports Centre at Holme Pierrepoint to await the arrival of the group;s leader and twenty-three teachers and instructors who were travelling from Germany in a coach. We visited sites in Nottinghamshire and Derbyshire, including the Board's research centre, making two underground visits and inspecting training centres. We ended the week with a visit to Chatsworth House.

By 1973, after I had finished organising the German tours, I was to get more involved with the creative work of producing training aids. I worked with Bob Roberts for a few months, travelling with him to Wakefield and other places. I appreciated that producing a training package was a collaborative effort. You took the lead in devising it, but you needed the expertise of the engineers in Mining Department, the customers who wanted the package, for their technical knowledge. Bob left in 1973 to work at Graham House, a Board residential training centre in Newcastle-upon-Tyne, and from this time until my retirement in 1984 I was responsible for the production of written texts, mostly hardback manuals – at last getting a chance to write as part of my paid full-time job. I began with some paper-back booklets describing how coal was moved out of a pit, and men and supplies brought in, called *Transport Underground* (Parts 1 and 2). After this came the hardbacks *Armoured Flexible Conveyors, Gate Belt Conveyor, Pumps and Pumping, Basic Mechanical Engineering, Fire-Fighting* and *Mechanical Transmission of Power.* None of these bore my name as author for they were all collaborative efforts, writ-ten under the guidance of engineers and trainers.

The subject to be covered was usually chosen by Mining Department, and an engineer was nominated with whom I would be working. My job was to discuss the subject with him, after which I would make site visits and discuss training needs at training centres. I would then devise a structure for the manual and write it in a style easily assimilated by a trainee. As anyone will appreciate who has bought domestic equipment supplied with a manual, it is all too easy to create a document that it is hard to grasp if not impossible. In my view, manual writing is an art demanding logic, clarity and good writing.

I discovered that most engineers did not naturally express them-selves through writing, tending to have visual minds capable of thinking in three dimensions. If I sent a draft text to an engineer at his office in The Lodge, Doncaster, where most were based, as often as not I would get a phone call asking me to come up. I would then sit beside the engineer while he pointed to places where I had got it wrong, usually clarifying the issue with diagrams. There were of course some who were equally good at prose and would make textual alterations. Eventually a text and illustrations were agreed, approved within the Mining and Training departments. The next step was to hand it over to John Quin, who had the task of designing and producing the publi-cation. Much discussion occurred during this period over line drawings, usually produced internally, often with the engineer giving his authoritative stamp. John with his charm and self-confidence made sure this important stage went smoothly, often visiting the printers to check all was correctly done.

One advantage of this work was that I met some great characters working at the different coalfields I visited. London with its pale office workers was always a stark contrast to the North of England with the forceful and assertive people I tended to meet in Yorkshire and Lancashire and elsewhere. I was to learn that many diverse people occupied the regions with their local traditions and their multitude of local dialects.

Reading my diary for 1973 I discover that I made twenty visits that year. In January I accompanied Bob to Kemball Training Centre in Staffordshire to discuss a package on report writing for maintenance craftsmen. In the same month I visited the Board's Bretby Research Centre in Derbyshire and then went down Fryston Colliery near Wakefield to look at a new machine called the Impact Ripper. This was a tunnelling machine undergoing trials, and a training package to introduce it would be needed; in the event the machine did not live up to expectations and the package was not required. In February I saw another Impact Ripper at work in Snowdown Colliery in Kent. Here the coalface temperature was 100 degrees Fahrenheit, adding to the discomfort of the miners, who had to cope with the tremendous machine noise, grease, oil and the constant shifting forward of the heavy hydraulic roof supports.

In March I visited Old Boston Training Centre in Lancashire to discuss a training package on a new Gullick machine. On this visit I was able to stay in St Helens with Cecil Pickavance, my LSE friend. The same month I was sent to Graham House in Newcastle to give a talk on training aids to newly appointed training officers. In April I went to Kemball Training Centre, to Gullick's mining machinery manufacturing firm in Wigan and to Trenton Colliery near Stoke-on-Trent. Just before Easter I attended the annual conference of the Association of Programmed Learning held at Brighton Polytechnic; I was able to arrange for Teresa to come with me because it was school holiday time.

In May I went to Lound Hall Training Centre, near Retford in Nottinghamshire. In June I travelled to Doncaster to discuss with engineers the booklets on *Transport Underground*. John Quin came with me, as he was involved with their design, and we worked with a charming engineer called David Allcock.

In July I was in Doncaster again to discuss with an engineer the package on report writing for machine maintenance operatives. The same month I went to Ellistown colliery with John Quin and Caroline Bradfield (who had been commissioned to do the illustrations) to meet up with David Allcock. While we were underground we took the opportunity to visit a coalface where a nuclear sensor shearer operated. In August I went to Kemball and Old Boston Training Centres regarding the Impact Ripper, and in November and December I visited Kemball to validate the craftsmen's report writing aids with the trainers.

Work on training aids was monitored by regular production meetings run by John Freeman. I have this compulsion within me to get things finished and out of the way, so I had no difficulty in carrying out a range of projects, even though I kept disappearing to review short films for my articles in *Films and Filming*. I never have had an office to myself, but fortunately I am blessed by being able to concentrate in even noisy situations, ignoring phone calls and conversations going on around me (helped no doubt by my poor hearing). John Freeman once said he could not understand how I could write manuals in such conditions and advocated working in the Board's library; I never found this necessary.

Work turook a turn for the better in 1972 when Film branch returned to Hobart House. After Dorset Square had closed, the chairman, Lord Robens, invited Francis Gysin to say where he would like the branch located. Francis chose Soho, and an office was secured in Wardour Street. This contained cutting rooms, film library and theatre. This meant that to approve rough cuts and show copies people had to travel from Hobart House. When Films returned, a theatre was built in the basement, alongside the cutting rooms. Francis had an office on the ground floor near some stairs to the basement. Another office was shared by Rita Gardner, still production manager, Kitty Marshall and Robert Kruger, both producers working for Francis. So every day I was able to call on him and discuss work; I was also responsible for seeing that Training branch's films were made, usually three a year. The usual drill was for Francis to say that he had capacity and to agree a subject from our list. He would then match it with a scriptwriter or director. An inaugural briefing meeting would be held, attended by a specialist from Training branch who knew the subject (usually head of mining training, mechanical training or electrical training) and often a Mining Department engineer. Sometimes these meetings were held in Doncaster. We would suggest suitable locations and set up area contacts, and the film-maker would get to work. I then remained in constant contact, either through Francis or directly with the film-maker, and watched as the subject was taken through all its stages, from script to location filming and then, after editing, to rough cut approval and finally a show copy. It then became a case of ensuring full distribution. Having worked as Francis's colleague I suspect I got some preferential treatment, and we had film after film made for us without delay.

Further visits to The Lodge, Doncaster, began to be made when John Freeman set up a working party on training aids. This was to ensure that there was national unity in our work, avoiding duplication of what was being done at Graham House residential training centre or by engineers. As committee members came from all parts of the country, Doncaster was the most convenient meeting point. Electrification meant that it was easy to get up and down from London in a day by rail.

Unions and others sometimes argued that the Board's headquarters should be in the coalfields and not in London. But this view was countered by the necessity of the Board members and chairman to be close to Westminster and government. Many services such as financial investments were best based in the capital. I was glad London was to remain the headquarters location, as I doubt if I would have left London for a job in the coalfields. This limited my choice in applying for higher-grade posts, as a stepping stone was often an area job. I did not want to uproot my family, alter my children's educational career, lose my wife her teaching job and neglect my widowed mother, living on her own. Nor did I want to lose a host of London friends and my film journalism.

10

MORE FILMS TO SEE

IN THE 1960s and 1970s the production of sponsored films expanded. More companies and institutions realised that visuals could make a greater impact than written texts. Target audiences were diverse. Prestige public relations films were made, especially by the oil industry outlining the ways they benefited the community, sometimes highlighting a medical or agricultural problem in a Third World country that they had helped alleviate. Others sought simply to emphasise their name or else describe the benefits of their product to increase sales. Some films were made to improve standards among employees or to teach them new techniques. In the 1970s the growth of management training helped provide a strong market dominated by about three film production companies, the most notable being Video Arts. The input of money from sponsors benefited everybody in the British film industry. The film laboratories had a steady flow of work, there were jobs for film-makers at all levels, and suppliers of equipment and film stock gained sales. This was largely unrecognised, the focus always being on feature films rather than shorts, with the media discussing the ups and downs of the British film industry in purely feature film terms.

The industry became organised by the British Industrial and Scientific Film Association (BISFA), which was run by a council and employed a full-time executive and other staff to negotiate common interests and, in particular, to run an annual industrial film festival at Brighton. Pre-selection film panels were run throughout the year to choose the best in each category to screen at Brighton, and I began to attend some of these as well as going to the festival itself. I was given formal permission to attend as a Board representative but did not have to pay the usual delegate fee, as I was also accredited as a press representative. I duly wrote an article in *Films and Filming* about the best of the films I had seen, as well as producing an internal Board report pointing out film developments in other industries.

I hold photocopies of my *Films and Filming* articles and dipping at random into these I find an article for September 1978. By now I have two pages, with four stills. I start off by recording the presentation of the British Film Institute's Grierson Award to David Rowan of Arbor Films for his fifty-minute film about the artist Tom Phillips, sponsored by the Arts Council, and then go on to record remarks made by Richard Cawston, head of the BBC's Documentary Department, who said that the BBC was making over a thousand documentaries a year compared with a mere dozen in the 1950s. The transfer of the classic line of British film documentary-making into the hands of the BBC and the independent television companies was of course a major development; it ran alongside the growth of sponsored documentaries and brought into prominence such talents as Philip Donnellen and Denis Mitchell.

My article then reports a British Petroleum film called *The Shetland Experience*, directed by Derek Williams, about their Sullom Voe oil terminal. I also report on an environment film festival at the Institute of Contemporary Arts, opened by John Schlesinger, with relevant film from across the world; on an interview film with F.E. Cleary, founder of the heritage-conscious property firm Haslemere Estates, made by Peter Bradford for World Wide Films; and on construction films by the Cement and Concrete Association, in which pre-stressed concrete was described as the single most significant development in the history of structural engineering. I then record the deaths of noted documentary film-makers Geoff Busby and Robert Vas.

Next I turn to the annual film festival, held that year in Birmingham rather than Brighton. Among the award-winners in different categories were the Royal Society for the Protection of Birds, Christian Aid (for a film about Bombay), Rank Audio Visual (for a sales training film), Video Arts (for films about finance, one of which featured John Cleese and Ronnie Corbett), British Airways Film Unit (for a film about Concorde), Mobil Oil (for a film called *Beneath the North Sea*), Cable and Wireless (for its *World of Communication*). A gold award went to a film entitled *Cashmere, the World's Rarest Natural Fibre*,

A film for Barclay's Bank called *Proudfoot's Last Stand* had Roy Kinnear playing a bumbling school teacher in a film scripted by Dick Clement and Ian La Frenais. *Food, A Cause for Concern* was made for the Dairy Council, intended to be used by teachers, and pointed out that children without a good breakfast or diet were unable to sustain concentration; it reminded audiences that 15 per cent of mothers were now men.

Sponsors had to get these films known if they were aimed at the general public rather than for internal use. Some had their own film distribution libraries, but all sought publicity in the press. Two national broadsheets, *The Times* and the *Financial Times*, ran regular columns about shorts written by freelances. Apart from *Films and Filming*, there was *Audio Visual*, which had begun as *Film User* and which catered for those who wanted comprehensive coverage of films available on 16mm as well as equipment and sponsors. In addition there were specialised magazines in the fields of photography, occupational safety, management and training which all printed reports of relevant new films. These were supplied by a small body of freelances when the magazine itself did not send a journalist.

In the nature of things we freelances turned up together at each press show, often two or three times a week, and began to share common concerns – for example, being irritated when two different sponsors announced press shows on the same day and at the same time. To represent our interests, Robert Rigg, founder and editor of a magazine, and John Chittock who, among other activities, wrote the *Financial Times* column, formed an Industrial Films Correspondents Group. This was subsequently seen as too limited a name and it became the Film and Video Press Group. By 1982 it had thirty-one members who varied in their attendance at press shows.

In the earlier years at least, sponsored films were made on 35mm, the format used in cinemas, and press screenings were held in theatres where they benefited from being projected on to a large screen in a darkened room. Distribution was mostly on 16mm, although some attempts were made on a small scale to provide 8mm copies to cater for those who had 8mm projectors. Distribution of films made for the government and its allied agencies was through the giant Central Film Library, run under the aegis of the Central Office of Information. It was the chronological descendant of wartime facilities when government messages were propagated through film.

Since sponsors sought publicity, distribution of films to applicants for loans was free. In the 1980s this policy was largely discontinued, under the influence of the Thatcher philosophy that services should be paid for and with the rise of industrial and staff training; many larger firms started to make their own training films and lend them out for a fee. With the appearance of video in the early 1980s this trend was reinforced.

As well as serving on BISPA selection panels and attending Press Group meetings, I was also a member of the National Panel for Film Festivals. This had its origins long ago in the Festivals Committee of the Association of Film Producers, which had the task of selecting British films to be entered in overseas film festivals that showed short films. The selection committee used to meet in the Central Office of Information offices in Norgeby House, Baker Street, in the 1950s, and I gained permission to be an observer at their evening screenings. This committee was superseded by a national panel, established in 1966 under the chairmanship of Professor, now Lord, Asa Briggs. It was set up under the aegis of the Foreign and Commonwealth Office, which appointed its chairman. The aim was to secure recognition for British film-makers at competitive festivals. The panel provided information to producers and sought to attract entries.

Selections were made at fortnightly evening screenings throughout the year in order to choose titles. Quarterly meetings were held to review the situation and to discuss results. Originally the secretariat was provided by the Central Office of Information, but from 1973 these facilities were provided by the British Council. The quarterly meetings took place at first in the Council's offices in Davis Street, but we transferred to their impressive new offices in Spring Gardens, close to St James's Park. I joined the panel, by invitation, just as Asa Briggs resigned, and my sole contact with him was a farewell handshake as we lined up to say goodbye. Next chairman was James Quinn, a former head of the British Film Institute, and the secretary was the capable John Stapleton, who after surviving dangerous military war service had worked on the Festival of Britain planning team. Membership was for three years, but I continued for five years until 1991. I found it an enjoyable occupation and very useful for me as a journalist in expanding the number of films I viewed and seeing films that won Britain prizes.

Short films, sponsored or otherwise, played their role in promoting our country but sometimes I pondered about my role in their promotion. By writing about sponsored films, you are inevitably supporting the sponsor and playing their tune – often that of a big corporation or a government department. Organisations such as Shell have produced first-class documentaries dealing with social problems or explaining the complexities of a technical subject for educational reasons, but the main motivation is to promote themselves. What is the attitude of the scriptwriters, directors and technicians who work on these sponsored films? Does it accord with their ideals? I often found that they were idealists in some way or other, in early years often imbued with zeal for social change. Perhaps the same is true of journalists working for newspapers with right-wing owners.

I discovered that W.H. Auden had discussed this problem while working for Grierson at the General Post Office Film Unit, where the pinnacle of his work was the verse commentary to the film *Night Mail*. This film was scripted by Basil Wright, directed by Harry Watt and featured music by Benjamin Britten. It was Basil Wright who had introduced Auden to the unit and this had led to his working there. In his biography *Early Auden* Edward Mendelson relates how Auden wrote an article, reviewing Paul Rotha's book *Documentary Film* (1936), in which he expressed his opinion that, although the documentary film-maker hopes to tell the truth about society, the truth rarely has 'advertisement' value for the governments and industries who pay the bills. Documentary film-makers would hesitate before offending the paymaster, he said. Mendelson argues that Auden's disillusionment with the documentary movement lay in his belief that bourgeois artists could not serve revolutionary purposes in a medium financed by government and big business. 'This contradiction was less malign than was the film-maker's refusal to acknowledge it.' Auden left the unit in 1936 to write the play *The Ascent of F6* and did not return.

Donald Alexander had worked in the documentary film movement before the Second World War and was certainly revolutionary in his attitude to social reform. But he was realist enough to recognise that there has to be a paymaster and that some compromise must be made, as I think did all the reforming documentary film-makers that I met during my work. Perhaps with the formation of the National Coal Board Film Unit Donald found the solution: the production of educational films of many kinds for a nationalised industry.

Although I found it difficult at times to be brutally frank about the shortcomings of a film after generous hospitality at a press show, I usually dealt with the problem by slotting the reviewed title in towards the end of my article, always trying to lead with a film that I thought was the best out of the batch I had viewed during the month. Being concise enough to cover as many films or related activities as I could was often the main problem as I toiled away on a Saturday or a Sunday. I posted or hand-delivered my monthly article and knew that it would not be edited but go into print just as I had written it. After Peter Baker left, Robin Bean became editor and continued so all the time that I contributed to *Films and Filming*.

All my chasing about and expenditure of energy seeing film shorts for little financial return was, I suppose, motivated by seeing my name in print in a magazine which sold internationally (I would occasionally get a letter from Australia or elsewhere about items I had reported). The good social life and friendships made were another motivation, and a third was love of film. As a boy I had gone to cinemas often three times a week, and film has a certain glamour not always shared by other art forms. Although the short film is usually seen as a lesser creative product than a feature, it has its own individuality, achieving through brevity, like a short story compared with a novel.

As documentary film has a chronological history I sought out the classic titles made in the past, often through attending shows organised by the National Film Theatre. In the 1950s there were few books on the cinema, but as they appeared I sought them out. Meeting other writers at press shows I came across Peter Cowie, then at the beginning of his career, who had established Tantivity Press to publish books about film. Peter was devising a book to be called *A Concise History of the Cinema* with a number of contributors, and he commissioned me to write a short history of documentary for it. The book was published in 1971 as a two-volume paperback, with my contribution split between the two volumes. Peter went on to write many good film books and to publish a valuable annual reference book called *The International Film Guide*, started in 1964 and still running in 1984 when I retired.

Sometimes a person who aims to make features finds making a short the best way to start. Perhaps this was true for Truffaut with *Les Mistons* and Polanski with his *Two Men and a Wardrobe* or Tony Simmons with his *Sunday by the Sea*. I saw Polanski's short at a screening at the Polish embassy and, standing in the group that encircled him, was astonished by his boyish stature. From there he went on to make his features.

Feature films came my way occasionally when the magazine editor asked me to review one, usually at an early evening show for magazines rather than at the daytime shows for newspaper dailies. I also went to the local cinema with my family as often as I could. Through my acquaintance from school with Bryan Forbes I was given the chance of visiting Pinewood Studios to see a feature film being made. He invited me to visit him there in November 1977 when he was directing *International Velvet*, released in 1978 and starring his wife Nanette Newman and Christopher Plummer. I sat in a corner and watched the rather slow process of taking some shots. Then we went off to the studio restaurant. Here I was impressed by the sight of Bette Davis sitting on her own having a meal. Bryan nodded his head in deference to one of the great names of cinema. After the meal we went to the theatre to see rushes. I sat beside Christopher Plummer, and when I got up to go he helped me on with my raincoat. Plummer seemed a really nice man, and every time since that I have seen him on the screen I have said to myself: He helped me on with my raincoat. There is a certain incongruity between the magic of the screen image and the informality of the stars.

I had a similar experience when John Chittock asked me to be one of the judges for the Grierson Trust panel that selected the best documentary of the year. I saw it as an honour to have lunch with Basil Wright, another juror, as well as with Derek Malcolm, then the *Guardian* film critic. The award was later presented at the London Film Festival. Derek Malcolm was an assiduous attender of the annual Festival on the South Bank, and here again, in the 'green room', one had the opportunity to see and talk to film-makers of renown. But I found its multitude of screenings too large to cover. Mostly it gave the chance to see shorts from overseas, especially from the United States where some great documentaries were made.

Although he invited me to lunch at Pinewood, my acquaintance with Bryan Forbes was never close, limited to occasional letters. Bryan's steps forward had been from acting into scriptwriting feature films, then to making some of the most distinguished British films of the 1960s, 1970s and 1980s. He formed a production company with Richard Attenborough and directed and produced. He was also an author, writing about eight novels as well as non-fiction books on the theatre and volumes of an autobiography. I have great admiration for what he has achieved from his West Ham beginnings. I also envied the fact that he had the enterprise to set up his own bookshop near where he lived, something that he recommended I did, too, appointing a manager to run it. But of course I didn't.

My life could never rival Bryan's in creativity but I enjoyed the many things I did, my enjoyment of conviviality always modifying my serious side. Also I am a creature of habit and I like to have a pattern to my life and to try constantly to improve what I am doing. I was fortunate to have as the background to my work activities a good home life. Teresa and I were lucky to have two children who, after they progressed through school, went to college, graduating in the 1970s. Like a good suburban man, I still walked to Wood Green tube station every morning, which gave me twenty minutes of exercise, and if there was nothing on in town I would be back by half-past six where a good meal would be waiting for me, Teresa being an excellent cook.

She and I continued to attend evening classes. Studying this way in the 1960s under the formidable Miss Neill at the City Literary Institute and elsewhere, I was rewarded after three years' attendance and three annual examinations by gaining a University of London Diploma in English Literature. In some ways I was more proud of this than my degree, which I had taken when I had no other responsibilities, neither work nor family.

Classical music and fine art have always fascinated me, and as a hobby I thought I would try my hand at creating my own art. First I did a year in a local evening class learning how to throw pots and mould figures. Then I took classes in oil painting, which I kept up for a few years. Gradually I formed the view that to be a good painter you had to give your whole life to it, and I knew that writing would always take precedence. So I dropped it, although I was to return to it after retirement. Painting myself gave me a greater appreciation of the wonderful pictures that I saw on my regular visits to art galleries.

Teresa and I read a good deal despite acquiring a television set in 1962, just in time to see the Russian astronaut in space. We read contemporary novelists such as Anthony Powell, Iris Murdoch, Kingsley Amis, Brian Moore, Alexander Solzhenitsyn and others. I read a fascinating book on the father of the Brontë children and worked my way through Leonard Woolf's five-volume autobiography as it was published. I also became enamoured of Balzac through translations of his novels.

Taking my children to Wood Green swimming baths on Saturday mornings, I rediscovered my love of water. Since then I have been every Saturday morning since. This expenditure of a couple of hours every week has, I am sure, made a positive contribution to my health, and it is something I still keep up in my eighties.

My main health problem has been deafness. I discovered this when I attended large meetings in a Hobart House conference room and the man next to me could hear what was being said by someone across the room but I could not. I began to think that deaf people should be issued with badges, equivalent to the white stick carried by the visually impaired, as deafness can be mistaken for stupidity. I took action by obtaining National Health Service hearing aids.

When the children were growing up we often took holidays in Ireland, the country of Teresa's birth. Pat, her brother, would come with us, hiring a car and driving us around. In 1961, when we first travelled there, the pony and trap were widely used for transport and the donkey for load carrying. I felt I had gone back in time. A few years later, when I visited again, the traps had been replaced by cars. Another change was that electricity was more widely used. This was before Ireland joined European Union, which changed it dramatically.

It was on the 1961 visit that we went to the small farm in County Clare that belonged to Teresa's family, now owned by her eldest brother. We sat in the old homestead, warmed by a peat fire used for cooking. The farm was away from a road, and the local postman used to complain back in the 1950s when I was writing almost daily to Teresa, who had come home here for the holidays.

In 1964 we stayed at Ballydehob, a small place in Kerry on the border with Cork, living in rooms over a shop, with old-fashioned petrol pumps outside. Everybody was friendly. One lunchtime in the nearby pub I was asked to sing a song. I came up with 'What Shall We Do with the Drunken Sailor', which seemed to go down well enough. We mounted the bus at Ballydehob to take our children to the coast. When we got off, the driver said to us, 'You're strangers here. Come along with me – you'll need some tea.' He knocked on a door of a nearby house and said: 'Hello, Mary. These people have just arrived. Give them a cup of tea.' Ireland was certainly a land of welcomes.

When the children left home in the 1970s, we started going abroad, to Bruges, Italy, including Trieste (where I saw a plaque to James Joyce), Greece, Hungary and Czechoslovakia, the last two still under Communist rule. After that it was Austria then the Soviet Union, visiting Leningrad (St Petersburg), Moscow, Kiev and Yalta. In the Yalta I was able to visit a small house where Anton Chekhov had lived in his later years. At other times we were to visit France, Germany, Spain and Denmark and also had three holidays in the United States.

Love of creative writing never died in me. Around 1967 I began to renew my interest in poetry once more and started to think that I could be a poet rather than a novelist. Well, we all have our dreams. My interest was stimulated by the annual summer Poetry Festival that began to be held on the South Bank. Teresa and I attended and were excited at seeing on stage such illustrious names as Robert Graves and W.H. Auden. We also saw American writers previously unknown to us such, as Alan Ginsburg, Robert Lowell and Stanley Kunitz, the latter two autographing volumes for us.

We went backstage to seek out Robert Graves for an autograph. Graves had been a hero for me, not only for his poetry but for that wonderful autobiographical account of the First World War called *Goodbye to All That*. He seemed a strange, detached sort of man, but he signed a book for me; by then he was in his seventies. Other admired poets who we heard included Charles Causley and Peter Porter. We also saw the then fashionable poet Yevgeny Yevtushenko and B.S. Johnson.

One of my journalist friends was young Gloria Tessler, who had heard of poetry readings arranged by *Tribune* magazine that were held in Robert Street, Camden Town. We went there a number of times together to hear poets such as Ian Hamilton, Alan Brownjohn and others. Sometimes people adjourned to a pub, and on one occasion I chatted with Dannie Abse, telling him I had known his wife Joan at LSE. He was hoping that Joan might turn up that night,but she did not make it, so there was no reunion for me. Joan had written a number of books about art and art galleries. Stanley Bloom was much more her friend than me when we were in Cambridge. Tragically she died in a road accident in 2007.

I began to write poetry and, influenced by Gielgud's records of Shakespearian speeches, then very popular, read my own poems on to a tape, with little introductory passages in between each effort.

Poetry writing became a matter for me of constant endeavour but no achievement. I sent some to Sid Chaplin, who returned them with a noncommittal 'reader's report' (Sid did reading for publishers), although he said later that his son, Michael, had liked them. Gathering courage I sent some to the *New Statesman, Tribune* and the *Times Literary Supplement*, but they were all turned down. As I did not like rejection, I gave up sending poems out. But I never gave up writing them. Well into the 1980s and 1990s I steadily wrote each Sunday morning between eight and nine in the morning while Teresa was at church. A few are reproduced as an appendix to this book.

In several places around the house I have pads of poems written in pencil, all of which need working on – as proper poets do, making poems out of verse, changing words and lines. Alas, I have not done much. I know that at the time I wrote them I enjoyed the experience of words coming from nowhere, appearing on paper and listening for some automatic music dictating their sound and rhythm. I am sure not all of them were bad, and they certainly meant something to me at the time, releasing emotions within me.

In 1973 I sought out creative writing classes, trying to make it part of my busy life of home, office and film reviewing. So that autumn I went to Morley College again, the place where I had attended the Randall Swingler lectures in the 1940s and 1950s. At the end of my day at Hobart House I walked to Victoria and took the bus across to Lambeth. There was a decent workman's café there that served a hot main course and dessert for about half a crown (15p). Then I would walk round the corner to the class. The one I joined had Ian Cochrane as tutor, a short, boyish man from Northern Ireland who had already published about four novels. I don't think he really knew what to do with a class of a dozen or so people. Like other tutors in this field he set us to write, we read out our work, and the group discussed it.

I liked Ian but had mixed feelings about his capacity to consume beer after beer. There was a bar at Morley College where we would gather first and then after a while head up to a classroom. At the end of the session some of us would join him in a pub. I have always enjoyed this social side of evening classes and indeed have made friends in this way; one of them, Bill Gates, I have kept in touch with ever since. But the college got somewhat concerned about Ian's use of the bar and his classes. In summer 1975 he moved on. Ian had a great capacity for friendship and encouraged us to write. Some of us used to meet him mid-week for advice. He lived in Kensington High Street, and local pubs would usually be the venue to meet, but, as I usually had to get back to Hobart House I had to cut things short and leave before too long. With his departure from the colleage, our acquaintanceship did not survive long.

Ian was succeeded by Rosalind Belben, who must have been in her thirties. She had known Lawrence Durrell and had published several novels. Her deep round eyes were very expressive and seemed to see right into you. She advocated a modern style of writing, fragmented perhaps, seen from different viewpoints, quite apart from the traditional novels of the nineteenth century, and this influenced the way we wrote our pieces. The custom was to bring in work we had written and to read it aloud to the group. For many of us this was a substitute for publication.

Under her influence I started work on another novel, which I was to call *Tube Train Home*. Needless to say this was based around the life of a suburban man and opens with him sitting in St James's Park in his lunch-hour. I set myself the target of writing at least a few paragraphs every night. I found that the novel can be a sort of dustbin into which you throw observations on aspects of life. I drew upon the remembrance of my father for one character, and I understood how writing draws upon what we have known or experienced but does not exactly replicate it.

I began to read it out at the weekly classes, and Rosalind expressed interest in it. I typed it out (although I don't think I ever wrote the final chapters), put it in a green ringbinder and lent it to her. She had been a publisher's reader (she recounted how she was one who had rejected Frederick Forsyth's *Day of the Jackal*, some fifteen firms having rejected the manuscript before its worldwide success); when she handed my novel back she was enigmatic and wrote me a letter that seemed to say she did not care for it, but I could never grasp from her letter exactly why. Rejection of written work never goes down well with me, although later I made another effort to try to write a novel (composing in longhand on the train coming back from coalfields assignments). However, I found that I did not have the drive to finish it. I think it was from that time that I gave up my ambition to be a novelist, even though I carried on with classes and story writing for some time. My conclusion is that I can write readable prose but that I am weak on plotting and creating believable characters, the essentials to story-telling.

As I continued with my life-long fascination with writers and the books they produced, I accepted the fact that people much younger than me had achieved fame through their work and admired their achievements. A chance to see some modern writers in the flesh came about from 1980 onwards when the Institute for Contemporary Arts put on a series of talks. These were held in the premises it had acquired in The Mall, at the foot of the Duke of York steps after moving out of Albemarle Street. I found this a useful venue, where you could meet friends for a meal, enjoy exhibitions of modern art and see films in its theatre.

One talk I particularly remember, given in the cinema, was by Margaret Atwood. This was in 1980 before she enjoyed the world-wide fame she was later to gain. She described her upbringing in Canada and the nineteenth-century books that were her first models. I was impressed by the lucidity of her talk.

Another memorable occasion was when Anthony Burgess was invited to speak. He seemed to be three men, not one, as he dazzled us with a range of subjects, carried away by fierce energy, the force behind his wide output. (Most of all I remember reading *Nothing Like the Sun*, his book about Shakespeare.)

Then there was Margaret Drabble, who had chaired the Atwood talk and who seemed to me very attractive. I had read her novels as they came out and once had won a small prize in a magazine short-story competition she had judged, and I think I spoke to her about this. Other talks I enjoyed were given by Emma Tennant, Marina Warner, Eva Figes, Arnold Wesker, John Osborne and Paul Theroux. I had read books by these authors and seen Wesker's plays. John Osborne signed one of his autobiographical volumes for me.

It was pleasant walking from Victoria past Buckingham Palace and through St James's Park (my favourite London Park) to the ICA. London seemed to me to have everything I wanted. I continued to go with Teresa to as many live plays in the West End as I could.

I realised in the 1970s, when I was in my fifties, that I had achieved no publication with my name on it, except for my writing on film in *Films and Filming* and for magazines such as *Audio Visual* or the *Times Educational Supplement*. Philip Dosse, founder of the group of arts magazines that included *Films and Filming*, had increasing financial problems and payments were usually late and never very generous. One lunch break I found him serving as an assistant in a newsagent near to Hobart House, presumably to increase his personal income. Finally in 1980 he went bankrupt and soon afterwards committed suicide.

Robin Bean, editor since 1968 of *Films and Filming*, saw that his only course was to set up another magazine to take its place and launched *Film*. He asked me to go on writing for him and used the last article I had sent in which had not been published. By the time he had set up *Film*, other people had taken over the Philip Dosse group of magazines, and *Films and Filming* was relaunched. Alan Eyles, whom I had known as a film journalist, was to be editor, and he asked me to write for it. I had the embarrassing task of telling him that I had already committed myself to Robin Bean and that it would not be appropriate to contribute to both. I continued to write for *Film* after 1984, when I left the coal industry, but this only carried on for a couple of years before the magazine disappeared. However, I was to continue to write about films in another capacity after retirement.

11

LAST YEARS IN THE COAL INDUSTRY

MARSHALL RIDDELL TOOK over as director of Industrial Training in 1975 after Duncan Rutter left to take charge of the food industry's industrial training board. Most people took to him immediately as a likeable leader. He had been a colliery manager, was easy to talk to, and was aware of what had to be done. Like Rutter he gave me a job escorting foreign visitors. They were from Europe and were coming to Britain to join the Health and Safety weekend the Board ran each year in Blackpool, which centred on a national first-aid competition.

The tour began on a Friday evening in November 1979, when I met Herr Obst at Heathrow and brought him to the Grosvenor, the mid-Victorian hotel next to Victoria Station. Marshall suggested I brought Teresa along for the weekend, and she booked in, too. Early next day we travelled north from Euston to stay at Blackpool's Imperial Hotel. Marshall held a reception, and I had to make sure everybody had a drink. I then escorted the European wives to an art exhibition that we had staged, followed by a beauty pageannt, before taking them to a seafood restaurant. I had drawn a large cash float and paid the bills and organised taxis. We finished at 2.30 on Sunday morning. On Sunday there was a fashion show and a safety quiz. Chairman Derek Ezra spoke and met the guests. The following day we returned to London, and I had to take some of them for a tour of the West End and Harrods.

One Saturday in 1982 Marshall was returning by car from a football match in his native Newcastle when he felt unwell, pulled over and died of a heart attack, a great loss. Kevan Hunt succeeded him as director. Starting life as a pit electrician, he had risen rapidly via Staff College. He was a strong character with a quick brain who would question a project down to its fine detail. Kevan was to be in the hot seat as director of Industrial Relations Department when the 1984 national strike erupted and to have a tough time. Sadly he died of leukaemia in 1966, aged sixty-one.

My social life continued to be pleasant at Hobart House. A film club had been set up, and one could stay on in the evening to see a feature. My friend Jack Reading retired in 1981, and I took his place as chairman of the A Circle, the staff club operating in the arts field. Joan Jerome, as secretary, organised many outings and events.

Staff Department was always considering job grading, especially after administrative grades were replaced by management grades. I felt that my job had been undergraded but got nowhere until a major examination of many jobs was undertaken. I spent about two days with a trained investigator seconded from an outpost department, detailing all my work and responsibilities, including that of the budget and controlling a vast stock of printed aids. John Freeman backed me heavily when my post came before the review panel, and I then went up a grade to Management 4. So from 1 January 1980 I got a considerably increased salary; this proved useful when I retired four years later, as my pension was based on salary lat retirement.

Soon after this, John Freeman gave up responsibility for overseeing my work and that of Training Aids section, and we reported to the head of Mining Training, Fred Gelder. So for my last four years at Hobart House I worked with Fred, whom I found very likeable. We had both worked for the Coal Board for a long time, and I knew him from the days when I was at No. 2 Grosvenor Place; Fred then worked in Method Study, which was based in the same building. He was a typical Lancastrian who brought northern warmth and humanity into the office and was generally liked. With so much to do, he did not have much time to give to Training Aids, but we had regular meetings and they proved helpful. He had a habit of ringing me up, calling me into his office a few doors down from mine and discussing at length a task that had been presented to us and asking me to take it over. At this point I usually had to say, 'Yes, of course, Fred. But would you like to let me know which job has priority?' I would then reel off a list of some half a dozen or so other tasks he had already passed over to me. To be fair on him, he could generally see that I had been overloaded with work and would try to rearrange things. Bosses don't always appreciate the amount of work their employees have to deal with.

In 1981 another change occurred when my faithful helpmate Peggy Bowker finally had to retire on age grounds, having somehow won another year past sixty. She was replaced by a young man called Steve

Wood, who took her desk opposite me. Caroline Bradfield also resigned from our design group at this time and was replaced by Philip Archer, who in his spare time was a painter and who was to have exhibitions of his work in London, before eventually becoming head of an art school in Leith, near Edinburgh. Caroline later returned, to work with John Quin, having realised it had been a mistake to leave.

Derek Ezra, whom I had admired for his clear, analytical mind, retired from his post as chairman of the National Coal Board in 1982. He was succeeded by Sir Norman Siddall, a mining engineer whom I also enormously respected, as did most other people in the Board. Unfortunately he had a heart condition by this time and was only in post for a year. This allowed Margaret Thatcher to appoint Ian MacGregor as chairman, who did not exactly prove a popular boss.

An additional enjoyable job in my last few years was helping run courses in fire-fighting training. This stemmed from my drafting the Board's training manual on fire-fighting, which I had undertaken around 1978, backing it up with other aids such as slides to form a training package. Fire is always a real and present danger in mining and the Board was anxious that everybody had training in this subject. To this end, an annual one-week training course was set up. The delegates were two representatives from each area drawn from their training centres. These area instructors would then pass on the results of their specialist training at their area courses. The lecturers at the annual course were area or national fire safety experts.

The location of the courses was Grassmoor Training Centre in Derbyshire, a purpose-built post-war centre with ample facilities for practical training: fire extinguishers and hoses could be tried out on real fires outside and classes held in the lecture rooms. I used to book rooms for about two dozen people at the Station Hotel, Chesterfield, and be responsible for their welfare and attendance. The hotel served very good meals in the evening, and friendships were made. I was astonished as I learned the variety of achievements these mining men (instructors were always ex-underground employees) had obtained. They all seemed to have mastery of complex subjects. I enjoyed their company very much. I also enjoyed the company of the course instructors, with whom I developed friendships. I tramped all over Chesterfield in those free summer evenings, watching some cricket if a match was being played, getting to know the local history and, if there was time, seeking out the bookshops. I also visited the twisted spire cathedral.

One distraction in February 1983 was an operation on my right ear, carried out at the Middlesex Hospital by the consultant Mr Garfield Davis, one of the most charming and understanding doctors I have ever met. I had transferred to the Middlesex from St George's, where I had first been tested and given NHS hearing aids, because it had moved out to Tooting and it took so much time getting there and back. I was admitted one Sunday to the Middlesex, put under general anaesthetic on Monday and woke up to find my son sitting at the end of my bed. 'Why are you not at work?' I asked him, for I had no idea of time. He explained that it was half past five. There was no bandage on my ear because it was all done by keyhole surgery. Three bones in the inner ear had fused together, and they had been replaced by plastic substitutes.

After discharge on Friday I found my sense of balance was affected and I kept stumbling. The noise of traffic was now so loud I wished I had not had the operation. In the event it took five weeks to get back to normal on sick leave, and when I did return to work I was sent home again straight away, as I was spotted stumbling along a corridor while trying to reach my office. I was better after a week, and I put my hearing aid away. Garfield Davis warned me that as I aged I would lose my hearing again, and he gave me ten years. He was almost exactly right, for in the mid-1990s I had to start wearing my hearing aid again. In due course I was to end up being prescribed two digital aids. They were supplied by the NHS and cost nothing, and I blessed again the Attlee government whose advances to the country in terms of health and education are seemingly forgotten.

I also considered the nationalisation of the coal industry by Attlee a great benefit, its technological achievements never being appreciated. But by the early 1980s the coal industry was contracting steadily, as the demand for its products was falling. Costs had to be contained, and collieries were being closed down in a planned way. It was this movement downwards that was to cause Arthur Scargill to lead the miners into the 1984 strike to prevent closures.

As the industry downsized, so administrative workers were reduced in number, and it became British Coal policy not to employ people over the age of sixty even though the retirement age was sixty-five. Eric Ross, my Training Aids colleague, proved an exception to this as he did not retire until 1982, aged sixty-three But we were all given discreet warnings by higher management that redundancy was coming for older workers. This was aided by government schemes that provided financial help to employers with redundancy problems.

I would be sixty in August 1983, and as this date came closer I knew I would not be working until sixty-five as I had anticipated. In 1983 I was sent on an internal pre-retirement course advising me on retirement problems, both practical and emotional, that I would have to contend with. At the end of February 1984 I was called into an office and told I was to leave the next day. So on 1 March 1984, aged sixty and a half, I finally left the coal industry. There was no time to organise a farewell party, just a few drinks in Kevan's office with my immediate colleagues. Made redundant on the same day was Irving Halle, also in Industrial Training branch. Sadly he was to die within two years of his retirement of a heart attack, which made me appreciate, when I heard of his death, of the enormous importance of good health. On parting, or some time after, I was given a certificate recording my thirty-nine years in the industry, dating back to late 1944 when I joined the Miners' Welfare Commission. My only wish was that Derek Ezra had still been in post to sign the certificate instead of Ian MacGregor, his successor.

I was glad I left the coal industry before it tore itself apart in a battle that devastated families and communities; another example of how personalities, in this case Scargill and Thatcher, can have tremendous effects on others, illustrating how people make history just as much as economic change. The privilege of power over others is so often misused. Violence leaves lasting scars.

12

BECOMING A
LOCAL HISTORIAN

I BECOME ATTACHED to places and everyday objects, and it was quite a wrench leaving my familiar room, desk and office files, as well as membership of a community. Fortunately it was not the end of work, which I need to be happy, but the beginning of new activities. These stemmed from my film journalism connections. I anticipated having more time to attend press shows and meetings of the Film and Video Press Group, so it seemed wise to renew my annual season ticket on the London Underground for the next two years so that I could travel into town freely.

I had already begun one activity before I left Hobart House. Fellow journalist and grand organiser, John Chittock, was active at the National Video Corporation, which supplied arts material to television companies, particularly filmed operas. John conceived the idea of selling the best of the sponsored shorts for television transmission. This meant choosing the better ones, and for this John set up a selection panel, calling on fellow journalists Clive Jones. Ken Roberts, Peter Cargin, Alec Hughes and myself, for which we were paid a fee. We looked through our files and submitted pages of suggestions. We then met at lunch-hour meetings, with sandwiches and wine in a Pimlico office, and argued our corner for different titles. This began shortly before my retirement, the meeting place being a short walk from Hobart House and my lunch-hour well used. When after a year or so the panel was temporarily suspended we were all paid a retainer, a welcome addition to my pension.

John was to put a more regular source of income and work my way a few months after I left the Board. As well as his journalism and the conferences he organised, John had started up two magazines. One was *Screen Digest* and the other was *Training Digest*. Both were monthlies, printed on stiff white paper without illustrations and available only by subscription. There was a short editorial but no articles. The content consisted of very short news items summarising developments in the worlds of film and training. The idea was to save time for busy executives who wanted to be up to date but did not have time to plough through long articles. Each news paragraph ended with an address and phone number to ease follow-up. They reached a market big enough to sustain publication and when John decided to divest himself of them, he sold them for large sums to other publishers.

My involvement began when John rang me one day to say, 'Ken, you've got nothing to do now you are retired. Would you like to free-lance for *Training Digest*?' I had to think about this offer. I had this dream of using my retirement to try again at creative writing – novels, short stories and poems – and try to make my name. Was my dream not demanding enough? Did I then take the right decision? I was turned sixty and fell for his idea, thinking a bird in the hand was worth two in the bush. It would give me regular paid work. The result was that, for the next ten years, until I turned seventy, I worked at home two weeks out of four for the magazine. The task was to take a lengthy press cutting or press hand-out and reduce the content to three sentences or thereabouts. I settled down over the years to doing eighty paragraphs a month, sitting at a table in my bay window in my front living-room, first drafting by hand and then typing the result.

The person I worked to was Christie Quinn, whom John had made editor of *Training Digest*. I had first met Christie in the 1960s at the BISFA film festivals in Brighton. This was where she lived; she was the daughter of James Quinn, former head of the British Film Institute, who also chaired the National Panel of Film Festivals on which I served. Christie was married to David Fisher, who edited *Screen Digest*, and they had two small children. I had known David some years as a fellow film journalist.

The drill was for Christie to send me fat envelopes containing the hand-outs and cuttings she wanted summarised. I would précis these and then often spend some time finding a contact address. In those days my letters usually arrived at half past eight in the morning so I was able to start by nine. Today I get my post towards midday – such is progress and mechanisation.

I went down to Brighton a few times to be briefed by Christie. I found these enjoyable excursions, as she is a charming person with a good deal of intelligence and willpower. She corrected some of my work in the early days, but, as with most jobs, I got better at it the more I did it. A benefit was the chance to continue attending press film shows now that *Film* magazine had folded. Under government encouragement, training became a UK growth industry. Work in this field, pioneered by the Industrial Society, was now expanded with industrial training boards for separate industries and an annual training competition launched by the appropriate ministry. Demand led to a growth in supply of training aids, either internal to an industry or by private enterprise. The leading film-making companies were Video Arts, Melrose, Longmans and Rank. I was invited to attend their press shows, seeking stories that might make news paragraphs; by an existing arrangement the films themselves were usually reviewed by freelance Ken Myer.

Video Arts was probably the most prolific of these film companies. I remember the launch of their first training film, which was at the preview theatre in Bowater House, which until recently stood overlooking Hyde Park by Knightsbridge. There were no refreshments of any kind at this show, which was attended by John Cleese. He was one of the founders of Video Arts, along with Anthony Jay and Derek Robinson. Cleese is known throughout the world; perhaps Jay is less well known, although he became famous for scripting the television series *Yes Minister*. Jay proved to have a clear, analytical mind, as shown by his introduction to the film at its press show, and he was among the best of their scriptwriters. Well-known actors such as Timothy West, Prunella Scales and Dinsdale Lansden were used, and opportunity was often given to meet them at the press shows. One film was directed by the veteran feature-film director Charles Crichton. Hospitality at their suite of offices in Oxford Street was of the first order. Similarly fine films and launches were given by Melrose, based in Clapham.

As well as film shows, I was also asked to cover training exhibitions held at the Barbican Centre or West End hotels. I would wander round the stands, gathering up armfuls of promotional literature and chatting to people to get stories, and stagger home with a pile of paper to sort through, select and write up. Exhibitions and their associated conferences, at which one has to sit through hours of often boring talk, are worlds of their own to which certain people devote their lives, often working ungodly hours. I always found them exhausting. Once or twice John and Christie asked me to attend the Birmingham Conference and Exhibition Centre; at first a hotel room was paid for so I could stay over, but I preferred travelling there and back in a day.

Being retired gave me more time for the Film and Video Press Group, for which I was honorary treasurer and membership secretary for some years. We published a booklet to aid sponsors run film shows and distribute their product and developed visits to production companies, film laboratories and the like from which members were able to write stories for their magazines and papers.

Change came with the invention of the video cassette. I think I knew the writing was on the wall in 1981 when the group were invited up to Peterborough to visit the long-established film library belonging to the Film Producers' Guild, a group of production companies making short films that used Merton Park Studios and which had offices in Upper St Martin's Lane. The Guild was now adding videos to the library. I wrote about this in a *Films and Filming* article, speculating about the future and drawing attention to a new phenomenon: shops on the high street renting out video cassettes. Before long the old world of 16mm film distribution began to disappear in favour of cassettes. Video Arts started screening films at press shows on video projectors, gradually managing to get good images on large screens. Critics could now see new films at home on videotapes sent by producers and need not attend press shows. They could settle down with a pile of them and rerun them if necessary. Another step was filming on video – easy to do and easy to get wrong. The founders of Video Arts sold up in July 1989, but the management buy-out was successful and standards were maintained. The world subtly changed.

In 1986 Francis Gysin retired from his post as films officer and began his practice of spending Tuesday lunchtimes in the Coach and Horses, the well-known pub next to the Palace Theatre in Soho. He encouraged ex-colleagues to join him, and a group would often assemble. Instead of dropping in to Hobart House to see him when I was in town, I would now – when I could – go to the Coach and Horses on Tuesdays, trying to avoid drinking more than was good for me. I continued to do this until his death in 1995.

The pub was famous for its landlord, Norman Ballon, known as the rudest landlord in London (he was not averse to telling people to leave in no uncertain terms if he took against them) and for its clientele from the arts world, particularly Jeffery Bernard, about whom Keith Waterhouse wrote the West End play *Jeffery Bernard Is Unwell*. Bernard would often sit at the bar until about one o clock before moving elsewhere. One day a fan of his, a woman from Wales, gave me her camera and asked me to photograph her standing next to him, which I duly did. Celebrities must have odd lives.

After commuting into the office every working day I found life at home very pleasant. Teresa had retired from teaching in 1980, enjoying having the house to herself before I turned up. Married couples sometimes find it a problem being thrown together all day by retirement, but we got along well. As I frequently went into town, she had some peace part at least part of the time. She was a great help in providing the right conditions when I was working at home on *Training Digest*, and we enjoyed the companionship, going together to adult evening classes on literature or social history. In addition we would attend each year a wonderful week-long event run by the Workers' Educational Association called 'Time on the Thames', based at university premises in Bloomsbury. Each day there were talks and seminars and other activities, all on the theme of London and its history. We were given organised visits to out-of-the-way places such as the Midland Hotel at St Pancras, the Red House at Bexhill, the home of the Woolfs at Rodmell and sewage and pumping stations, such as the marvellous building at Abbey Mills. We explored Hackney and its wonderful Victorian swimming baths, went down to Kew, visited the disused Battersea Power Station (before it was made derelict) and had meals together to celebrate. Held in July, it always seemed to be the hottest week of the year.

Keeping up my interest in creative writing, I joined a local evening class on this subject that met in a Crouch End school. A change of lecturer in the second year disappointed many in the class, and it folded. Out of this grew a small private group of six to eight people meeting once a fortnight in the home of Maria Scott, who had been one of the class members. We used to gather together to read out work that we had written or alternatively write something in the class on a set subject that we then read out. I wrote many short stories in this way. The chief need of unpublished writers is for people to read or hear their work and react to it; creative writing classes all over the country help meet this need, reading out your own work being a form of publishing. We became a group of good friends, and I went along for several years until in about 1990 it slowly fizzled out.

I suppose that I should have persevered at writing stories and done something with the verses I wrote steadily every Sunday morning but life was full of interest and I was not as passionate about creative writing as a dedicated author must be to succeed. An entirely new interest, that of local history, had become an important part of my life by the 1980s, and it was through this that eventually I was to have texts published and to see my name on the covers of several books. It was an unexpected way of fulfilling my life-long ambition to be a writer.

Teresa and I came across the Hornsey Historical Society in 1976 when it ran a stall at a Muswell Hill Festival, set up in the car park off the Broadway. Teresa thought membership might help her with her primary school teaching, and so we joined on 22 September 1976 at the first meeting of the society's new season. At the next monthly event we attended the launch of the society's first history publication. This was *Memories of Hornsey* by Edwin Monck, a man of ninety-seven who had spent much of his life in Hornsey and who had accumulated a collection of historic postcards that were drawn upon to illustrate his text.

Today conservation and heritage matters are of wide interest, but this movement did not really take off until the 1970s. In the post-war years the emphasis in the UK was on reconstruction, sweeping away war-damaged properties and building a brave new environment. This gathered strength as prefabricated building systems were introduced and tower blocks and walkways became the fashion, and new towns were built out in the countryside.

Legislation in the 1970s reflected changing attitudes as tower blocks became unpopular, the architecture of New Brutalism was disliked, and visionary town planning seemed to result in another kind of mess. A law made provision for councils to create conservation areas to protect historic built environments deemed worthy of protection on aesthetic or historic grounds. People became more interested in local history, and across the country history societies were formed. There had always been parish histories – one of the first, for example, being written in 1631 about Tottenham by the local vicar Reverend William Bedwell (a scholar of great distinction involved in the translation of the King James's Bible). But a wider interest, beyond the antiquarian and linked to conservation, now developed.

Hornsey Historical Society had been founded in 1971 as an educational charity 'to promote local studies in an area of the London Borough of Haringey not previously covered, the former Parish and later Borough of Hornsey', as stated in the preamble to *Memories of*

Hornsey. It is interesting to note that the society was dedicated to Hornsey and not to Haringey, and I think this stems from basic human concepts of neighbourhood. The 1965 Act of Parliament that replaced the London County Council with the Greater London Council created a ring of new large London boroughs. These replaced the smaller authorities covering more limited areas. Hornsey had been added to Wood Green and to Tottenham, all former borough councils, to create the London Borough of Haringey. Similar changes occurred in the creation of Brent, Barnet, Camden and the other London boroughs. In cost saving and specialisation these larger units of administration have obviously had financial benefits, but I have never thought them an ideal structure for governing people locally. The old boroughs had usually been based on ancient parishes dating back mostly to Norman times. They had endured as units over the centuries because, in my view, the scale was one that the average local resident could comprehend. It was his or her neighbourhood. Once this local area is enlarged to cover places that the resident rarely visits, that person loses a sense of connection and loyalty to his local authority.

In my view this is definitely the case with Haringey, which joined together east–west rather than north–south authorities. From time immemorial the roads into London have created a natural orientation towards the centre. East–west routes are limited and less used. Thus the east side of Haringey is remote to those in the west and the west remote to those in the east. The situation is exacerbated by the poverty of Tottenham, which is now substantially populated by immigrants of all nationalities who tend to be at the bottom of the social scale. This contrasts with the middle-class and mostly comparatively rich areas in the west of Highgate, Muswell Hill and Crouch End. Councillors for rich wards and poor wards must sometimes struggle to take an all-borough attitude against the needs of their own wards.

For some time after the creation of Haringey in 1965, there was nostalgia for the lost Borough of Hornsey, and I think that this must have been one factor that led to the founders of the society devoting it to Hornsey. Another was that a neighbouring society, called the Edmonton Hundred History Society, already covered Tottenham, which had been within the old Saxon Hundred of that name. Hornsey had been in Ossulstone Hundred and outside its coverage. In due course, following parliamentary boundary changes, Hornsey

Historical Society defined its area as covering the parliamentary constituency of Hornsey and Wood Green.

Involvement as a volunteer helping to run the society was to follow. In the summer of 1977 I got a call at the Board in my lunch-hour from Bridget Cherry, the architectural historian who was one of the founders, asking me whether I was prepared to stand for the Executive Committee and act as assistant conservation officer. I said yes and was elected in July at the AGM. At the same time I was invited to become a member of the Publications Committee, which was headed by Bridget and met in her house. This I gladly accepted, joining Joan Schwitzer (then chairman of the society), Harold Robins and Reg Aldir. The group brought out a newsletter, which was to evolve into an annual printed bulletin of illustrated articles with a separate newsletter. Owing to the pressures of her professional life, editing the Pevsner architectural guidebooks, Bridget gave up running the Publications Committee the following year, and I was asked to take over the chair. This I gladly did.

In 1979 I also became the society's representative on the Muswell Hill, Fortis Green and Rookfield Estate Conservation Area Advisory Committee, taking the place of Ruth Rogers, another member, who sadly had been killed in a road accident. This I still serve on, many years later, and I am also still chair of the society's Publications Committee.

In 1979 I was also to begin my involvement with Alexandra Palace, which Haringey Council acquired from the Greater London Council on 1 January 1980. Just before that date the council set up a consultative committee with representatives from residents' associations and societies such as ourselves to advise on plans to convert the Victorian building into a modern exhibition building, vying with Olympia and the other exhibition halls. As the society's representative I began to attend rather fractious meetings, at which local people expressed their dislike of the exhibition centre idea because of the threat of increased traffic and crowds. They formed an organisation called Save Our Space (SOS). In July 1980 a fire consumed half the building, and plans were put on hold until an official government planning inquiry. After deliberating for six months, the inspector recommended that planning permission be given for exhibitions. Throughout the 1980s, under the admirable chairmanship of Councillor Robin Young, chair of the Palace Trustees, and following the advice of the architect Peter Smith the consultative committee regularly examined the proposals and plans and gave their input from local knowledge – a good example of local democracy. Unfortunately the insurance and other monies available for restoration after the fire proved insufficient and parts of the Palace have remained unrestored. Finance has always been the problem with the Palace ever since it was built.

In the last few years the Palace has attracted wider interest as the place where public television broadcasts to domestic receivers first began in November 1936 – an event of world importance, although little has been made of it. Curiously one of the press events I attended in 1986 was a visit to the National Museum of Photography, Film and Television, a branch of the Science Museum opened in Bradford, Yorkshire. The occasion was the opening of a new gallery devoted to television. I went as a member of the Film and Video Press Group. The day was to be marked by an opening ceremony and a buffet lunch for visitors, including surviving pioneers of television who had worked at Alexandra Palace. A party went by train from Kings Cross, and drank champagne as they passed Alexandra Palace. Unfortunately just outside Bradford the train came to a halt, and waited there, so that we eventually arrived at the museum half an hour late. The local guests stood by the buffet tables anxiously awaiting our arrival.

The galleries were opened by Cliff Michelmore, with whom I had sat and talked for a while on the train. Chief among the elderly television pioneers was Cecil Madden. I remember the return train journey because, in a jovial mood, I began to speak to someone sitting alone in a carriage whom I was sure I knew but could not place. He was disconcerted when I asked him his name; he replied that he was Michael Fish, the television weatherman.

A founder member of the Hornsey Historical Society is Joan Schwitzer, who became chairman in 1974 and continued in this post until 1985. In 1979 I became vice-chairman and began a long period of working with Joan, which continues to this day. Joan proved a decisive chairman in 1981 when Haringey offered us the shell of an old 1848 church school as the nucleus of a headquarters building. At that time it existed as a vandalised bus shelter and public toilet block. Joan's persuasive powers with the committee led to a decision being made to take the plunge and accept the offer. Conversion was needed, but fortunately one of the members of the society was an architect and he redesigned the building and oversaw the work, which was supported by a Haringey grant. This gave the society a place to stock and sell publications, house its growing archive and its office and hold meetings, exhibitions and receptions. The story is told by Joan Schwitzer in the society publication *Making History Together*, issued in 1998. It is fair to say that Hornsey is now one of the leading local history societies in the country, and its publications are regularly praised. It has a steady membership of about 450 people with around fifty attending the monthly lectures.

In the 1980s concern was expressed by the Hornsey and Crouch End Conservation Area Committee about the state of the medieval church tower surviving in the old churchyard, a relic of Hornsey parish church whose congregation now attended elsewhere in the parish. Conservation Area members, along with the church and Hornsey Historical Society, set up a new charity called the Friends of Hornsey Church Tower, with the aim of preserving and restoring it. Bridget Cherry was one of the founder members, and a committee was set up on which I served in the role of membership secretary and nNewsletter – another enjoyable little writing job. Grants were obtained for supporting girders and the like, and restoration was brought to the point at which open days could be held, when the public were allowed to ascend the old stone spiral staircase to the top of the tower for the view. A recently acquired lottery grant is aiding the restoration of the graveyard.

In this way my leisure time began to be taken up with committees, serving on the general and publications committees of the society, the Conservation Area committee, the Alexandra Palace consultative committee and the Friends of Hornsey Church Tower committee, each of which generated tasks of one kind or another. The most interesting of these was writing texts about local history and giving talks when invited by groups. My life had always revolved around work and activities carried out in the West End, and I had paid little attention to my local environment, so at first I knew nothing about the history of Muswell Hill, the place I was mostly to write about. Reginald Smith, a solicitor who was our society's vice-president, had given a talk and led a walk in Muswell Hill, and he kindly gave me his outline lecture. Two small booklets by F.W. Draper filled out my knowledge, along with other reading. In consequence, in April 1982 I was able to give a talk on the history of Muswell Hill at one of our monthly lecture meetings, with an audience of about a hundred. Before that in 1979 and 1980 I had led walks around Muswell Hill for the society, with attendances of some fifty to seventy people. I discovered I enjoyed standing up and talking to audiences, perhaps a late expression of my earlier ambition to be an actor, based on an innate exhibitionism. From then on I was invited to give talks to local groups across north London, on Muswell Hill, Hornsey, Alexandra Palace or Crouch End. I illustrated these with 35mm slides, photography having always been a hobby, and eventually I accumulated a library of 35mm slides, numbering about a thousand. I also bought a slide projector and screen, graduating in due course to a Kodak Carousel. Teresa accompanied me on our talks and outings, helping to carry equipment and selling society publications. This became a fun part of life in retirement.

Helping produce publications was another pleasant activity. In the early days of the Publications Committee, Bridget Cherry and Joan Schwitzer had conceived the idea of producing a series of pocket–sized walking guides covering the different areas of the old borough of Hornsey, pointing out buildings of historic interest. Bridget drafted Crouch End, Joan covered Highgate, Reg Aldir did draft walks on Hornsey Village and Stroud Green, and I devised walks around Muswell Hill. In the event, the project was long and drawn out, and I was asked to supervise the whole series, editing as necessary, and it was some years before all the walks were published. Sadly Reg Aldir, a retired printer, died, and I found myself taking over his texts and expanding them; I also became joint author of the Crouch End walk with Bridget Cherry. *A Walk Around Muswell Hill*, issued in 1987, was the first to come out and was the first publication by me written for the society and the first ever publication with my name on the cover on sale in bookshops. The series has sold consistently, with other walks added, such as Malcolm Stokes's trail around the parish boundary stones to be found in Kenwood estate and Albert Pinching's *Old Wood Green*. The walks are constantly reprinted to meet demand.

My first printed local history work took the form of some entries in *The London Encyclopaedia*, edited by Ben Weinreb and Christopher Hibbert, published in 1983. Christopher Hibbert had written to the society inviting someone to contribute entries on a number of local areas, and the job fell to me. This book has proved very popular, going on to appear in paperback and regularly being reprinted; I am always pleased to see my name among the list of contributors.

My next two publications came as the result of representations made to the committee by the late George Halse, our sales manager who often held the fort at the Old Schoolhouse when it was open to the public for sales, particularly of historic postcards, which the society began to reproduce, and of early Ordnance Survey maps, of which we had had copies in quantity. George said that visitors enquired about Hornsey's history, and he suggested that someone write something about it that could be sold, so easing the problem of dealing with queries. The result was the launch in October 1986 of a 48-page booklet entitled *From Forest to Suburb*, which summarised Hornsey's history and provided illustrations. I undertook research, but I have always seen my role as a populariser, making facts more widely known in a readable form with respect to chronology and logical presentation. I felt my training for this had been with the manuals and packages I had written for the coal industry. My task was made easier with the publication in 1980 of Volume VI of *The Victoria County History of Middlesex*, covering Hornsey, one of a series of volumes covering the country under the aegis of the University of London's Institute of Historical Research. Launched over a hundred years ago, the *Victoria County History* series brings together a wealth of historical facts of all kinds relevant to each area, the work being done by professional researchers. The volumes have become invaluable for local historians, although they tend to be reference volumes.

George Halse next suggested a text giving a history of Alexandra Palace and Park, about which there was also a steady stream of enquiries. Again I took this on, and the result was published in 1992 under the title of *Palace on the Hill*. I got much information from the only book about it that seemed to have been published previously: Ron Carrington's *Alexandra Palace: A History*, which had been commissioned by the GLC, the owners, for the hundredth anniversary of the opening of the existing Palace in 1975. Carrington's book was out of print and not generally available. From this and other sources I created a short, chronological narrative giving the history of the enterprise; for a long time it was the only available text on the subject.

I had been able to include photographs of Alexandra Palace in a earlier volume, published in 1989, called *Highgate to Hornsey*. This came about because one of our members, Dick Whetstone, who was a collector of historic postcards, had been approached at a postcard fair by publisher Stanley Benz, who wanted to issue a picture book on the Hornsey area based on Dick's collection. I worked with him on this, selecting appropriate views and writing the captions to provide a geographical journey through the old borough of Hornsey. It made a landscape-shaped volume with 105 views and was published by S.B. Publications. It sold well but has been out of print recently and with the death of Stanley Benz is unlikely to be reissued.

The society's archive contains a good collection of old cards, some of them donated by Edwin Monk, and these provided the basis for a regular weekly series of captioned views of historic interest, which I supplied to the local paper, the *Hornsey Journal*, from 1994 to 1997. I also supplied for some years a short report of each lecture given at our monthly society meetings, both to the *Journal* and to the *Hampstead & Highgate Express*, until both papers changed their style and dropped society reports, that old standby of local journalism. I took no fee for any of this work, nor for the serialisation by the *Journal* of my Muswell Hill walk.

At this time several national publishers discovered, like Stanley Benz, that there was a market for picture books reproducing historic views. These came to be published for virtually every place, sometimes with rival books from different publishers covering the same town. Publishers began to seek out local historians with access to archives and our society was approached by Chalford Publishing, soon to be renamed Tempus Publishing, as a possible source. Joan Schwitzer and I agreed to do a joint book called *Highgate and Muswell Hill*, Joan to cover Highgate and I to cover Muswell Hill. The book was published in May 1995 and has been in print and ever since.

This gave me the idea of doing a book to be called *Hornsey and Crouch End*, having become familiar with the archive pictures through doing the weekly items for the *Hornsey Journal* and having written captions for them. I rang the publisher, and Tempus agreed that I should do the book, which they published in 1998. That, too, has been constantly in demand and in print since.

Soon after I produced a short pamphlet called *Finsbury Park*, which was rushed out for a festival in the park for which the society had booked a sales stall. My most detailed research was done for a chapter in *People and Places: The Lost Estates of Highgate, Hornsey and Wood Green*. This society publication had been masterminded by Joan Schwitzer. Ten authors each contributed one or more chapters on lost estates or buildings. My choice was to research the history of a house latterly known as The Limes, over which the new suburb of Muswell Hill, with its shopping parades and Edwardian domestic terraced houses, had been built from 1896. Delving in the Guildhall, London Metropolitan and other archives I was able to trace its origins back to the late seventeenth century and to identify the occupants; many of the names, such as Gurney, Marshall and Mudie, connected with the world of books. Looking at old copperplate handwriting in the Hornsey manor rolls recording copyhold tenure evoked thoughts of past times and of people long gone. The book came out in 1996.

This research led me on to write *A History of Muswell Hill*, published in 1999. Muswell Hill's history had been covered in a short volume of 1984 by David E.D. Freeman and in a fuller work from 1995 by Jack Whitehead called *The Growth of Muswell Hill*. But I wanted to do my own straightforward chronological history, and I was supported in this aim by the society, which agreed to publish my book. Soon after, I was approached by Tempus Publishing, who asked me to write a volume on Muswell Hill for their History and Guide series. This was published in 2002 as *Muswell Hill: A History and Guide*. It turned out to be a handsome volume in larger format with a colour cover and an inset of colour photographs, many of which I had taken myself. In due course I agreed to produce a further picture book on Muswell Hill for Tempus, which was published in 2006, called *Muswell Hill Revisited*. In preparing this I tried not to use pictures I had already used in previous books and found that I had to carry more than 300 images in my head when researching views for the new book. Again I devised a chronological structure but stretched the time period up to the last years of the twentieth century in order to accommodate some good recent photographs I had found in Haringey's archives at Bruce Castle. I had been working there as a volunteer helper for the curator, Deborah Hedgecock, and she encouraged me to compile the book. I was helped by the generosity of Hugh Garnsworthy and David Dell, who both allowed me access to their extensive collection of historic postcards.

The society also issues an annual printed publication called the *Hornsey Historical Society Bulletin*, containing illustrated research and reminiscences about the local area and its people. I have been able to contribute quite a few articles for this over the years and enjoyed writing on personalities such as J.S. Alder, the local church architect, and Robert Paul, the British film pioneer who built a studio on the northern fringes of Muswell Hill. The society acts as its own small publisher and has issued over thirty titles, making it one of the most prolific of the country's local history associations.

The Hornsey Historical Society has enriched my life in my last three decades with many lectures, visits, exhibitions, creative outlets and a host of friends. After serving as chairman for five years, I had the honour of being appointed president, the main task being to preside at the annual general meeting.

Teresa was active with me at society events, but sadly in February 1997 she suddenly died without warning. She woke up feeling unwell one Tuesday morning and took to her bed to rest. I went to see her in the bedroom in the early afternoon and she seemed to be asleep. How do you recognise death? Sadly it was so. She had died in her sleep in the forty-fourth year of our marriage. I had lost my best friend. Departed was the woman who had given me years of affection and companionship, who had a keen intelligence, tremendous energy and who was a first-class organiser and an excellent mother.

A dozen years have passed since she died. My mother always urged me to look forward to the future and not regret the past, and this is the advice I have followed. I knew Teresa would not want me to give up and retreat into a shell or become isolated. So I took the initiative and went out and found new friends who would accompany me to theatre, opera and concerts with me or just enjoy a pleasant lunch in a restaurant. My son Richard and daughter Oonagh and their spouses and children (my five granddaughters, most of them now at college) have been my greatest support. I can never thank them enough for their love and care. My existing friends, whom I do not name, know how much I depend on their company for a balanced life. Friendship is perhaps the most important thing in life. It keeps you sane. Now all I have to do is to live to be a hundred.

Come on year 2023!

APPENDIX

SOME POEMS

A Walk from Helston

If I should go three hundred miles
And walk the road to Breage,
There I'd find the self same streams
That I heard when I was a lad.

Fifty years ago this spring
I heard those waters run,
Solitary on a Cornish road,
When I was very young.

What journeys have I made since then,
Since I was a student lad,
Have I been where I wanted to go,
Or has it been irretrievably sad?

Smilingly I enjoy again,
The life that I led for a while,
I see the faces all too plain,
And memories which make me smile.

I think again of Cornish streams,
Hedges built of age old rock,
Tiny fields and our dreaming,
When all those lives interlocked.

Carried on a Current

Distantly the river runs,
Ultimately it feeds the sea,
If I could travel on it
Would it make me free?

Standing on the river bridge
I look towards the coast,
No, I cannot see it now,
To reach it, just a sad boast.

At the place where the river dies,
In the eddies, where the sea begins,
Would I cross a final barrier,
Join the spaces where I'd live?

Sorrowfully I turn away,
Join the people walking by,
Leave the bridge where the future was,
And let my life stutlify.

Young Clerk Going to Work in London

In and out of the station
The tube trains come and go,
Is anyone a relation?
Crammed inside so full.

This bustling world of thousands
Contains so many names,
Will I link with these mouse men
Join the stream without fame?

No one knows their destiny
Even when on a train,
Not from rationality
But by chance we make our name.

Lost

Will I hear it if I stand in your garden,
Hear what is in your head?
I want to know, I cannot ask
Here in the shadows, wondering.

It is a long time since we met,
Summer, when fields embraced us,
Under the hawthorn hedge, I loved you;
You quivered then, long ago.

I lay somnolent as the sun died,
Quietly, slowly you stroked my hair,
I did not ask then your meaning,
In the hedge shade, at summer end,
It was understood, then.

At Home

Idly I stare at distant roofs,
Laid out in rows upon the hill,
Count their tile tops as they move
Back from my window view.

On a corner stands a tree,
What is it connects tree and me?
Oak it is and long established,
Is it true we are neither free?

For oak and I are rooted here,
This place is where we must be,
From this spot's soil we take our strength
Unmoving, bound, set here permanently.

In the House

Neither wind nor rain,
Nothing but this quiet grey,
I wake to it each morning,
I end with it each day

Terrace bound I look across
To a low line of distant hills,
Will I see the sun at last?
Or will the grey still distil?

Within the house I sit in chairs,
Look out of windows at monotonous skies,
Restlessly walk from room to room,
Sit still again and stultify

At last I turn my back upon it,
Take up what work I have,
I shall use my fingers profitably,
Dull greyness shall be my life

Irresolute still I look
At where once brightness was,
Is it what my mind still seeks?
You, and laughter, on the lawns?

Roaring with Laughter

Lastly I said, as I stood there,
Arguing on the corner of the road,
What will you do with the honey bees?
Once they begin to sneeze?

He stared at me with open mouth,
'Have you gone completely mad?'
I laughed back at his attitude,
His pomposity was utterly sad.

'I don't quite understand you.'
Suddenly he was faltering now,
The birds will fly with silver wings,
I shall ride on the horns of a cow.

My words made him grow paler,
A frightened look came to his eyes,
I shall fly over the roof tops,
And tickle pigeons in the skies.

He didn't say any more when
I said that but turned and walked away,
I slapped my thighs and laughed then,
For my words had won the day.

Then I put my hand into a passing angel's,
Was lifted up off the ground,
I looked down at the roadside spinney,
Knew I was beyond it all now.

Bonds

Say 'Enough' to me, under this tree,
Turn away from me, say 'Let be',
You would no more of my love,
Lie back, watch those clouds above.

So spring ran into summer,
I suppose it was some years ago,
It was more than you wanted,
You were not sorry to see me go.

But still within in each other's eyes,
Each saw those sad, strong bonds,
It would not be enough to say 'Goodbye',
There would be love still, beyond.

Easter Sunday

Grey light lies within the morning,
Breaks this special day,
Will the sun come fawning,
Wiping its light upon our way?

I stand alone on the doorstep,
Peering out over the land,
Nothing has changed this morning,
When will you show your hand?

Turn back within the house,
Walk between grey lit rooms,
Listen for the sounds around us
That will mark the day's rich bloom.

Birds that seek the bread ends,
A cock that crows not far,
The sound of traffic that descends
Upon this urban road of cars.

Sit a while and contemplate
Before this fair day begins,
I would live before it is too late
And all my ambitions win.

Afterwards

Do you remember how pleasant it was?
There, talking in the party corner,
Did I put my hand upon your arm?
I don't remember, or do I,
Looking at each other, laughing,
Telling jokes one after the other.
Was it outside that we kissed?
When foolishly we went into the garden?

I don't remember, or is it
A warm soft form I feel,
Is it you, your eyes dancing,
That now I remember?
I sit among the empty glasses,
Your coat has gone from the hall,
The bed is warm and thrown open.
It is morning, empty morning.

Up the Long Road

Walk up this long road
Of bays and bricks and lawns.
Ignore the passing traffic,
It is a world that is forlorn.

So many evenings desolate
Sweep week by week across its way,
Nobody moves in the windows,
Some curtains here are drawn all day.

These people obviously hide their lives,
Barriered within their gates,
Seeking some internal mischief,
Lives as private as their place.

At the top of the hill I turn and look,
Along the dull road I've come,
How many houses are shut up?
How many lives have gone?

Has my time been like the roadway?
Full of private shut-up cells?
Is that how they all see me?
A nowhere man, all sealed?

Speaking

Nothing but the dark morning
Am I aware of in this house,
You could sound some warning,
I would not hear it as I converse

Speaking not to another human here
But to myself in this frosty winter air,
Lying this pencil, across this page,
Committing fresh follies as I age.

For who is himself but he who speaks,
Who knows what he thinks till he says,
Who can define himself to another?
Until words he can resolutely utter?

Tourist

The hard shape of the end house
Crunches in the sunlight,
Showing its plaster fragments
To the full glare of the sun.

I walk along this street
Quite taken by the light,
The old walls and doors,
Entrances for those long dead,
Invite me to stand and stare,
To merge present and past,
To be alive and alone
Where it was and is,
To enter courtyards full of ghosts,
Savage to me.

Bones on the Shore

Nor on the sea bay can I escape
This remorseless time tick.
If I look on aeons of history
As the water laps the shore
It will not take away what is,
Will not stop what will be.
Pace restlessly as I will
The movement comes, devours,
And skeletons will lie around me
As I hear the sea's last roar.

Sunlight

In such sunlight as I see
All good things come to me
Watch it paint with yellow hands
Early morning streaking bands
Slowly where warm fingers lie
It will come this way, by and by.

Look upon the sunlit scene,
The best there is or ever been,
In this now I take my all,
Warmth and light at my call.

Smilingly I sit upon the grassy ground,
Admire all that grows around,
Think of days yet to come,
Smile my face up to the sun.

Who says old age is time gone by?
For me and now the sun is nigh,
Laughing I love the daily round,
And tomorrow I will make a bound.

Encounter

She looks at me with uncertain eyes,
Is it her life's husband that she spies?
Or should she wearily cast me off,
Telling herself if enough's enough

Disenchanted in the darkened room
We hear the tree boughs turn and boom,
Wondering if nature is altogether fair,
Bringing us together as a sexual pair.

Autumn Years

Give me not the dark night
Which ahead I now see,
I would stay within the bright lights,
Spirit of life, have pity on me.

Do not end suddenly my mature years,
For much I have yet to do,
Termination is now among my fears,
I am not yet ready for my life to be through.

Cast myself still heartedly into my tasks,
A full life's cunning I can now deploy,
Why should I waste this accumulated craft
And put away for ever my main joy?

Mature years let me enjoy your strength,
I would battle on in greatest vigour,
To which such knowledge is lent
Old men can yet be victors.

Oak Tree

I suppose these are the years of my maturity,
Why do they come in with such fury?
Sweeping along to my disgust,
Why cannot my youth always last?

Sit down and watch the ladscape's line,
Remember to yourself the infinity of time,
Look and gaze on nature's wonder,
Ripening stalks, seeds sent asunder.

So I look on this old oak tree,
Its acorn beginning, its sky so free,
Spreading wide its multiple boughs,
Tremendous with strength, the world it endows.

Yet here upon the wizened earth
The timber lies that once was strength,
The life of oak trees is not all that long,
Set against time's binding thong.

Beginning and end are part of me,
I cannot change what I see,
Though strong, an oak must fall,
Only acorns left to mark its all.

The End of March

Sweet light which brings me morning
Give me the best of days,
Let me enjoy your loving,
The heat, the wonder and the haze.

For I would turn my palms up,
To catch the loving warmth,
In my hands I would cup
The sun's devoted breath.

Advice to Another

Go not down to the deep river
Wait till the tide rises to you,
The cold of God will make you shiver
He will ask you for his due.

Do not lift up that handy blade
Or see how far would be the fall,
Sit still yet in your chair,
God will be waiting always there.

Do not go to meet him in the water,
Do not find him in self-slaughter,
Do not go to join him before your time,
There is another way, another line.

Travel on around some corners,
Against self-death he did warn us,
Enjoy what yet you might today,
God gave you life, heed and stay.

An Elderly Man in His Corner

Beauty of mine you were for a moment,
Loved you were in the youngest of days,
Captured for ever, totally solvent
Treasure which I hoarded always.

Out of its closet my memory mind
Draws out now its silver and sheen,
The youthful beauty which I once worshipped,
The body so caressed and clean.

Nobody thieves a man's old memories,
Old as he ultimately might get,
Memories excite still his frenzies,
Reviving his lusts and dreams.

Peace now in the early mornings,
Dark hair conjured sweetly up,
Round breasts stroked in dear memory,
On you and your beauty still I sup.

Thames Time

Stumble down to the shores of the Thames,
Stout wide river flowing grey,
Watch the buildings on the banks,
How they've changed since yesterday.

Yet still stand true other piles
Upright in the misty airs,
Faces born throughout my life,
Architecture for which I care.

St Paul's great dome and the forties bridge,
Cutting a line so right,
Shadowy face of Somerset House,
Shell Mex House standing bright,
Institute of Electrical Engineers,
London Transport's little line.

Across them face the South Bank follies,
Once I saw them being built,
Then they were the world's tomorrows,
Now they are often called its sorrows.

Love is what this old view brings,
Seen as I stand on Hungerford Bridge,
Each tells me of so many things,
Memories firm like an unshiftable ridge.

Black Overcoat

Ready for winter funerals,
The old black coat on the door,
The only times that
I wear it are the times that I deplore.

Symbol it is of what must be,
Token of the days to come,
Would I shut it from reverie,
With that sadness I would be done.

Accept it yet I must do,
A man who had had his life,
For entwined in others we know.
The meaning of love and strife.

Belgravia

I walked these roads when I was younger,
I thought they were my own, you see,
I had my desk away down yonder,
For the lunch-hour I was free

Every turning I knew quite well,
Faces I often recognized,
The shops were once my glory,
Everywhere goods in a rising swell.

Back I've come in the years long after,
Now it no longer belongs to me,
There's no desk to which I can wander,
My time now is wholly free.

Changes I see in every vista,
Shops I knew have disappeared,
As for the faces, I say I miss them,
Their bright glances no longer sear.

This is no longer my little country,
No more do I rightly journey here,
Others have taken the shape of the pavements,
It is up to me to disappear.

The Stub

The pencil becomes a stub,
And the pad is nearly down,
Little I have left to say,
Except that I'm nearly gone.

Kiss my soft lips at last,
Forget what might be,
You and I cannot hold fast
Once we reach eternity.

Day's End

Nothing I saw but starlight,
At the end of this average day,
I thought they were so very bright,
Pinpoints of joy in the sky.

I sat alone in my garden,
Silence covered an urban dark,
No one was heard at day down,
And I had found peace at last.

Life Journey

Infinite the horizon as you walk,
The further you go, the further off,
So it is with things you want
You march for days and end in dark.

Mainspring is it, of our lives?
Trying to attain the impossible prize,
Without the walk what's the arrival,
Sitting down is mere survival.

So we know we are never done,
Forward we walk to a retreating sun,
Age will clip our speeding legs
And little will remain but a final bed.
Sad stories beguile such ageing ones
But laughter relieves their failing walk.

Telling Stories to a Child

Tell some of the old stories
Into your ever listening ear,
The words will be passed on then,
We join with tradition, dear.

They heard these stories long before,
So many centuries ago,
Old stories never fade away,
On and on they flow.

So you and I link memories
Across the decades of time,
What once was mine alone, dear,
Now is your inheritance sublime.

So Long and No Longer

Will the night?
Yes, the night will fall,
Stars will shine, moon be full,
The dark envelop all this world.

Will the cold?
Yes, the cold will come,
The sun will end.
The cold come with the dark.
Songsters of such nights
Also now are still,
There can be no more day delights,
The earth has grown too full.

Using Up Life

Tides of the day flush up the work,
These low efforts I must not shirk,
It is better, is it not, to toil,
Than idle about with thoughts that soil.
But in the oblivion hours of labour
Pause, now and then, dreams to savour,
Give up not wholly the inner self,
Be human as in work you delve.

There is more to me than doing things,
In my ears some anthem rings,
And at the tip of my silent tongue
Words stand tiptoe on the rung.

Would they come out in magic lines,
Beauty in corners they would define,
And lying living on a page
They'd seek to live beyond this age.

Dies Off Our Life

Now ends one day and then another,
Imperceptively we grow older,
Dies away all our desire,
Wilting like a forgotten flower

Some green stalk, turning brown
Lies forlorn upon the ground,
Once it grew magnificently
Blooms that gave it majesty

Such sweet days when summer was,
And all the world was bright across,
Blossoms colouring all the way,
Sunshine brightening every day

Dies off our life and our flower,
Nestles soon in some dark bower,
Lives only now in memory's world,
All blossoms faded and life all furled.

Retired

In such unsuitable ways
Do we spend uncounted days,
Losing them time after time.

Can you remember much at all?
The moments spread out in a line
From morning bed to late-night sleep,
What in between can you keep?

I sit here wondering about my days,
The days I had, days without delays,
Remorseless, onwards, moving like a clock,
Now is, now isn't, now it is forgot.

In the mirror I can count the years,
Fortunately I have lost some fears,
What job to have, wife to take,
What horizon to reach for, all too late
Past, the going down now;
Serene, one can become, old sun.